GIULIA BER TACCHINI
PAOLO CALCAGNI
LUCIO LUZO LAZZARA
RICCARDO RINETTI

THE
OFFICIAL
POINT OF
VIEW

a POINT.

DESIGN MOVES US EMOTIONALLY.

WE HAVE NEVER UNDERSTOOD WHY, OR ELSE, PERHAPS, WE HAVE NEVER REALLY ASKED OURSELVES THE QUESTION. WHATEVER THE REASON, THE FACT REMAINS THAT CERTAIN SHAPES GIVE OUT A SENSE OF 'RESISTANCE', AND TEND TO SUBVERT THE ESTABLISHED ORDER OF THINGS.

THESE SHAPES AROUSE DESIRES. AT TIMES GENTLE, AT TIMES ARROGANT, THEY REMIND US THAT THE THOUGHT OF AN INDIVIDUAL CAN STILL MANAGE TO MAKE ITSELF HEARD, RISING ABOVE THE HUBBUB AND DIN WHICH WE TEND TO GET USED TO.

EVERY YEAR THE MILAN FURNITURE FAIR BRINGS THE CITY A WEEK OF "RESISTANCE", DISORDER, AND VOICES; THERE ARE MANY DIFFERENT VOICES, SO DIFFERENT THEY ACTUALLY MANAGE TO COMMUNICATE.

WE HAVE CALLED OUR VOICE 'THE OFFICIAL POINT OF VIEW'. THIS VOICE WILL GUIDE YOU THROUGH A WEEK OF HUMAN "RESISTANCE", IN THE SHAPE OF TRANSGRESSIVE FORMS.

THE OFFICIAL POINT OF VIEW IS OUR POINT OF VIEW AND WE HAVE TRIED TO KEEP IT AS CLOSE AS POSSIBLE TO OUR CONCEPT OF DESIGN.

THIS POINT OF VIEW IS A HIGHLY SUBJECTIVE ONE, AND IS AT TIMES HASTY OR BIASED, OR EVEN ABSENT-MINDED. IT IS NOT ONLY SINCERE, GLUTTONOUS AND JEALOUS BUT ALSO LOUD, OBSESSIVE, INSTINCTIVE AND SUPERFICIAL.

IN SHORT, IT IS A HUMAN WAY OF SEEING, CONSTANTLY RESISTING THE TEMPTATION TO BECOME OVERLY SPECIALIZED.

THE OFFICIAL POINT OF VIEW WILL NOT HIGHLIGHT THE MOST AMAZING NEW DEPARTURES ON SHOW AT THE FAIR, NOR WILL IT REPORT FROM THE MOST EXCLUSIVE PARTIES THAT WE WERE INVITED TO AND YOU WEREN'T. IT WON'T HELP YOU FIND YOUR WAY AROUND THE NEW PHANTASMAGORICAL TRENDS, NOR DOES IT AIM TO SOLVE YOUR FURNISHING PROBLEMS.

THE OFFICIAL POINT OF VIEW IS A VOICE WHICH AIMS TO TELL THE STORY OF MANY VOICES, WITHOUT ANY DOUBLING UP OR OVERLAPPING.

THE OFFICIAL POINT OF VIEW IS AN EYE WHICH HAS BEEN AROUND AND TAKEN A LOOK AND IS NOW HERE TO BE SEEN IN TURN.

DEDICATED TO ALL THOSE WHO WANT TO VIEW AND TO RE-VIEW WITHOUT HAVING TO HEAR WHISPERED JUDGEMENTS OR PREJUDICES.

THE OFFICIAL POINT OF VIEW IS AN INDEPENDENT PUBLISHING PROJECT DESIGNED AND BROUGHT TO YOU BY GIULIA BER TACCHINI, PAOLO CALCAGNI, LUCIO LUZO LAZZARA, RICCARDO RINETTI.

TIMETABLE.

THE OFFICIAL POINT OF VIEW

specials.

GL

WAR 304
336 HOTEL DROOG
SWEET HOME 330
BATH ANIMALS 374
CATALOGUES 400
402 ESTERNI
RUSSIAN ROULETTE 416
POLITICS 446
ANGELS 490
CREDITS 502
THE OFFICIAL POINT OF VIEW
007

an orange.

BRUNO MUNARI

"THIS OBJECT CONSISTS OF A SERIES OF MODULAR, THREE-DIMENSIONAL SEGMENTS GROUPED VERTICALLY AROUND A CENTRAL AXIS. THE STRAIGHT SIDE OF EACH SEGMENT RESTS ON THAT AXIS, WHILE THE CURVED SIDE IS TO THE EXTERIOR. THE FINISHED OBJECT IS SPHERICAL. THE SEGMENTS COME WRAPPED IN A HIGHLY-DISTINCTIVE PACKAGE, BOTH IN TERMS OF MATERIAL AND COLOUR. THIS PACKAGING HAS AN OUTER COATING THAT AFFORDS EFFECTIVE PROTECTION FROM THE ELEMENTS.

THE HARAHNESS OF THIS OUTER SKIN IS MITIGATED AND THE DELICATE CONTENTS ARE PROTECTED BY THE APPLICATION OF A SOFT LINING TO THE INSIDE.

THE MATERIAL IS ALL OF THE SAME TYPE, BUT VARIES ACCORDING TO THE PURPOSE. OPENING THE PACKAGE IS VERY SIMPLE. WRITTEN INSTRUCTIONS WOULD BE QUITE SUPERFLUOUS. THE LINING LAYER ALSO SERVES TO CREATE A BUFFER ZONE BETWEEN THE OUTSIDE SURFACE AND THE CONTAINERS. THIS ENSURES THAT IF ONE EXERTS A LITTLE TOO MUCH PRESSURE WHEN PIERCING THE SKIN - NOT DIFFICULT SINCE ONE HAS NO IDEA HOW THICK IT ACTUALLY IS - ONE DOES NOT RISK DAMAGING ANY OF THE CONTAINERS WHITIN.

EACH OF THE CONTAINERS IS FORMED OF A PLASTIC FILM THAT IS JUST LARGE ENOUGH TO HOLD THE JUICE, WHILE OF COURSE, BEING EASY TO HANDLE. ALTHOUGH THE SEGMENTS ARE HELD TOGETHER BY AN ADHESIVE, THIS IS WEAK AND EASILY GIVES WAY TO ALLOW THE SEGMENTS TO SPLIT APART.

AS USED TODAY, THE PACKAGING IS NON-RETURNABLE, AND CAN BE THROWN AWAY. SOMETHING DESERVES TO BE SAID HERE ON THE FORM OF THE SEGMENTS. EACH IS IN THE EXACT SHAPE OF THE HUMAN MOUTH.

THUS, ONCE REMOVED FROM ITS PACKAGING, A SEGMENT CAN BE PLACED BETWEEN THE TEETH. BY BITING DOWN GENTLY, ONE BREAKS THE OUTER WRAPPING AND CAN DRINK THE JUICE. SPEAKING OF THIS, SO-CALLED MANDARIN ORANGES MIGHT BE CONSIDERED A LINE EXTENSION, WHOSE SMALLER SEGMENTS MAKE THEM PARTICULARLY SUITABLE FOR CHILDREN. (THESE DAYS, THE ADVENT OF JUICERS MEANS THAT CONFUSION REIGNS, AND ADULTS EAT WHAT MIGHT BE CALLED CHILDREN'S FOOD AND VICE VERSA.)

OVER AND ABOVE THE JUICE, THE SEGMENTS USUALLY CONTAIN A SMALL SEED FROM THE SAME TREE. THIS IS A TOKEN GIFT FROM THE MANUFACTURER TO THE CONSUMER WHO MAY JUST WISH TO GO INTO PRODUCTION OF THESE OBJECTS ON A PERSONAL BASIS.

PLEASE NOTE THE ECONOMIC ALTRUISM OF A SUCH AN IDEA, AND THE

PSYCHOLOGICAL BOND THAT IS THUS ENGENDERED BETWEEN CONSUMER AND PRODUCER. HARDLY ANYONE IS GOING TO PLANT THE SEEDS, BUT THIS SELFLESS MOVE, AND THE FACT THAT ONE COULD DO IT IF ONE WANTED TO, FREES ONE FROM FEELING BEHOLDEN IN ANY WAY TO THE PRODUCER, WHILST ESTABLISHING A RELATIONSHIP OF TRUST. A THOUGHTFUL AND GRACIOUS GESTURE, WHICH CERTAINLY CANNOT BE COMPARED TO THAT OF THOSE PRODUCERS WHO OFFER A COW TO ANYONE WHO BUYS 250 GRAMS OF CHEESE.

AN ORANGE, THEREFORE, IS ALMOST PERFECT. FORM, FUNCTION, AND CONSUMPTION COME TOGETHER. EVEN THE COLOUR IS EXACTLY RIGHT. IN BLUE, IT WOULD BE ABSOLUTELY WRONG. THIS IS A TYPICAL OF AN OBJECT THAT IS MASS-PRODUCED ON AN INTERNATIONAL LEVEL. THE ABSENCE OF ANY SYMBOLIC OR EXPRESSIVE ELEMENT INFORMED BY STYLE FADS OR ESTHETIQUE INDUSTRIELLE, DEMONSTRATE A DESIGN CONSCIOUSNESS THA IS EXTREMELY HARD TO FIND IN THE AVERAGE DESIGNER.

THE ONLY CONCESSION TO DECORATION IS WHAT WE MIGHT CALL THE "ORANGE-PEEL" TEXTURING EFFECT. PERHAPS THIS WAS DONE TO CALL ATTENTION TO THE PULP WITHIN THE SEGMENT-SHAPED CONTAINERS. THAT SAID, SUCH A LITTLE DECORATIVE TOUCH, JUSTIFIED AS IT IS IN THIS CASE, IS MORE THAN ACCEPTABLE".

(COURTESY OF COSMIT 1999; CORRADINI EDITORE 1998)

THE OFFICIAL POINT OF VIEW

010

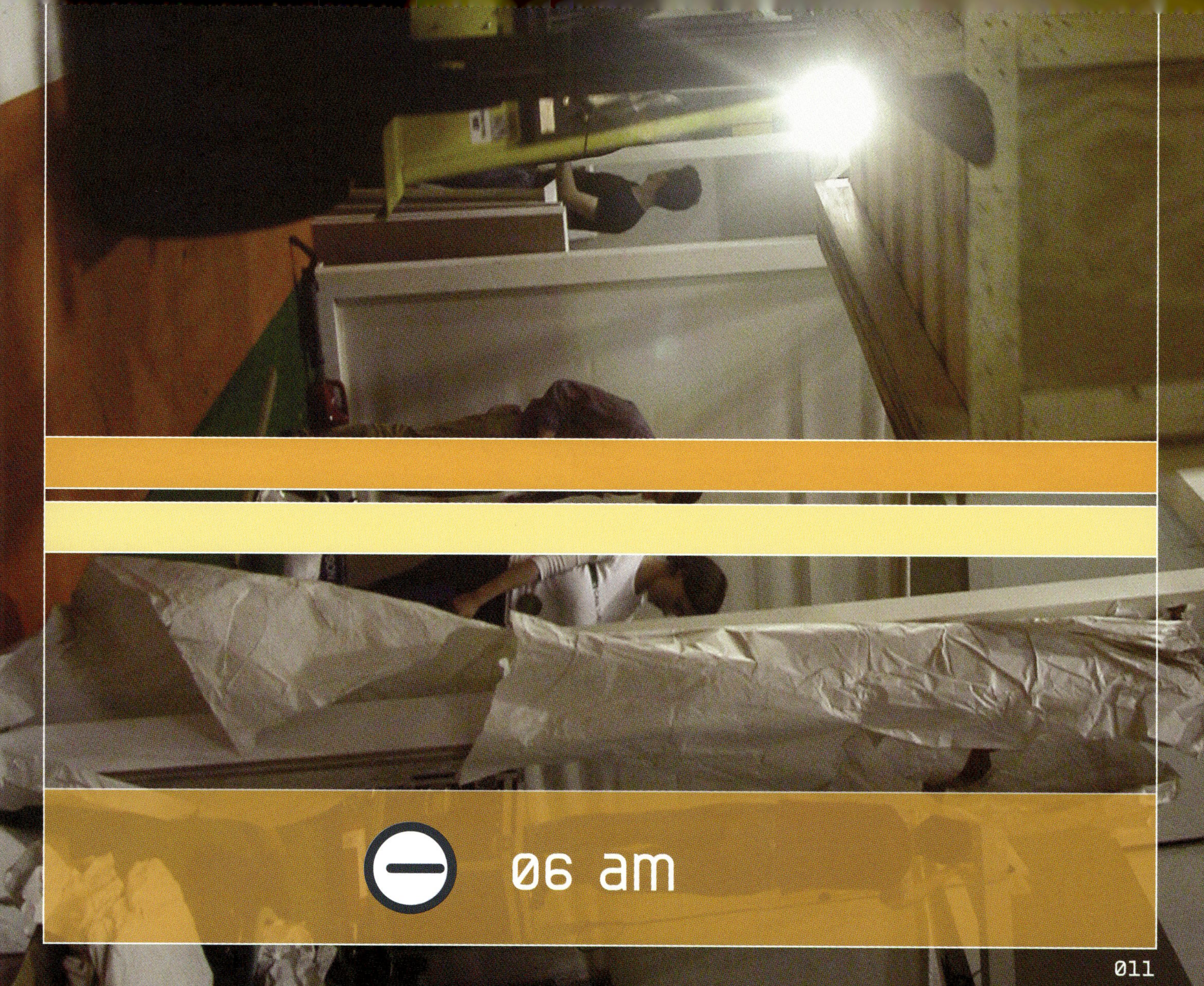

06 am

06 am

013
"ITALY IS INCREASINGLY THE CENTRE OF GRAVITY NOT ONLY FOR BUYING AND SELLING FURNITURE, BUT ALSO FOR PRODUCING IT"
MANLIO ARMELLINI - CEO COSMIT
COSMIT SPA
THE OFFICIAL POINT OF VIEW

014
06 am

FRAGILE
B & B
SALONE DEL MOBILE
EDIZIONE 2002
MILANO
DESCRIZIONE DEL MATERIALE:

取扱注意
FUJIMA
FORM ASH
SHOP
TOKYO
2-5-16,JINGUMAE,SHIBUYA
TEL:03-5775-6412 FAX
E-mail:k-emura@form
OSAKA
2-11-18,KITAHORIE,NISHI-KU
TEL:06-6578-7881 FAX
ORANGE POINT
203,3-4-4,MINAMI-AOYA
TOKYO,JAPAN
TEL:03-5413-6563 FAX
THE OFFICIAL POINT OF VIEW

06 am

e; qualunque forma è

nenti storici che si possono

nell'oggetto lì esiste "

Ettore Sottsass

Satellite 2002

THE OFFICIAL POINT OF VIEW

NORWAY SAYS

TUTTI DESIGNERS

norway says
27
sataco takashi
satellite
A.K.I.S.
THE OFFICIAL POINT OF VIEW

07 am BATHROOM

024
BATHROOM
A BEAUTIFUL OBJECT
IS SIMPLY DESIGNED

GIULIANA CIVELLO FOR SURFACE-TAG TEAM 2002
"MOP CHAIR"

FERNANDO E HUMBERTO CAMPANA FOR EDRA
"SUSHI" SOFA

THE OFFICIAL POINT OF VIEW

250
BATHROOM

027
NORIKO YASUDA FOR HOTEL DROOG
"FOOTREST"
THE OFFICIAL POINT OF VIEW

cappellini

AATTAK

GRUPPO AUREA

THE OFFICIAL POINT OF VIEW

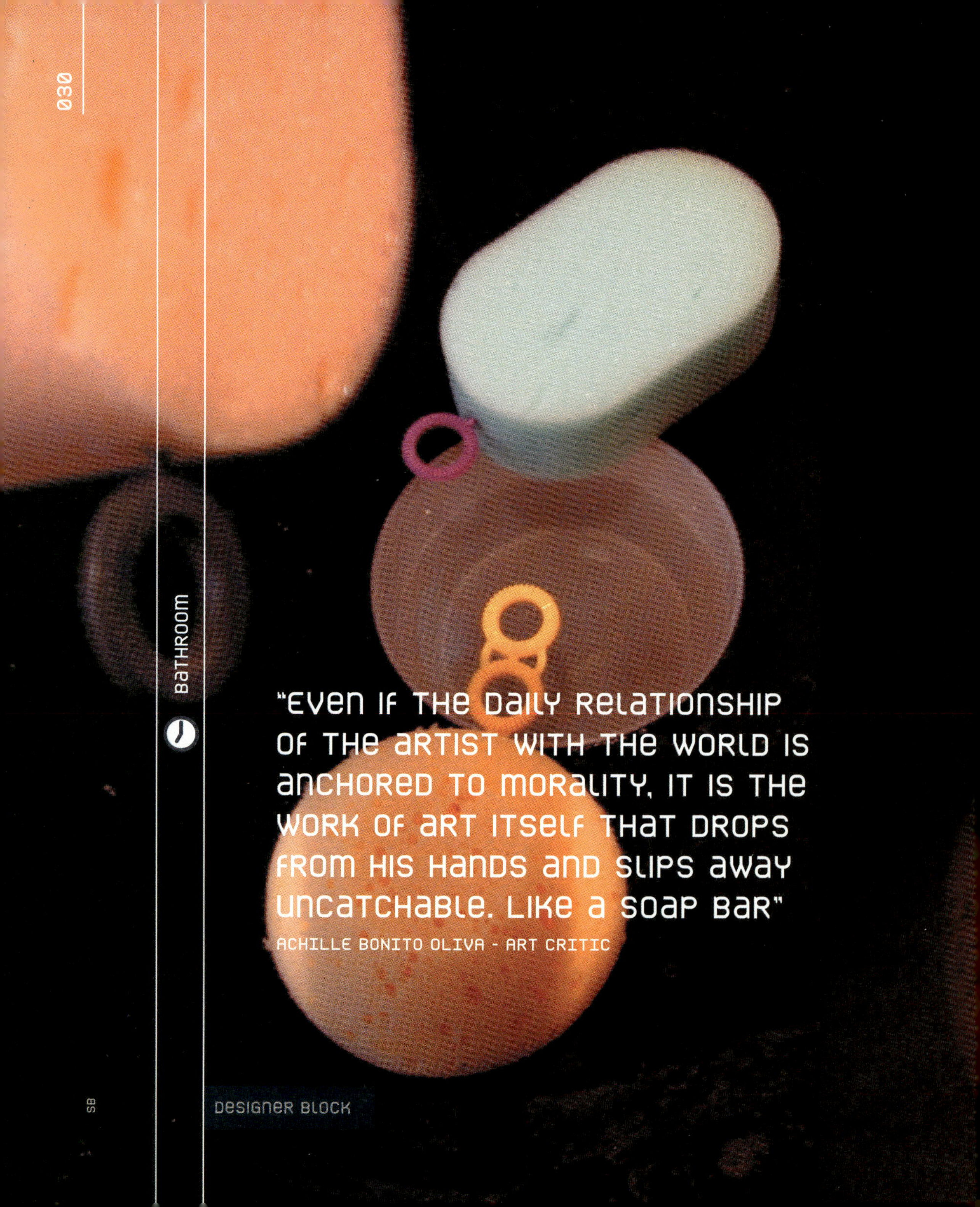

"Even if the daily relationship of the artist with the world is anchored to morality, it is the work of art itself that drops from his hands and slips away uncatchable. Like a soap bar"

ACHILLE BONITO OLIVA - ART CRITIC

031
ALESSI
SB
SB
SB
ADI
THE OFFICIAL POINT OF VIEW

BATHROOM

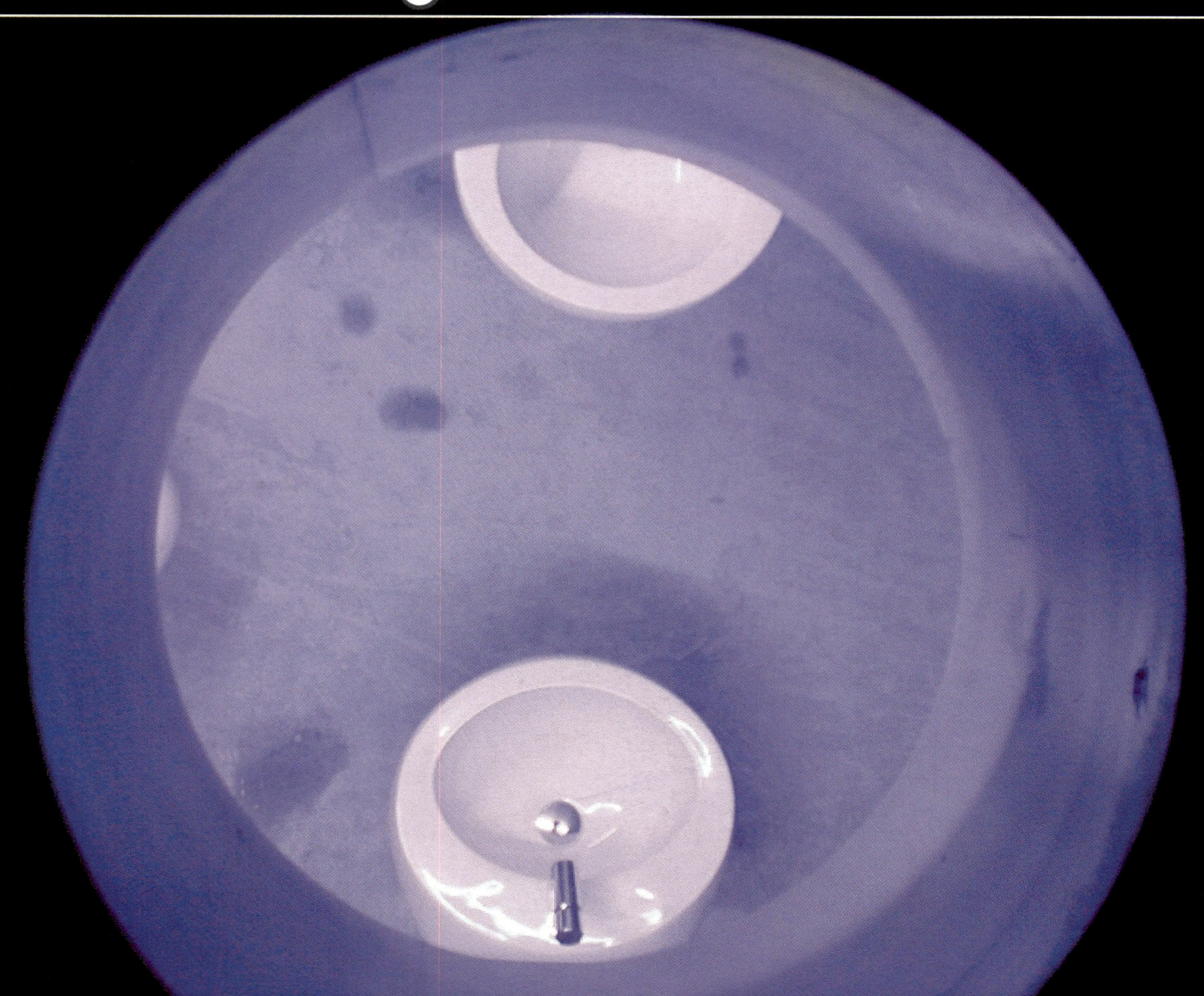

STEFANO GIOVANNONI FOR ALESSI

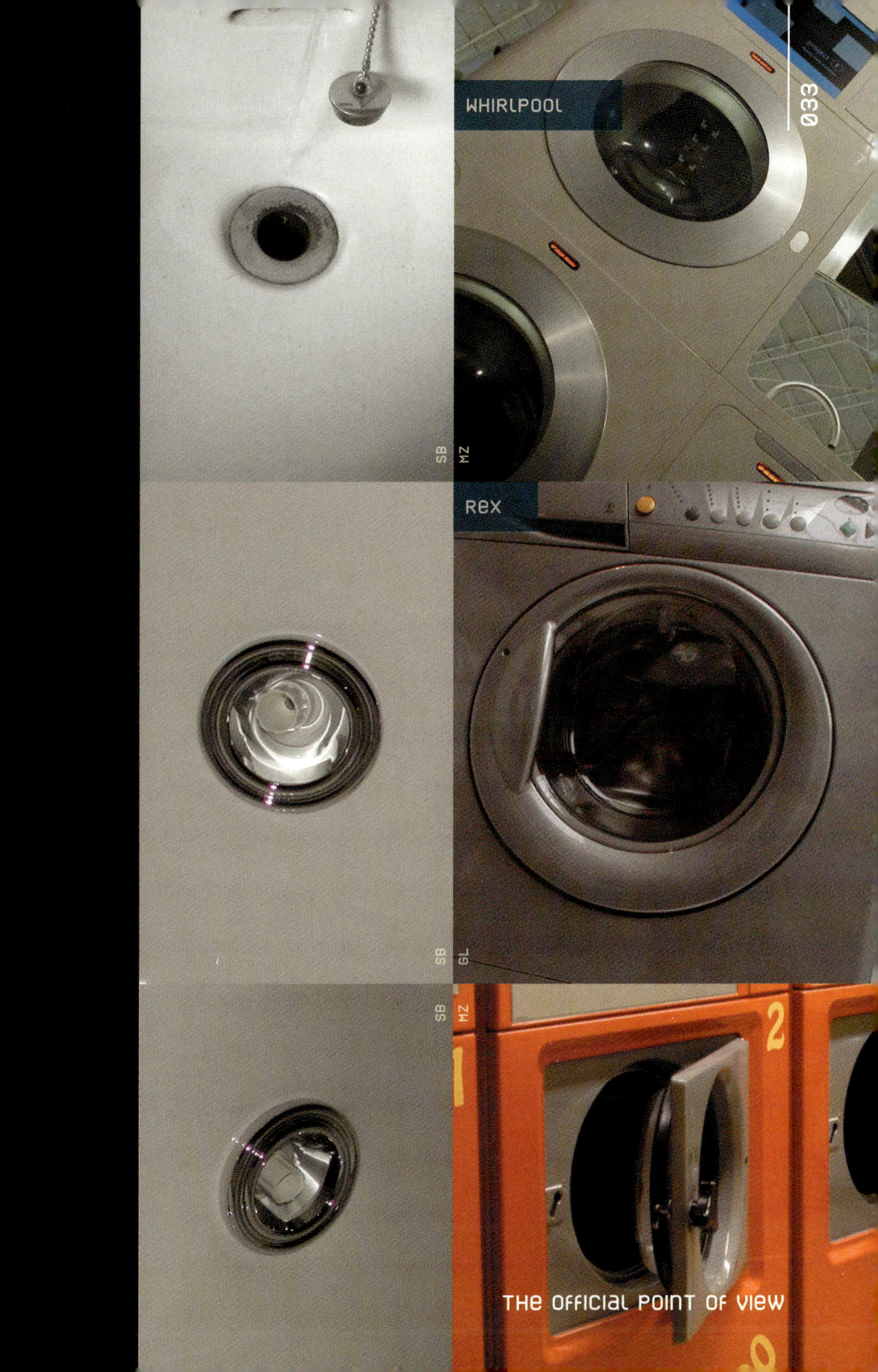
WHIRLPOOL
033
SB MZ
Rex
SB GL
SB MZ
1
2
THE OFFICIAL POINT OF VIEW

034
BATHROOM
innovating form is
an urgency of man

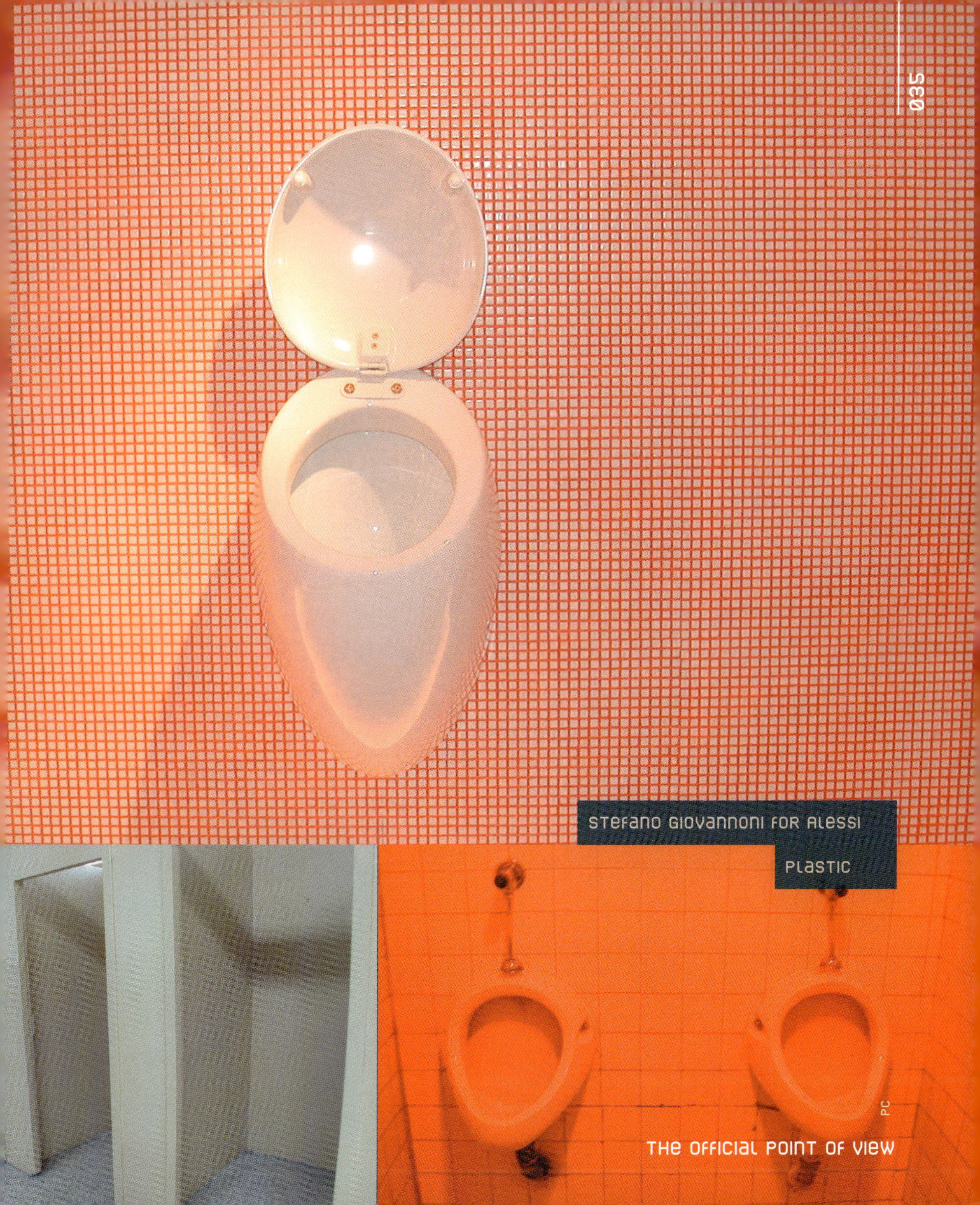
STEFANO GIOVANNONI FOR ALESSI
PLASTIC
PC
THE OFFICIAL POINT OF VIEW

036
ARTEMIDE
"PIPE"
BATHROOM

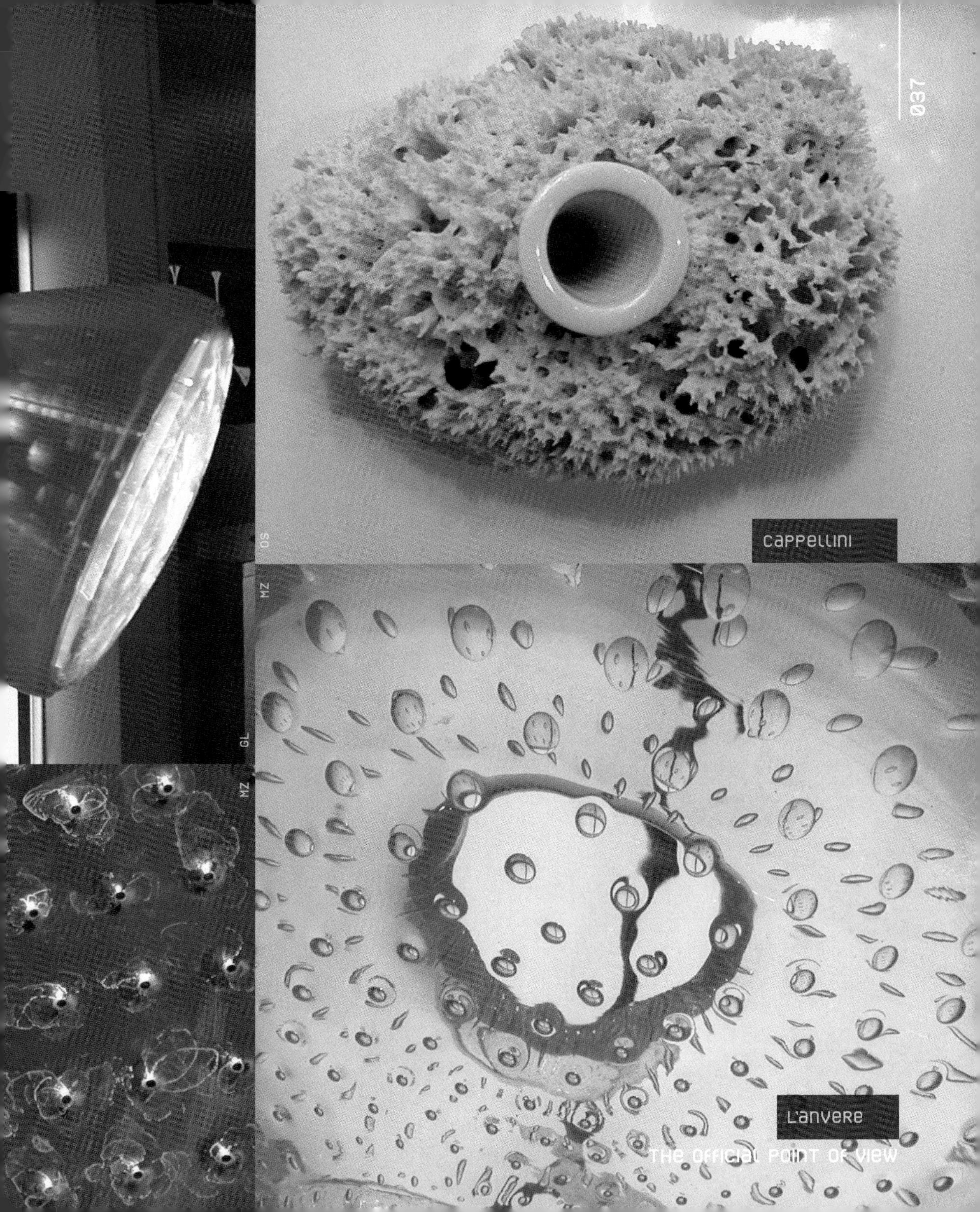

037
CAPPELLINI
L'ANVERE
THE OFFICIAL POINT OF VIEW

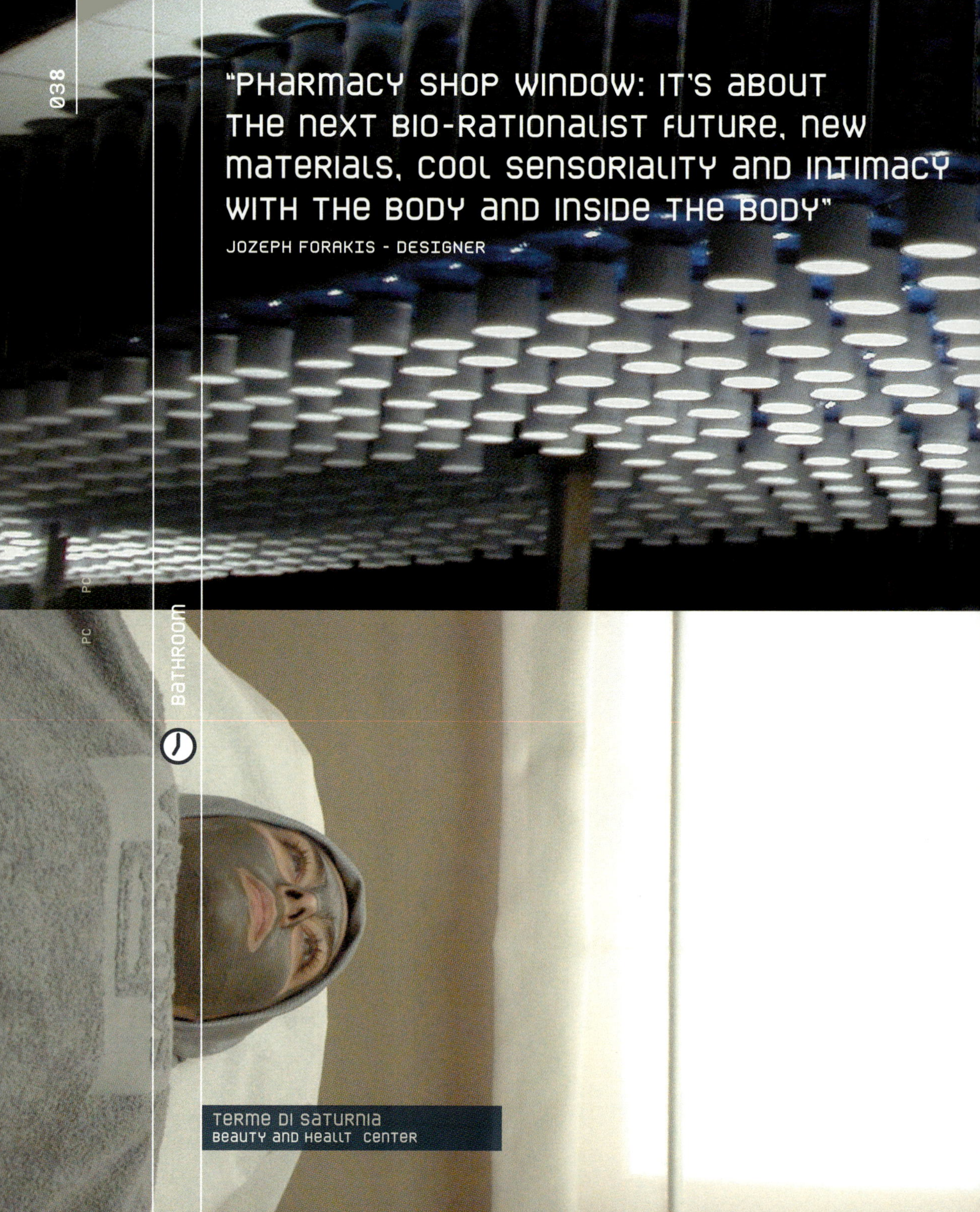

"PHARMACY SHOP WINDOW: IT'S ABOUT THE NEXT BIO-RATIONALIST FUTURE, NEW MATERIALS, COOL SENSORIALITY AND INTIMACY WITH THE BODY AND INSIDE THE BODY"

JOZEPH FORAKIS - DESIGNER

TERME DI SATURNIA
BEAUTY AND HEALLT CENTER

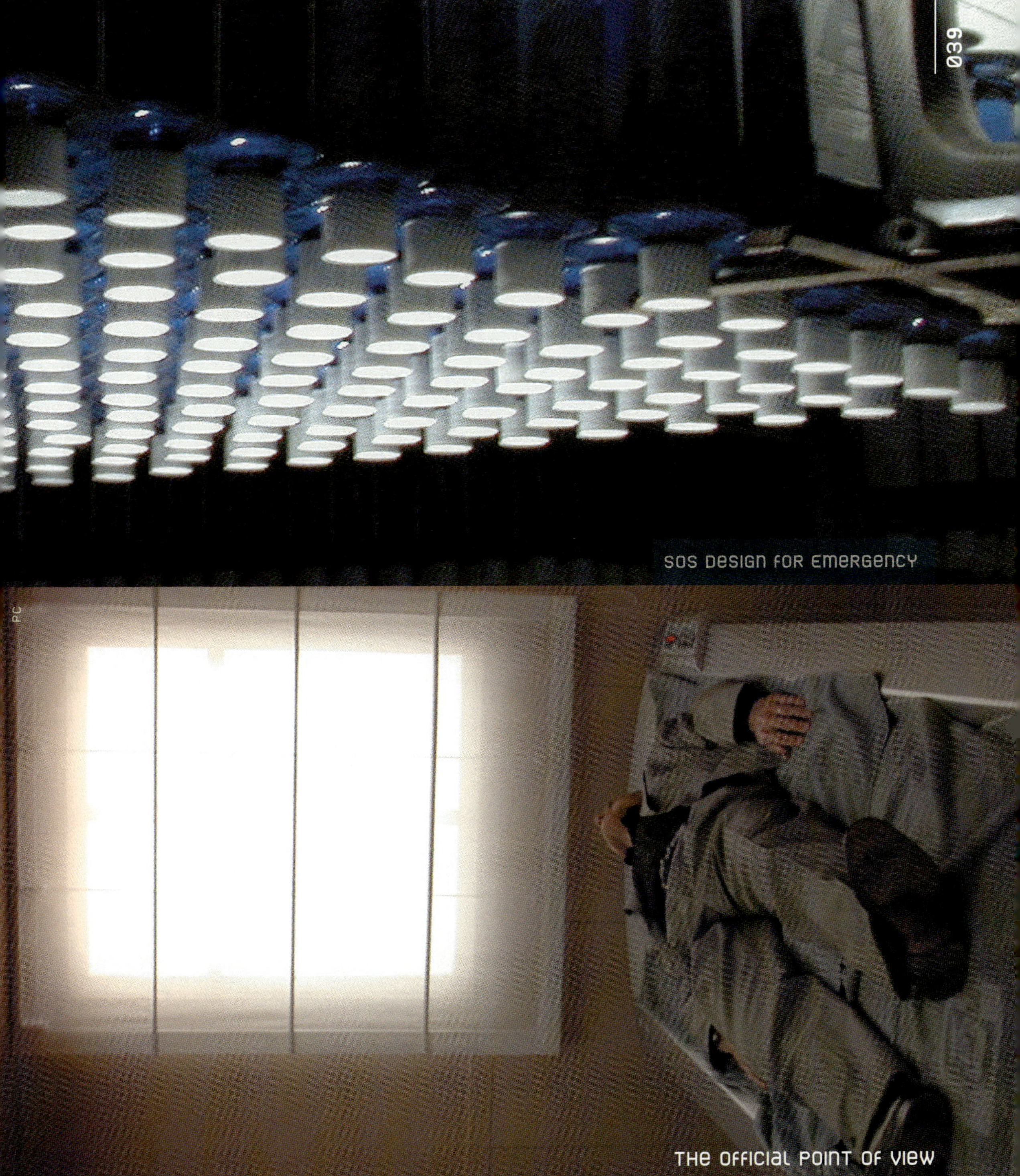
039
SOS DESIGN FOR EMERGENCY
PC
THE OFFICIAL POINT OF VIEW

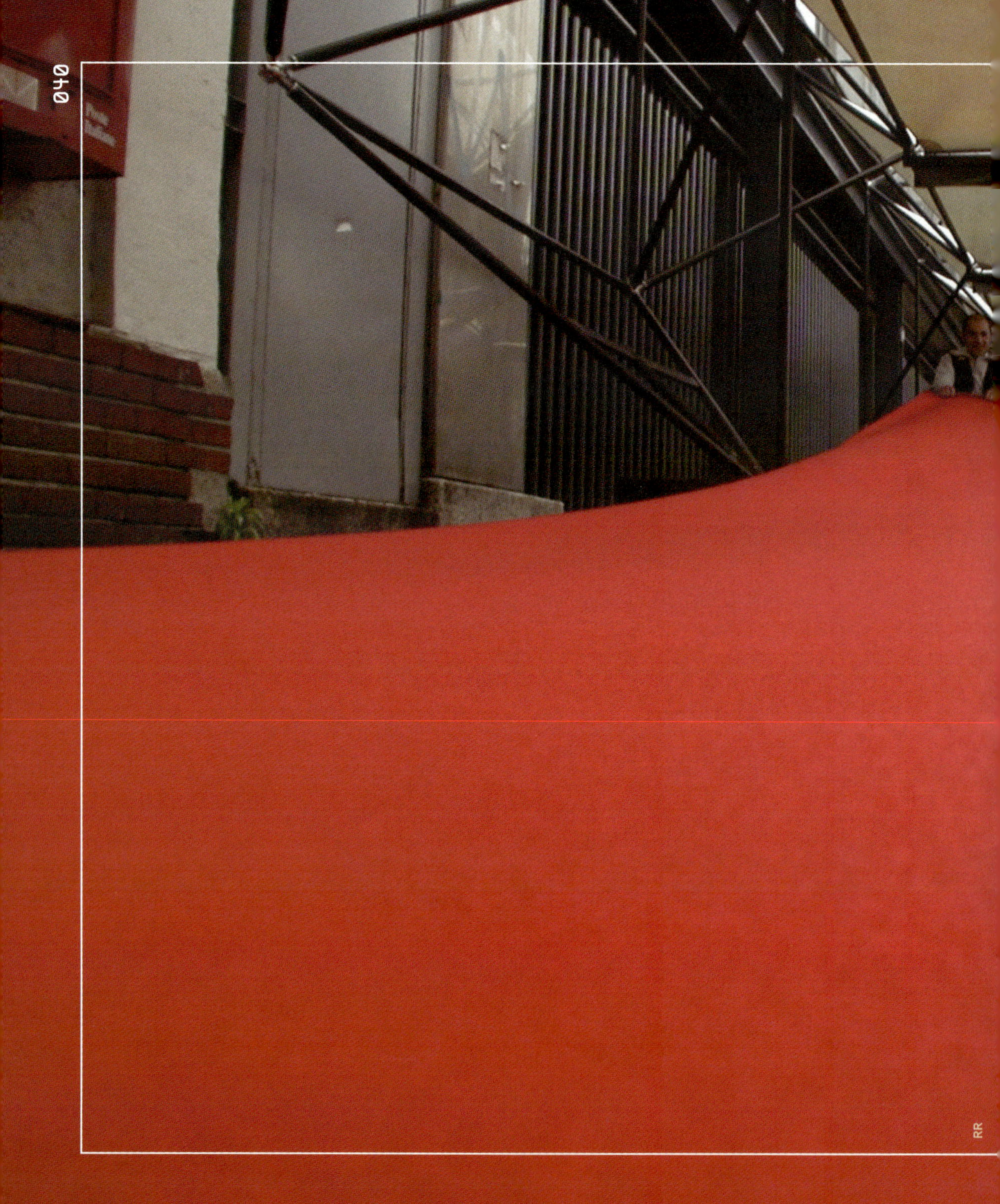

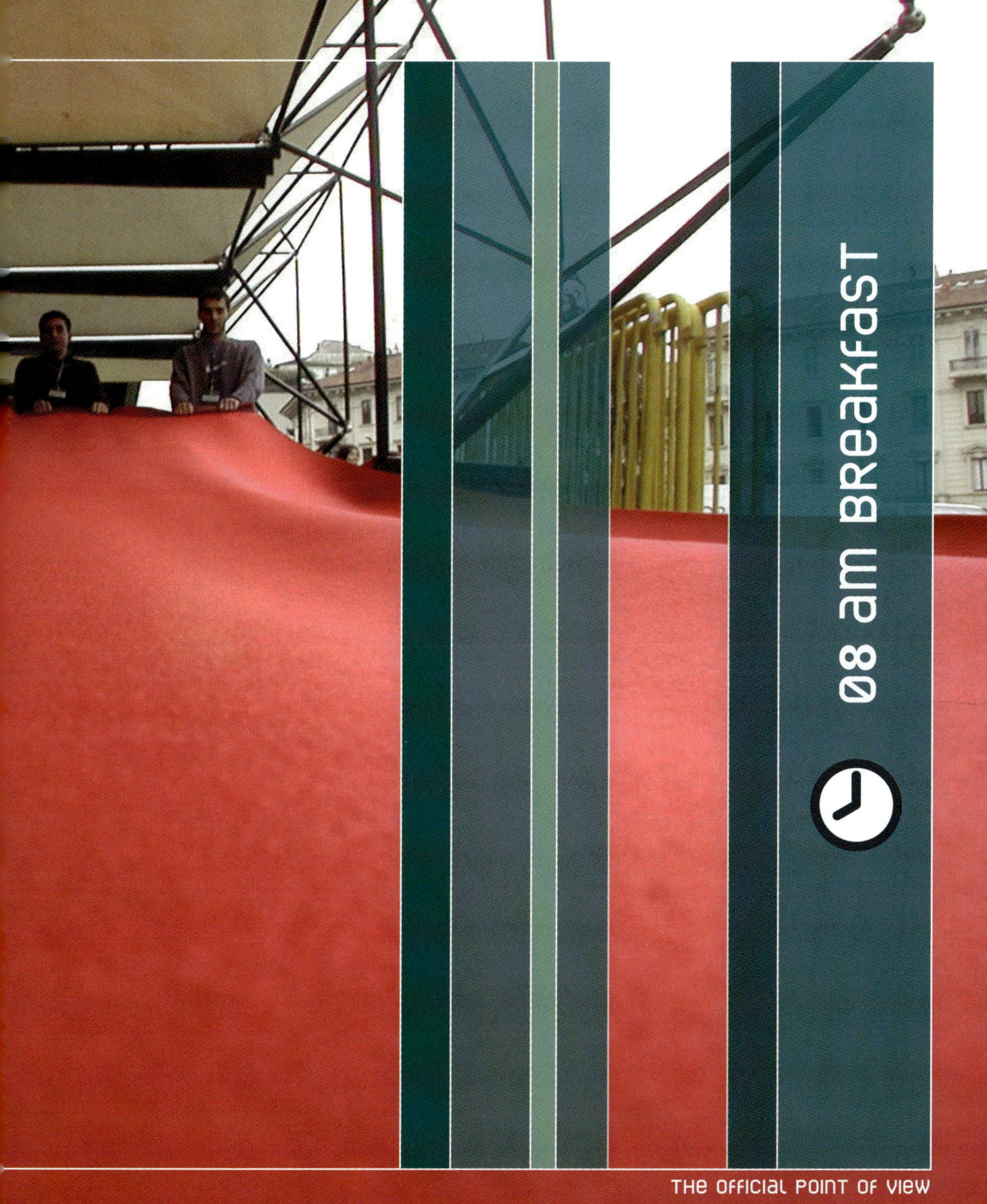

08 am BREAKFAST
THE OFFICIAL POINT OF VIEW

HOW ARE YOU TODAY?
BREAKFAST
BOFFI
GL
GL
LZ
GL
GL

MILANO SUBWAY
THE OFFICIAL POINT OF VIEW

MR.BROWN
KAFFEE
INHALT 250ml
MR.BROWN
BREAKFAST
Qualità
Qualità
Qualità
Qualità

045
BIALETTI
BIALETTI
ADI
ARTENDGALLERY
THE OFFICIAL POINT OF VIEW

046
BREAKFAST
cafe senza

illy

MZ
AV
THE OFFICIAL POINT OF VIEW

BREAKFAST

"DOES THE CREATION OF A DESIGNER
RESEMBLE ITS MASTER
AS IS THE CASE FOR DOGS?
NO, IT VERY OFTEN RESEMBLES
THE PERSON WHO COMMISSIONED IT"

MATTIA FRIGNANI FOR WUNDERKAMMER STUDIO

MZ
SB
PC

PANDORA
THE OFFICIAL POINT OF VIEW

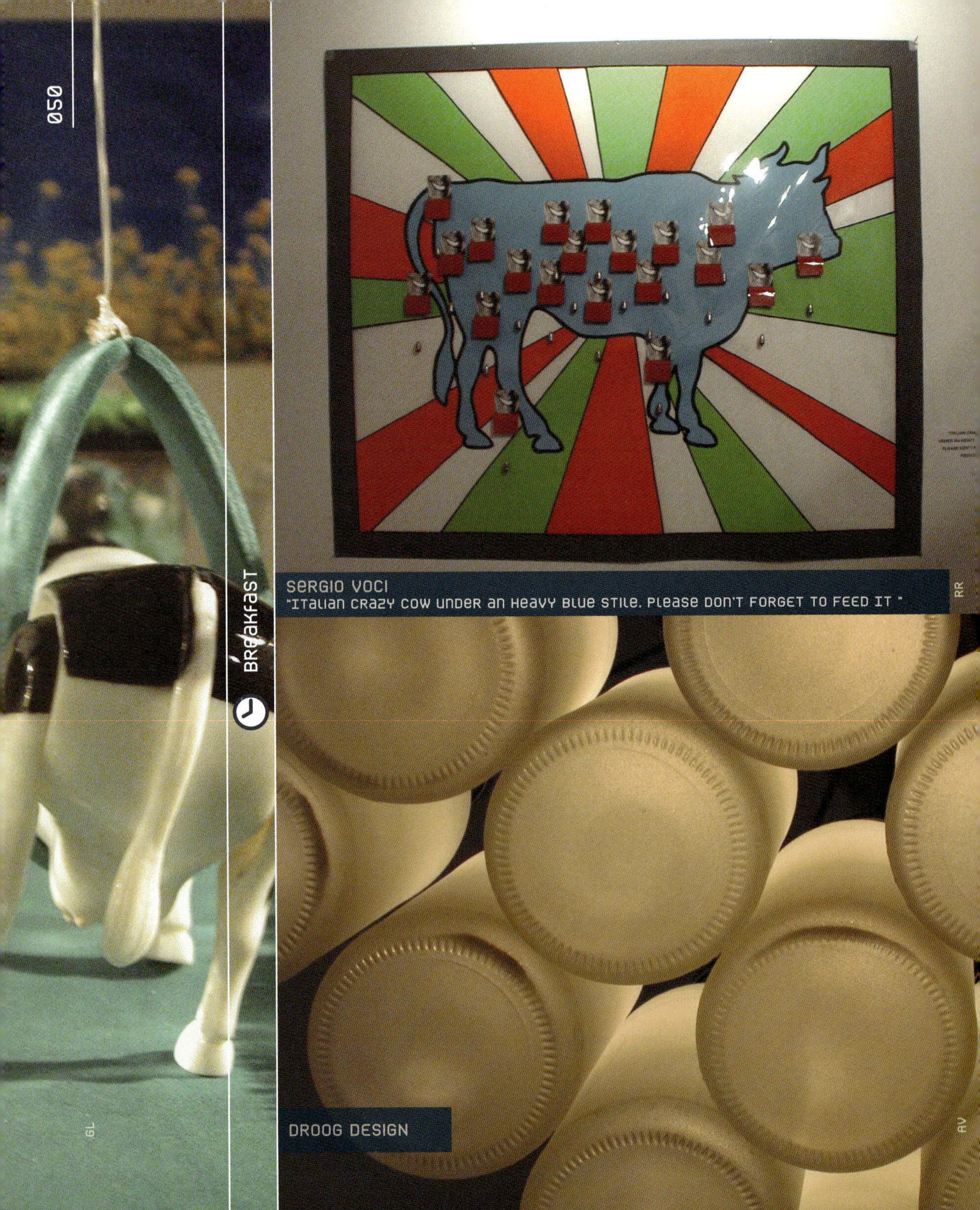
SERGIO VOCI
"Italian crazy cow under an heavy blue stile. Please don't forget to feed it "
RR
GL
DROOG DESIGN
AV

PC
SHIT DESIGN
VIA
PC
THE OFFICIAL POINT OF VIEW

052
BRAZIL FAZ DESIGN
AV
SB
AV
SB
BREAKFAST
C.C.S.
RECAPITO MILANESE

Latte
parzialmente scremato
C.C.S.
VITRA DESIGN MUSEUM
SCULPTURAL DESIGN
AV
RR

MATTEO THUN

BREAKFAST
BAUBAU'S

055
AV RR
SHIT DESIGN
FELICE ROSSI
GRAND HOTEL SALONE
THE OFFICIAL POINT OF VIEW

056
DESIGNERSBLOCK
BREAKFAST
C.C.S.
SB
AV

057
ANTONIO CITTERIO FOR MAXALTO
ARK TECHNOLOGIES
THE OFFICIAL POINT OF VIEW

Brea
GABRIELE DE VECCHI
INGO MAURER INSTALLATION

WUNDERKAMMER STUDIO

THE OFFICIAL POINT OF VIEW

060
BREAKFAST
GAETANO PESCE
ZERODISEGNO

JACOPO FOGGINI
THE OFFICIAL POINT OF VIEW

breakfast
SB
RECAPITO MILANESE
SB

PHILIPPE STARCK FOR KARTELL
TM
THE OFFICIAL POINT OF VIEW

064
TM
PC
BREAKFAST
"THERE ARE NO MIRACLES
IN THE WORLD OF DESIGN, OTHERWISE
STARK'S CITRUS SQUEEZER
WOULD WORK"
FILIPPO MAZZARELLA - JOURNALIST AND FILM CRITIC
TM
CAMBIOFACCIA

065
JOHANNA GRAWUNDER
"PILLOW TALK"
THE OFFICIAL POINT OF VIEW

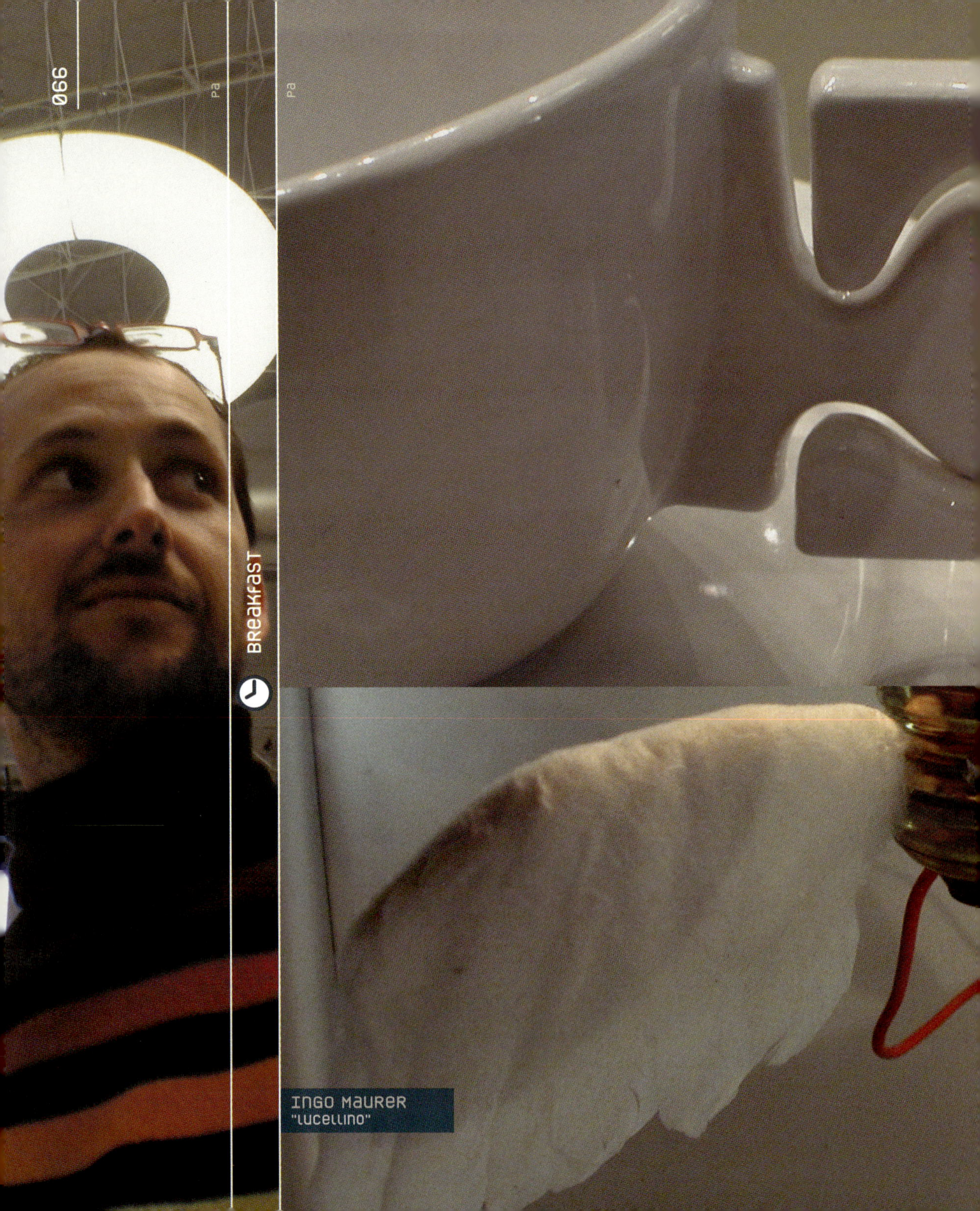

Pa
Pa
BREAKFAST
INGO MAURER
"lucellino"

067
antoine fenoglio & frédéric lecourt
sismo design
the official point of view

098

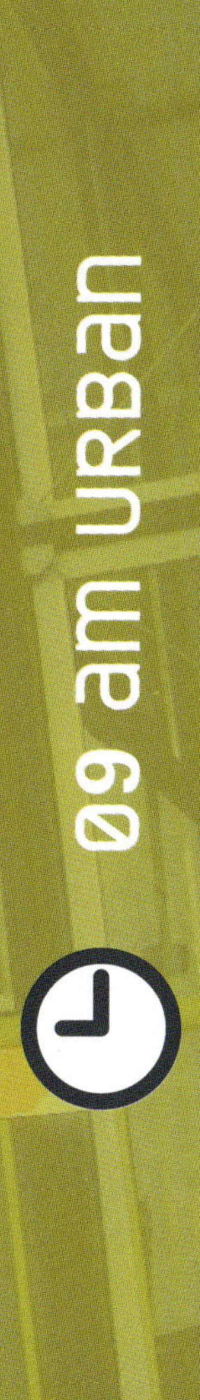

09 am URBan

URBAN
"THE FURNITURE FAIR PROVES THAT MILAN
IS A CITY WHERE PARALLEL SOCIETIES THAT
DO NOT INTERMINGLE EXIST - IF YOU LIVE
OUTSIDE OF THE WORLD OF DESIGN YOU
DON'T REALLY REALISE THAT SOMETHING IS
HAPPENING - APART FROM THE FACT THAT IT
TAKES YOU NEARLY TWICE AS LONG TO GET
TO THE OFFICE IN THE MORNING"
VALENTINA SACHERO - ENGINEER

THE OFFICIAL POINT OF VIEW

URBan

DILMOS

Pa

DILMOS
DILMOS
THE OFFICIAL POINT OF VIEW

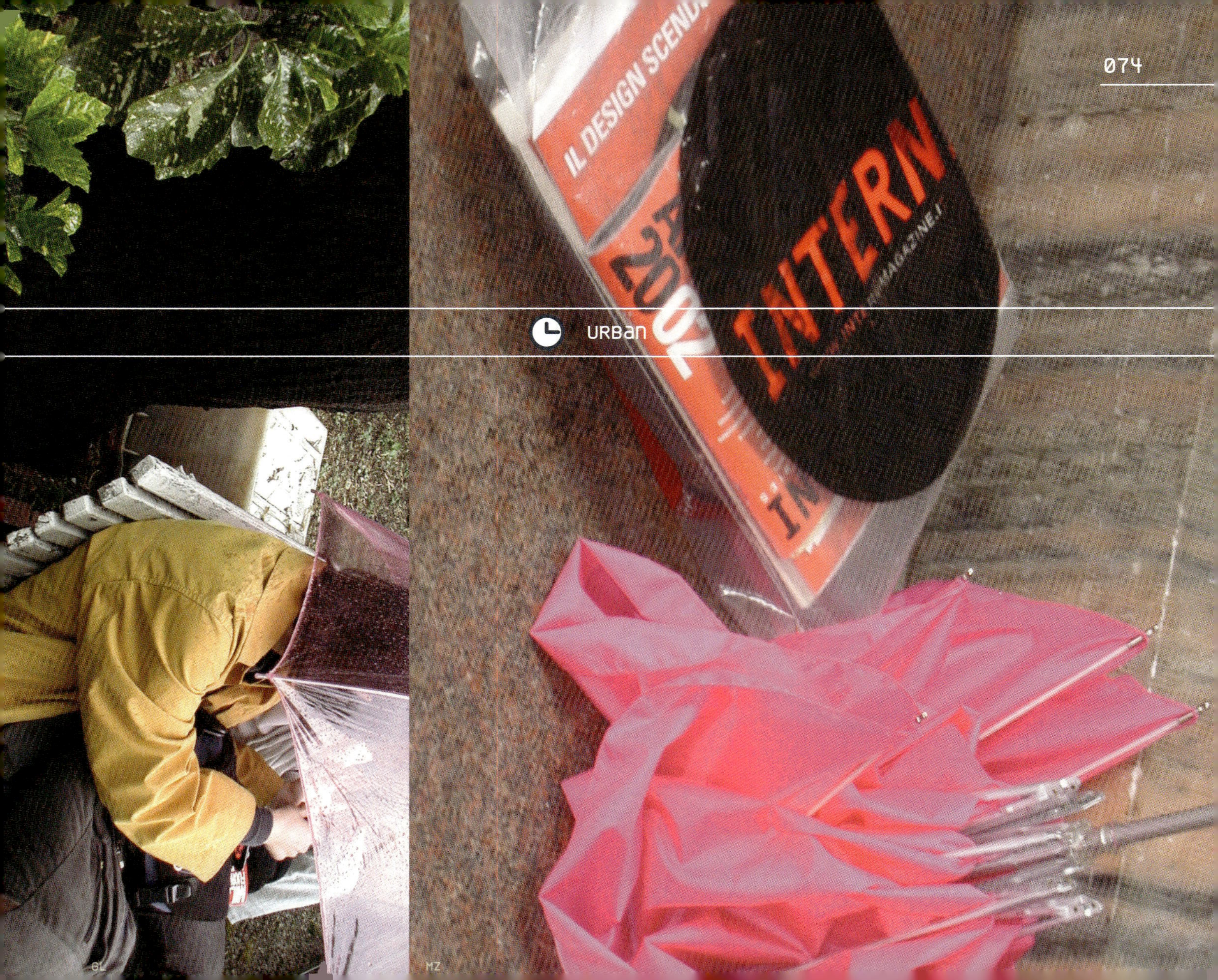
IL DESIGN SCEND
INTERN
2002
URBAN
MZ

TSINGTAO BEER
THE OFFICIAL POINT OF VIEW

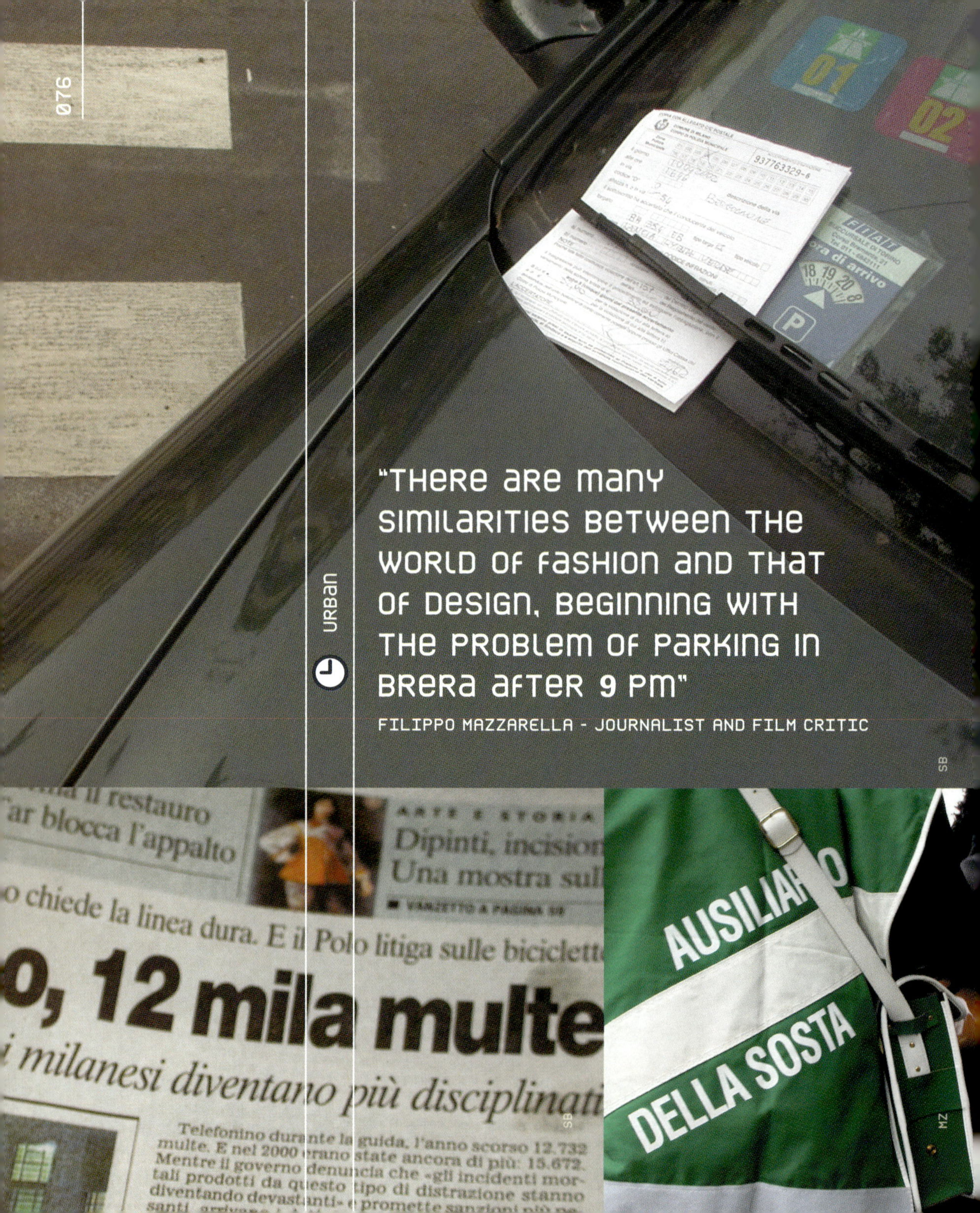

URBAN
"THERE ARE MANY SIMILARITIES BETWEEN THE WORLD OF FASHION AND THAT OF DESIGN, BEGINNING WITH THE PROBLEM OF PARKING IN BRERA AFTER 9 PM"
FILIPPO MAZZARELLA - JOURNALIST AND FILM CRITIC
SB
il restauro
ar blocca l'appalto
ARTE E STORIA
Dipinti, incision
Una mostra sull
o chiede la linea dura. E il Polo litiga sulle biciclett
O, 12 mila multe
i milanesi diventano più disciplinat
Telefonino durante la guida, l'anno scorso 12.732
multe. E nel 2000 erano state ancora di più: 15.672.
Mentre il governo denuncia che «gli incidenti mor-
tali prodotti da questo tipo di distrazione stanno
diventando devastanti» e promette sanzioni più ra
SB
AUSILIARIO
DELLA SOSTA
MZ

MZ
RR
SB
DIVIETO
SOSTA
DAL 7 APRILE
AL 9 APRILE
937765327-1
THE OFFICIAL POINT OF VIEW

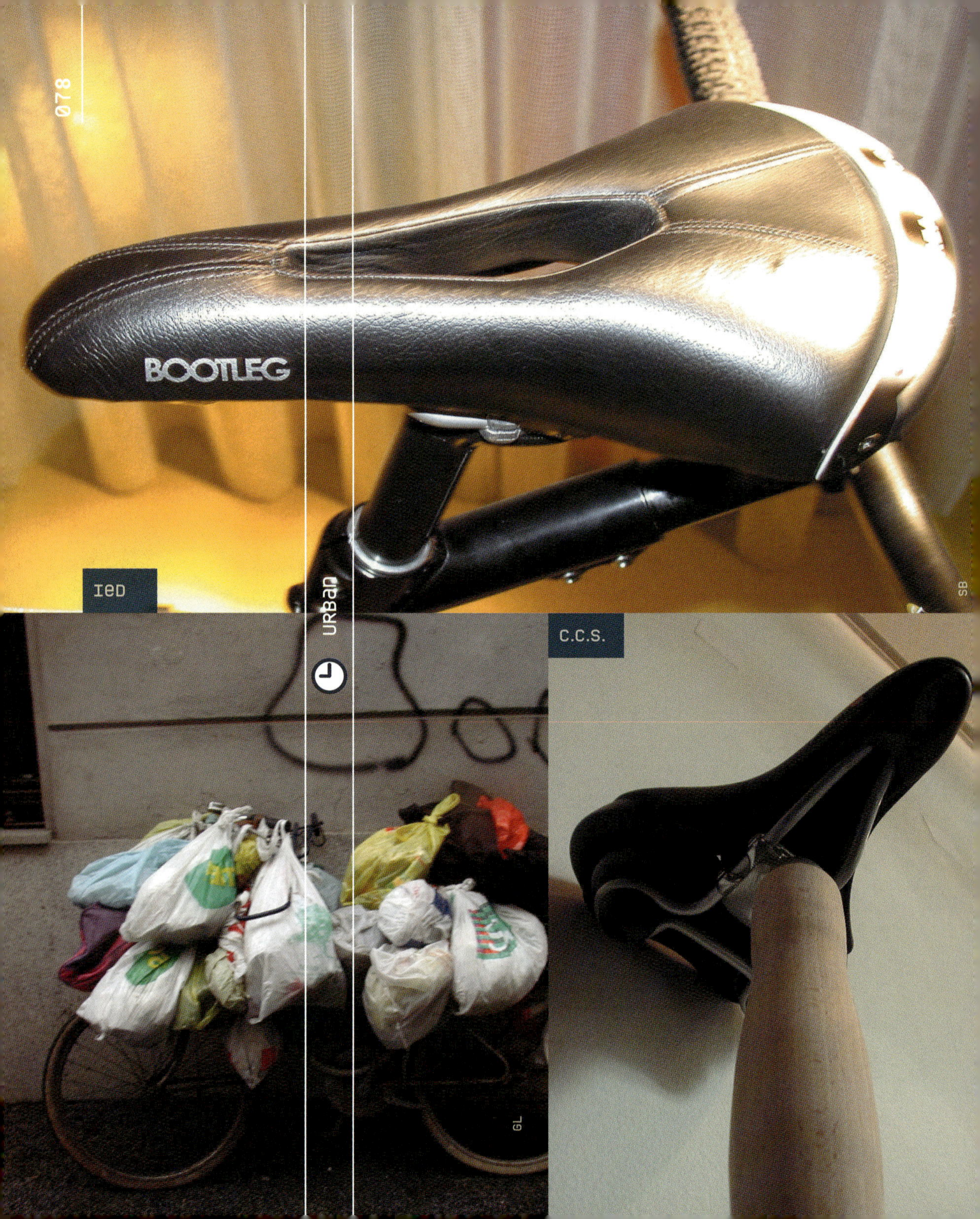
078
BOOTLEG
IED
URBAN
C.C.S.
SB
GL

MZ

"DESIGN COULD BE A WAY OF ADAPTING THE ENVIRONMENT IN WHICH WE LIVE ACCORDING TO AESTHETIC AND PRACTICAL CRITERIA"
ALBERTO MORELLI - MUSICIAN

PC

THE OFFICIAL POINT OF VIEW

moooi weer
urban

moooi weer
moooi weer
081
moooi weer
THE OFFICIAL POINT OF VIEW

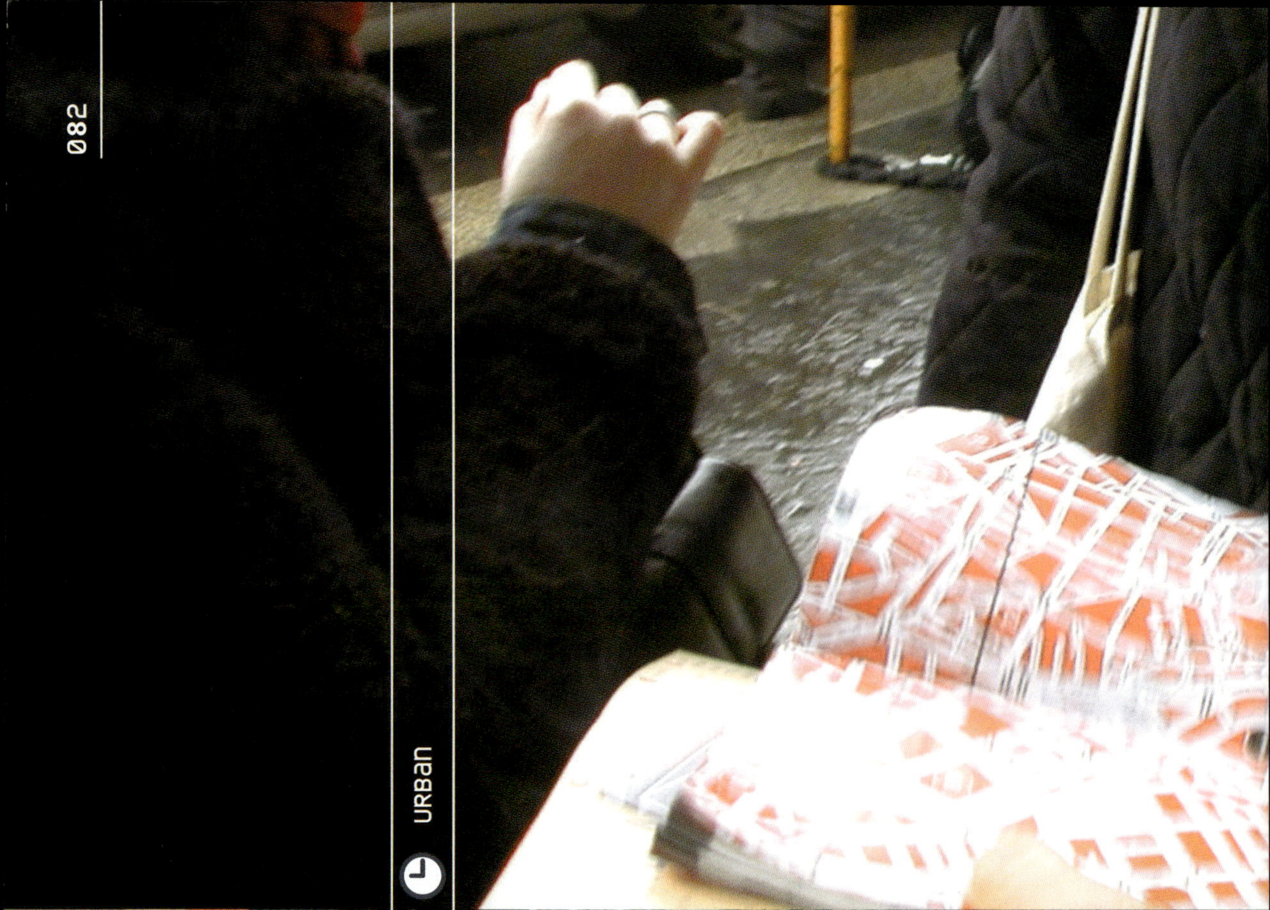

NAVETTA
SHUTTLE
DESIGNCONNECTION2002
SUPERSTUDIO PIÙ'
RECAPITO
SPAZI & SERVIZI PER LE AZIENDE
MILANESE
RR

GL

ZONA
TORTONA
MILANO E DESIGN
10-15
ZONA

LEGGO
THE OFFICIAL POINT OF VIEW

URBAN

"IN MY HOUSE THE WALLS ARE COMPLETELY WHITE. I HAVE NO WORKS OF ART ON THEM BECAUSE I'M LIKE A SURGEON WHO, ON ARRIVING BACK HOME, DOESN'T WANT TO SEE BLOOD ON HIS WALLS"

ACHILLE BONITO OLIVA - ART CRITIC

THE OFFICIAL POINT OF VIEW

INTERNI D'AUTORE IN PIAZZA

An exhibition of temporary architecture, built
around the city, by seven internationally
renowned architects invited to design their ideas
of living space.
Alessandro & Francesco Mendini, Peter Eisenman,
Massimiliano & Doriana Fuksas, Astrid Klein &
Mark Dytham, Leon Krier, Bernard Tschumi,
Oscar Tusquets Blanca, active in the fields of
architecture, design and urban and territorial
planning, have created seven microarchitectures.
Complete works introduced in the city, as an
opportunity for three-dimensional reflection on
our present and our possible futures.

Peter Eisenman "A Void"

THE OFFICIAL POINT OF VIEW

BERNARD TSCHUMI "THE ACTIVE ENCLOSURE"

OSCAR TUSQUETS BLANCA "THE IDEAL HOUSE"

MASSIMILIANO E DORIANA FUKSAS "THE HABITATION CAPSULE"
ASTRID KLEIN & MARK DYTHAM "THE SOFT BATH"
THE OFFICIAL POINT OF VIEW

TAXI

Salone Internazionale del Mobile
Eimu 2002 Comfort & Technology
10 am OFFICE

Ø92
to
office
MZ

DOWN ▶

093

edizione straordinaria

salone satellite

the official point of view

094
KUNDALINI
3D CARPET
OFFICE
MONKEY BOY

KONSTANTIN GRCIC FOR MOROSO
"OFF SCALE"

THE OFFICIAL POINT OF VIEW

096
OFFICE
EILEEN GRAY
"BLACK BOARD 1923/30"
FOR ECAR

SACHIO HIHARA
Salone Satellite

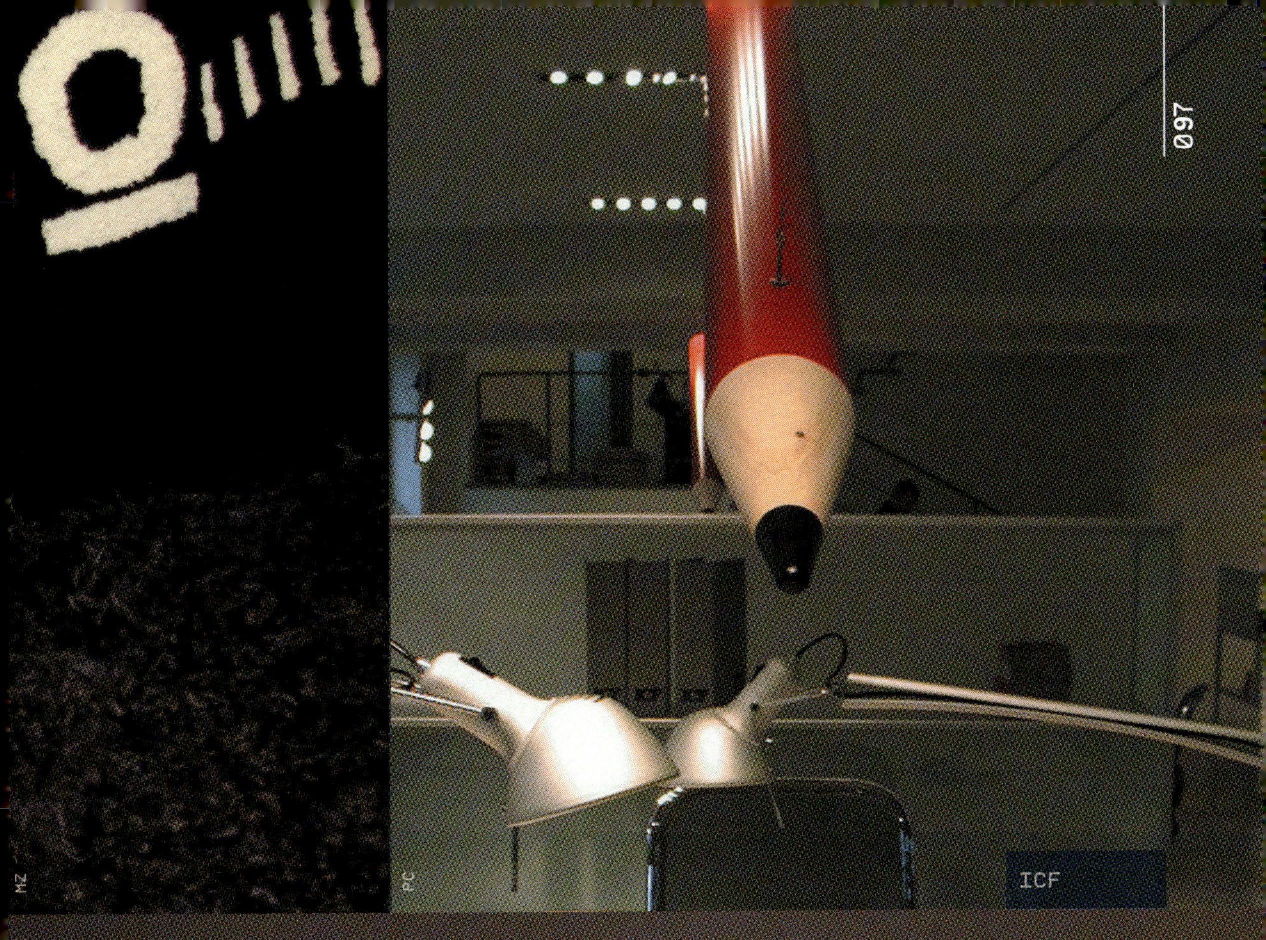

dis**ORDINE**
dis **ORDER**

THE OFFICIAL POINT OF VIEW

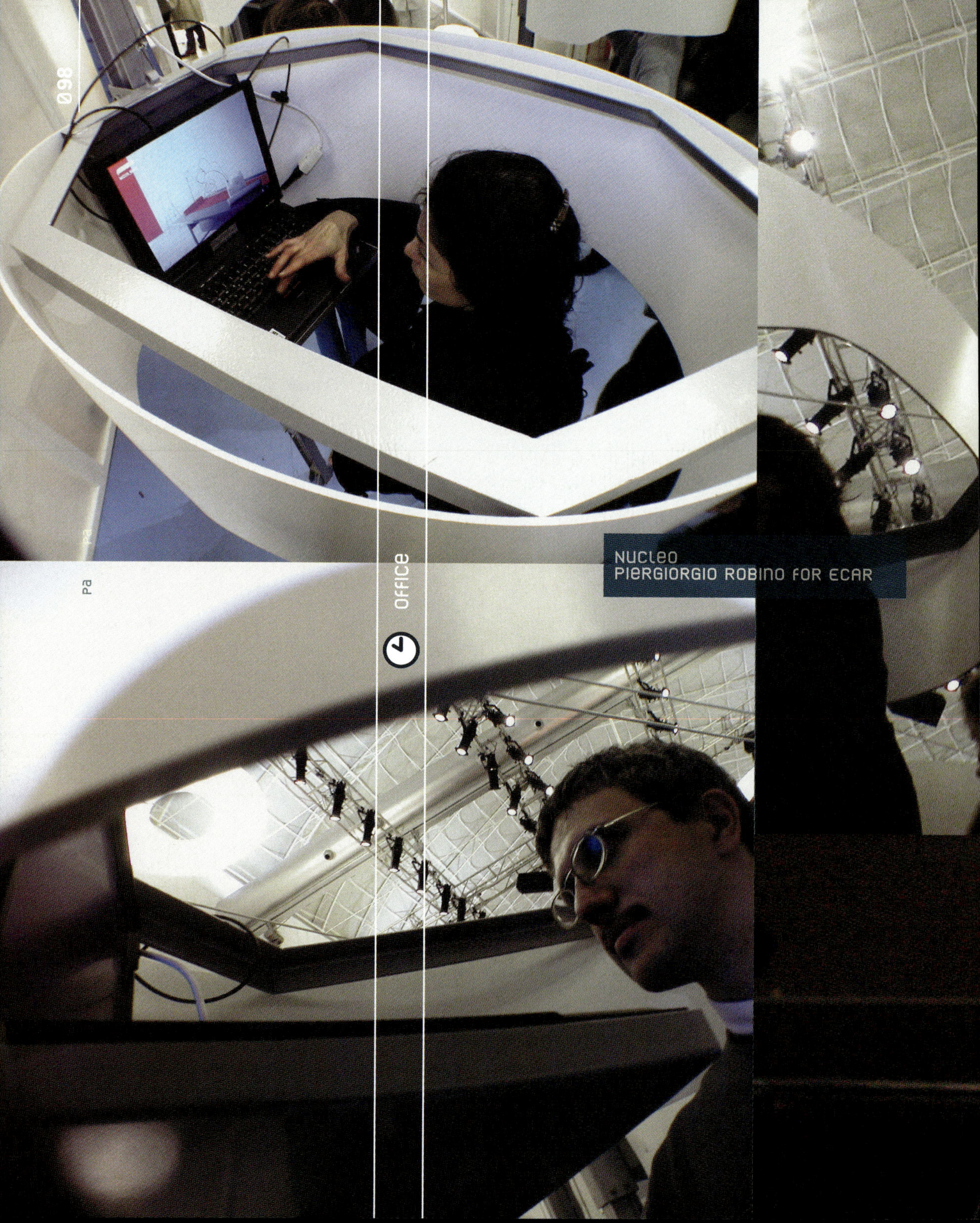
098
office
Nucleo
PIERGIORGIO ROBINO FOR ECAR

099
BOFFI
GL
Pa
kitchenology
demolink → security integrated → theft
THE OFFICIAL POINT OF VIEW

100
Gaetano Pesce "Broadway 1993"
Linea
OFFICE
FRÉDÉRIC SCHAUMBURG

101
ALL MANAGERS HAVE DAZZLING
SMILES BECAUSE THEIR DENTAL
EXPENSES ARE REIMBURSED
sedus
THE OFFICIAL POINT OF VIEW

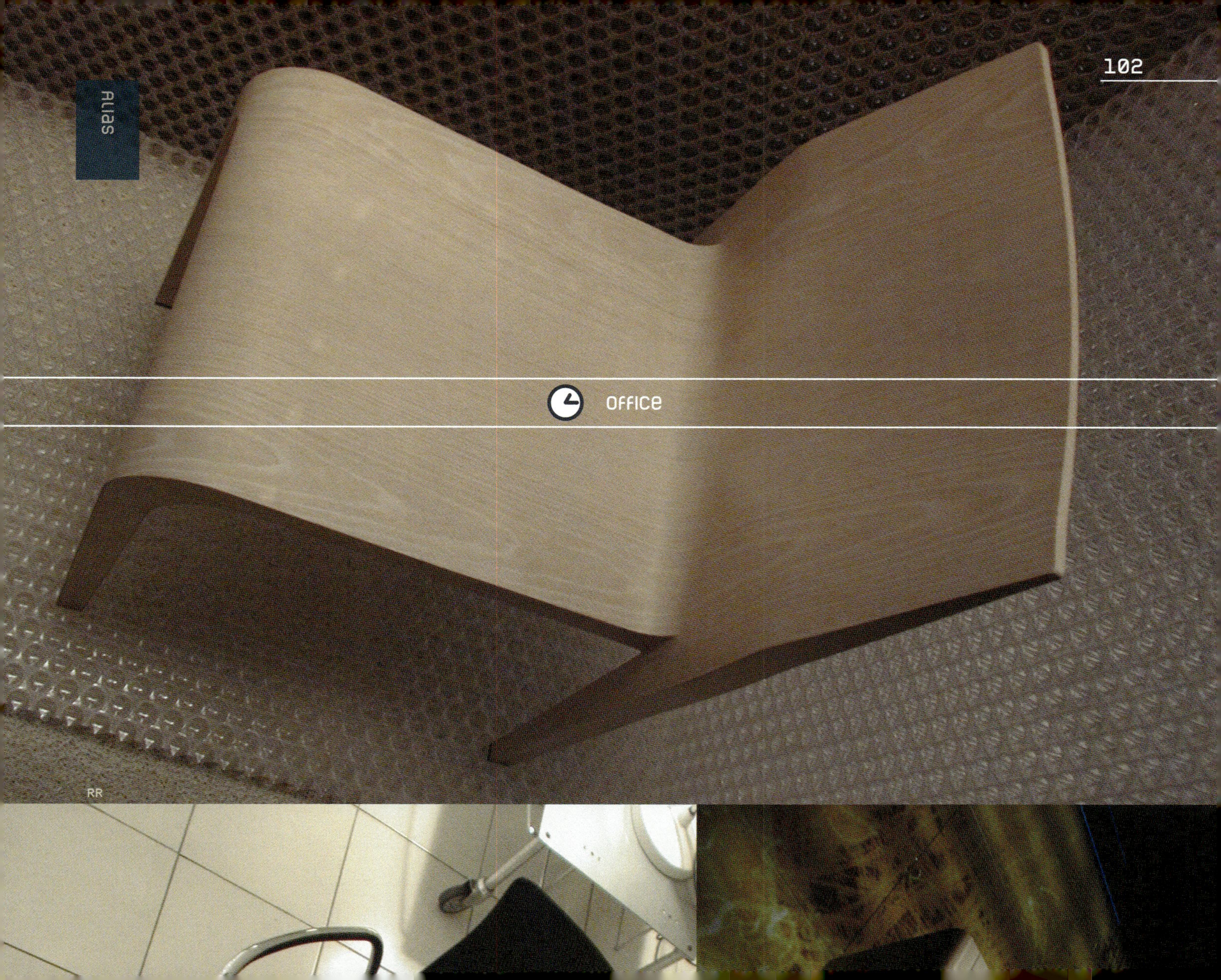
Alias
office
RR

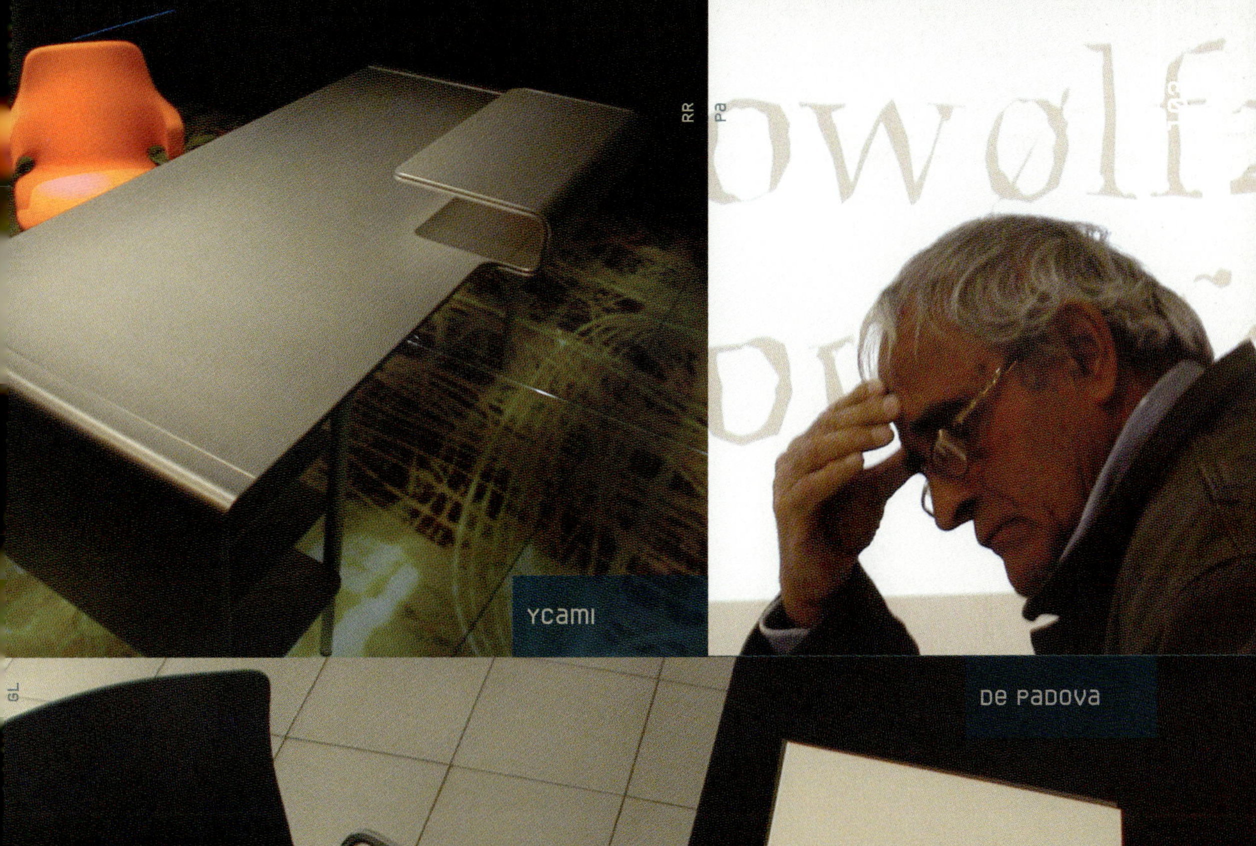
RR
pa
ycami
owolf
De PaDOVa
GL
THE OFFICIAL POINT OF VIEW

104
office
OFFECCT
FAC-SIMILE GALLERY

D-NISC
cambiofaccia
THE OFFICIAL POINT OF VIEW

B&B ITALIA
BenJamin SHAFFer
SurFace TaGTeam 2002

sedus
DOMODINAMICA
"DESIGN IS A GOOD THING
BECAUSE IT DOES GOOD TO THE
COMMUNITY, TO THOSE WHO
HAVE SIT OR LIE.
IT IS GOOD BECAUSE IT
INCREASES THE NUMBER OF
BIRTHS"
DAVIDE FACCIOLI - GALLERY OWNER -
THE OFFICIAL POINT OF VIEW

Home Office
Office at Home
Bau Baus
APT. 5 DESIGN
satellite
OFFICE
TM
RR

SENSE OF WONDER

THE OFFICIAL POINT OF VIEW

office
Pa
SB
FRAME

111
SB
MZ
THE OFFICIAL POINT OF VIEW

OFFICE
MOTOROLA
JOZEPH FORAKIS FOR MOTOROLA
ationship tall
lk talk talk ta
k talk talk tal

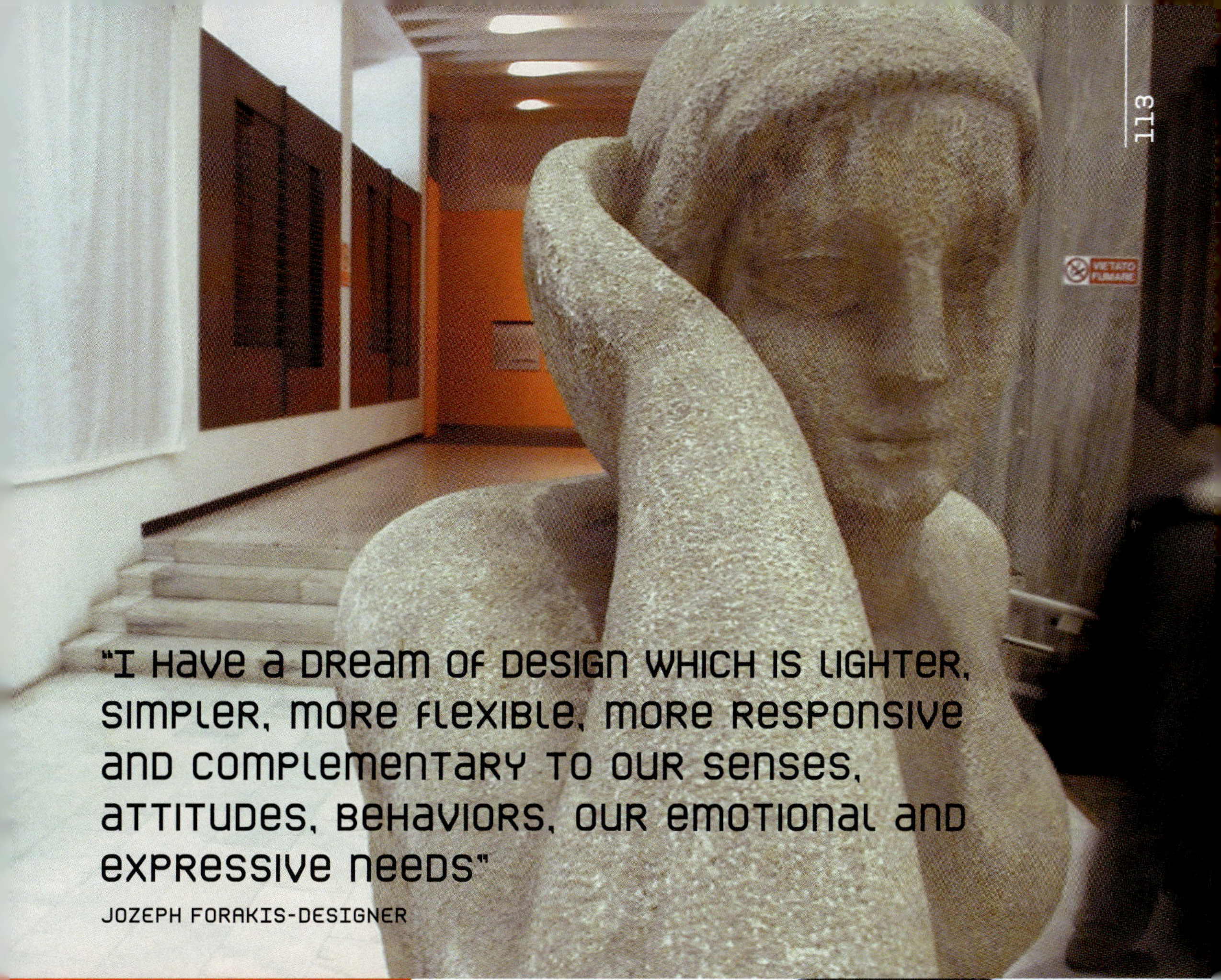

"I Have a Dream of Design WHICH IS LIGHTER, SIMPLER, MORE FLEXIBLE, MORE RESPONSIVE AND COMPLEMENTARY TO OUR SENSES, ATTITUDES, BEHAVIORS, OUR EMOTIONAL AND EXPRESSIVE NEEDS"

JOZEPH FORAKIS-DESIGNER

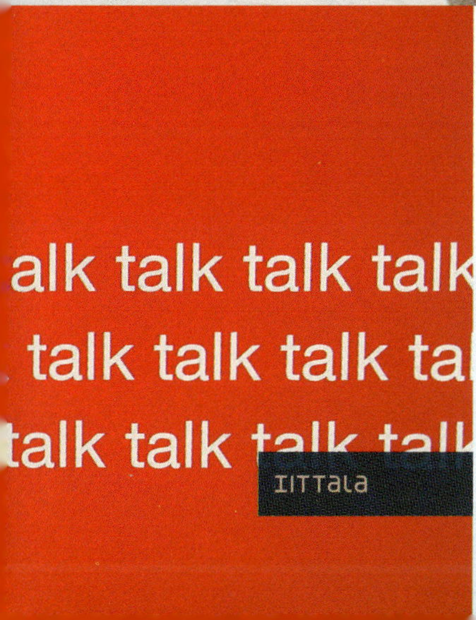

Raffaele Iannello
Office
pa pa

SENSE OF WONDER

GOLDFINGER?

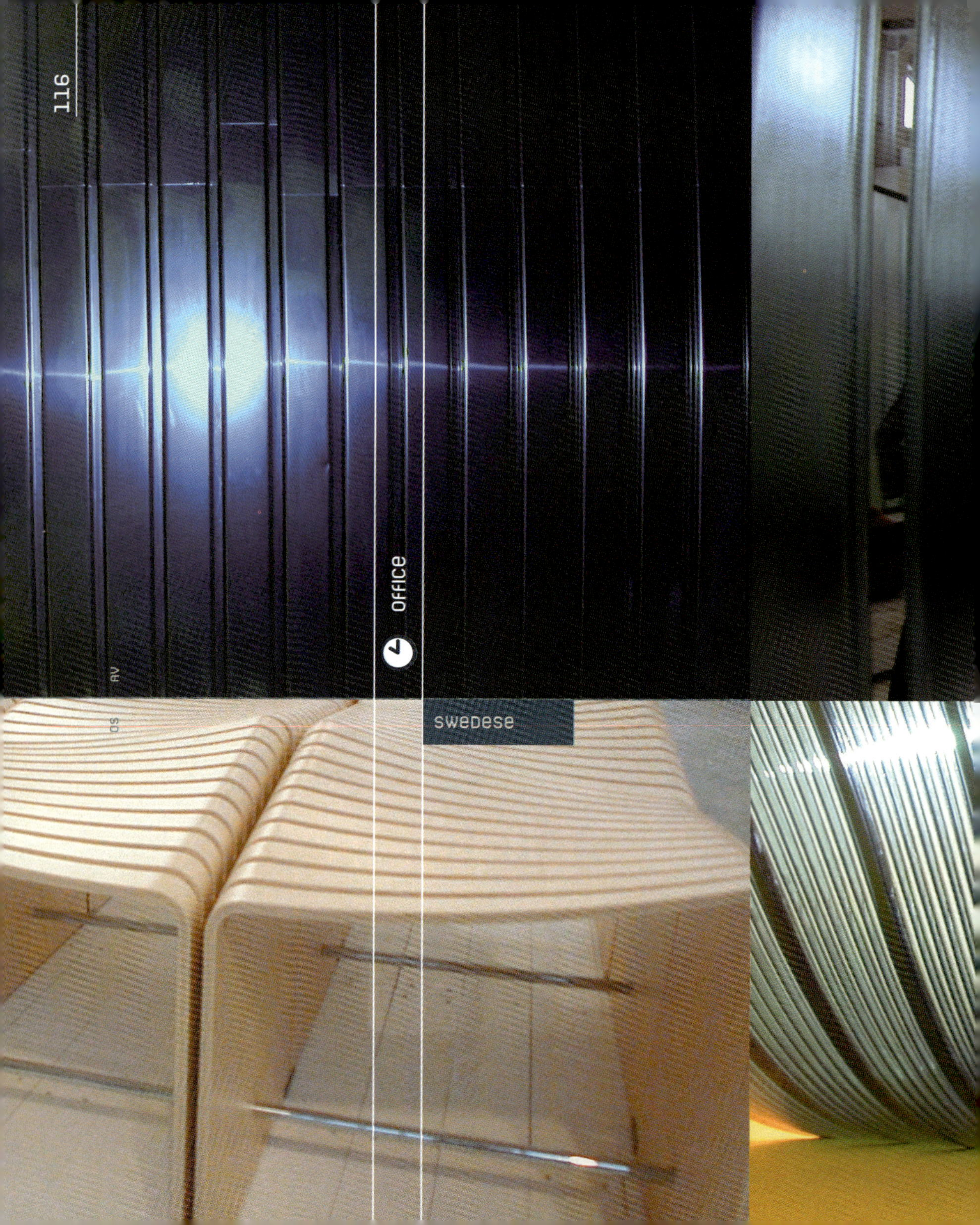

office
swedese

117
surface
IED
THE OFFICIAL POINT OF VIEW

FLYING DUTCH DESIGN
GRAZIA NERI
GIANCARLO VEGNI "EFFETTI"
FOR CAPPELLINI
THE OFFICIAL POINT OF VIEW

DUSI
SOLZI
Pa

121
GAETANO PESCE
GRAN HOTEL SALONE
YCAMI
MARKUS BENESCH
MONEY FOR MILAN
THE OFFICIAL POINT OF VIEW

Adesso puoi collegarti con Sony.

OFFICE
Adesso puoi collegarti con Sony.
go create
SONY

SONY
PELOTA

Aattak
de Padova
THE OFFICIAL POINT OF VIEW

124
OFFICE
CORSO COMO 10
Linea
SB

125
ACERBIS
SEDUS
THE OFFICIAL POINT OF VIEW

office
SB

DESIGNERS BLOCK
THE OFFICIAL POINT OF VIEW

openspace
kartell
office

DeTaILs
aRe noT
a DeTaIL

THE OFFICIaL POINT OF VIEW

OFFICE
LIGHTNESS IS A
QUALITY IN DESIGN 
BANG&OLUFSEN
INSTALLATION, ARCHIVIO DI STATO
SEDIE
TAVO
FURNITURE SHOP
MILANO, VIA CORELLI

131
PETER BOTTAZZI
DESIGNER
PAUL SMITH
SHOP
CAMBIOFACCIA
THE OFFICIAL POINT OF VIEW

SB
office

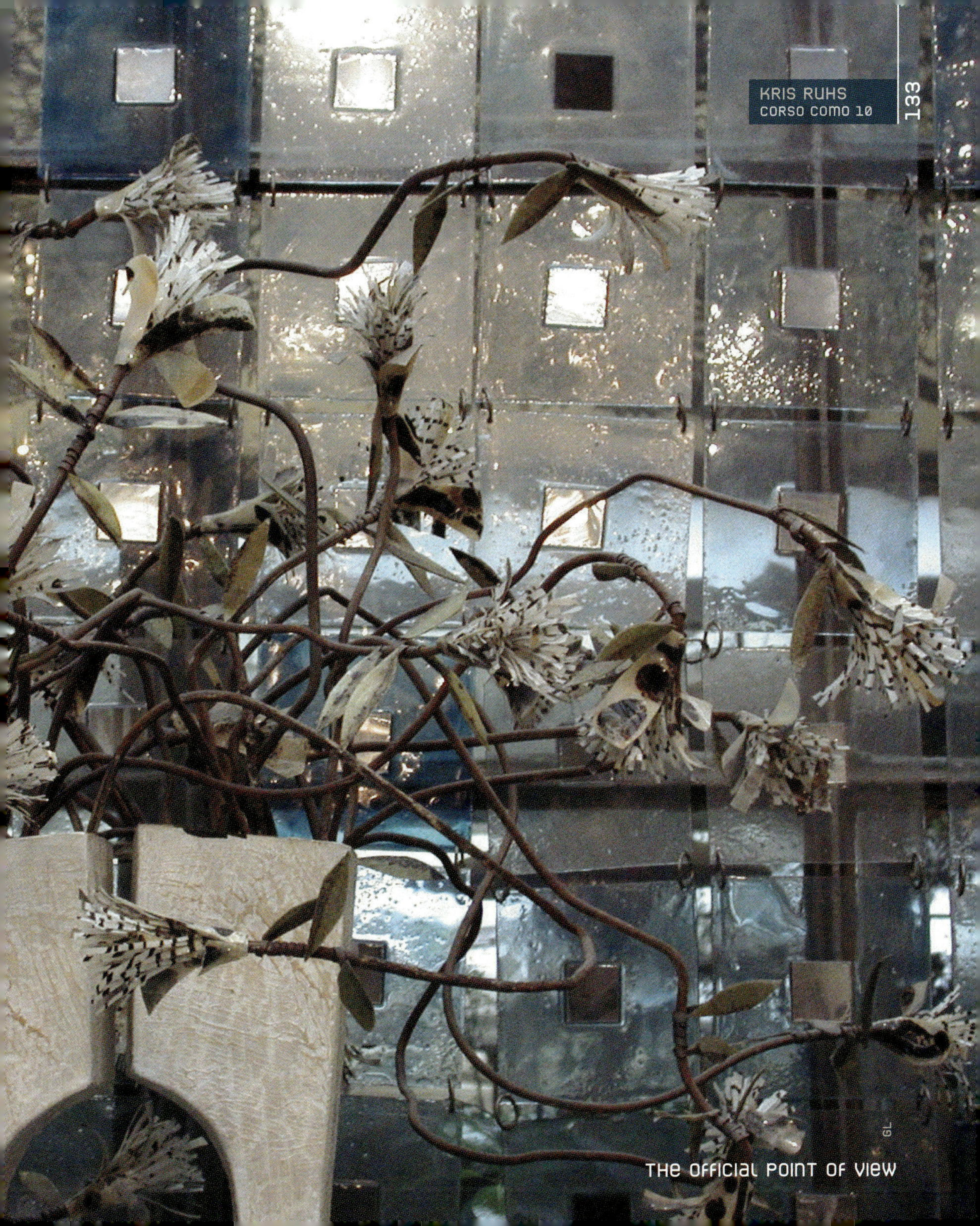

KRIS RUHS
CORSO COMO 10
133
THE OFFICIAL POINT OF VIEW

mandarina duck

MANDARINA DUCK
ISTITUTO CE...RA
MANDARINA DUCK PRESENTS THE "MURANO BAG",
INNOVATIVE DESIGN PIECE BY MARCEL WANDERS

E09

137
11 am THE FaIR
THE OFFICIAL POINT OF VIEW

138
THE FAIR
RR
ROLLINGFRAME

22
THE OFFICIAL POINT OF VIEW

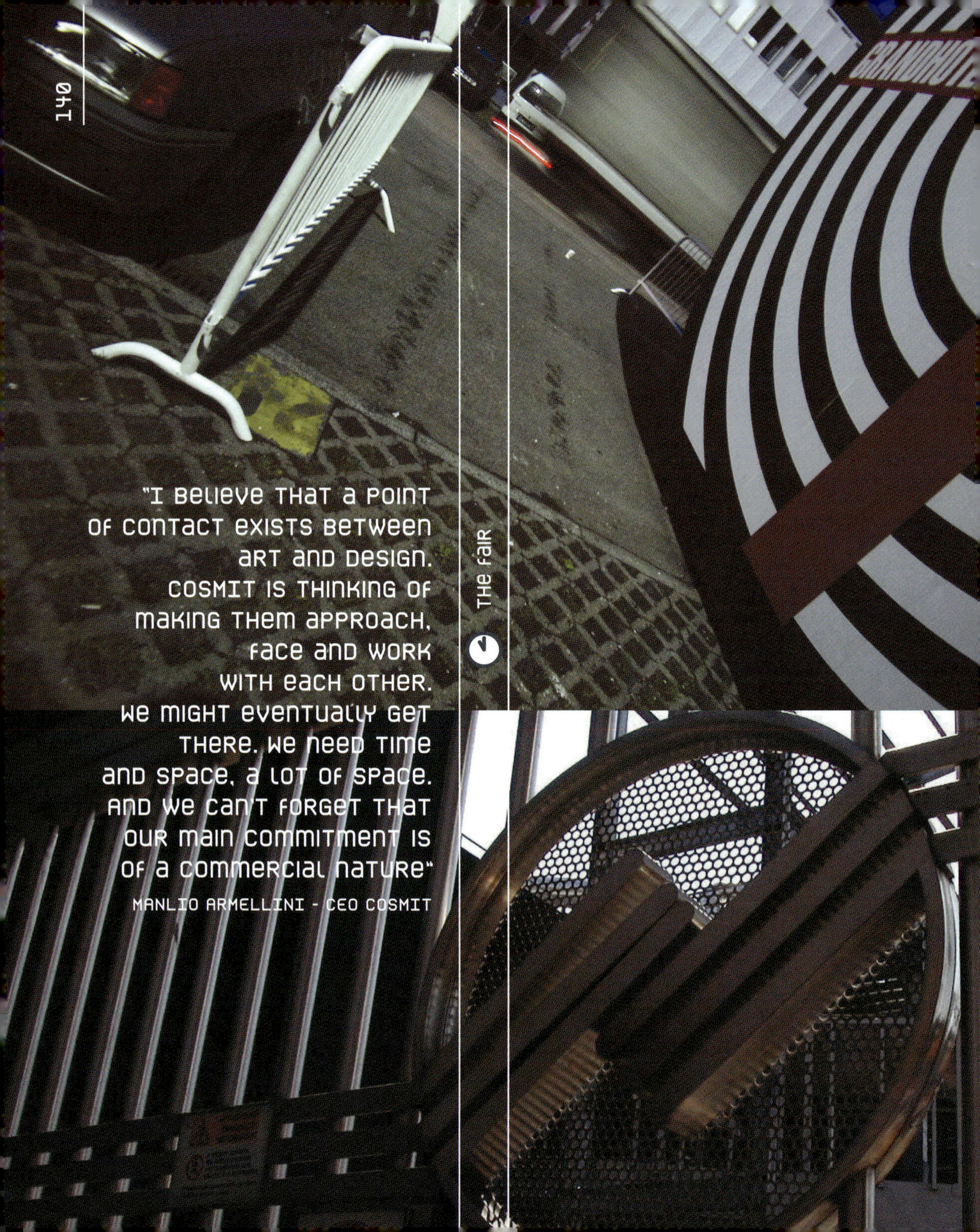

THE FAIR

"I BELIEVE THAT A POINT
OF CONTACT EXISTS BETWEEN
ART AND DESIGN.
COSMIT IS THINKING OF
MAKING THEM APPROACH,
FACE AND WORK
WITH EACH OTHER.
WE MIGHT EVENTUALLY GET
THERE. WE NEED TIME
AND SPACE, A LOT OF SPACE.
AND WE CAN'T FORGET THAT
OUR MAIN COMMITMENT IS
OF A COMMERCIAL NATURE"

MANLIO ARMELLINI - CEO COSMIT

THE OffICIaL POINT Of VIEW

HIDDen
THE FAIR
GL
JU

THE OFFICIAL POINT OF VIEW

Kartell
Kartell

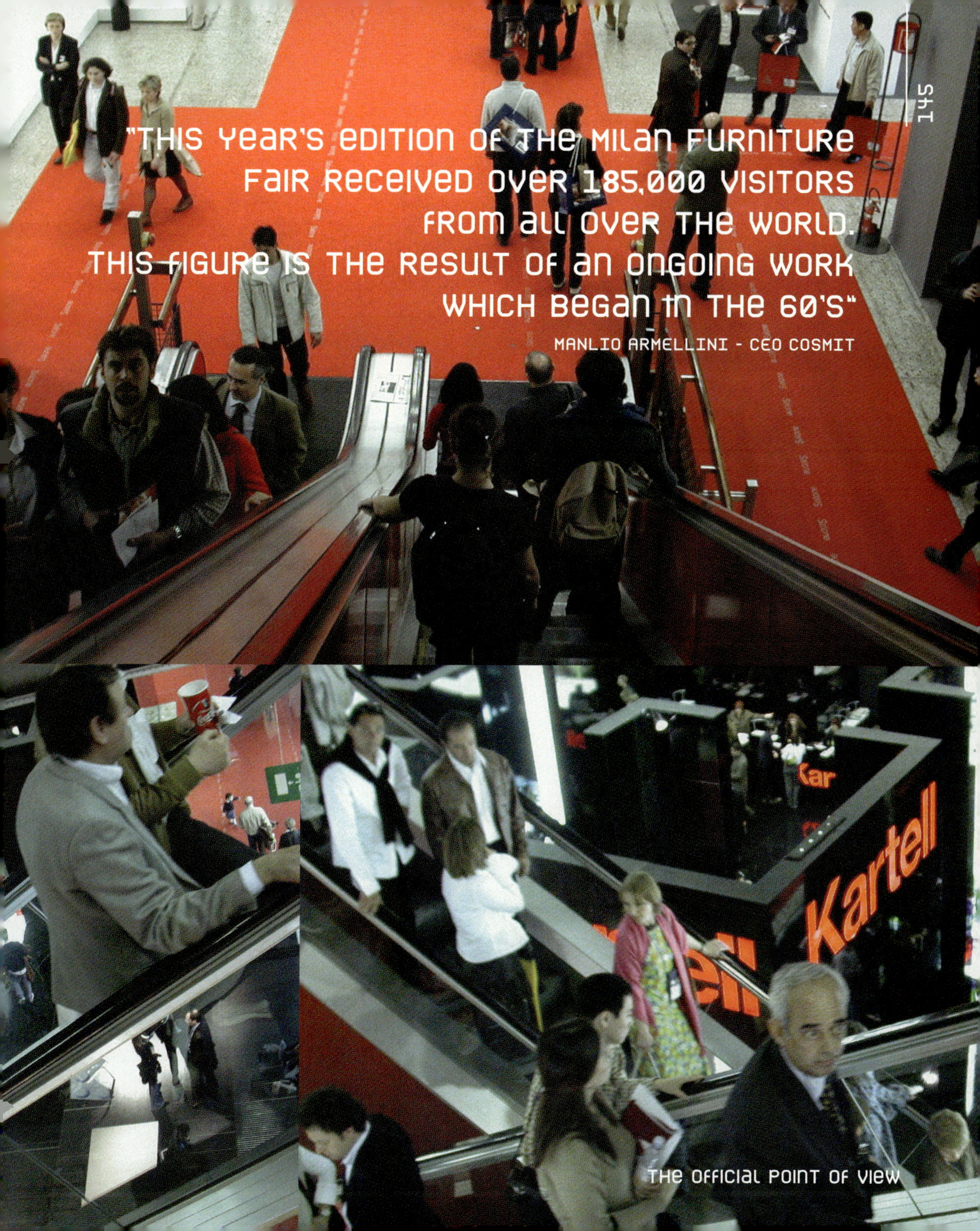

"THIS YEAR'S EDITION OF THE MILAN FURNITURE
FAIR RECEIVED OVER 185,000 VISITORS
FROM ALL OVER THE WORLD.
THIS FIGURE IS THE RESULT OF AN ONGOING WORK
WHICH BEGAN IN THE 60'S"
MANLIO ARMELLINI - CEO COSMIT
145
Kartell
THE OFFICIAL POINT OF VIEW

MILANO
KITCHEN

KITCHEN
ROSS LOVEGROVE
TY NANT

DOMUS ACADEMY
149
THE OFFICIAL POINT OF VIEW

MANDARINA DUCK

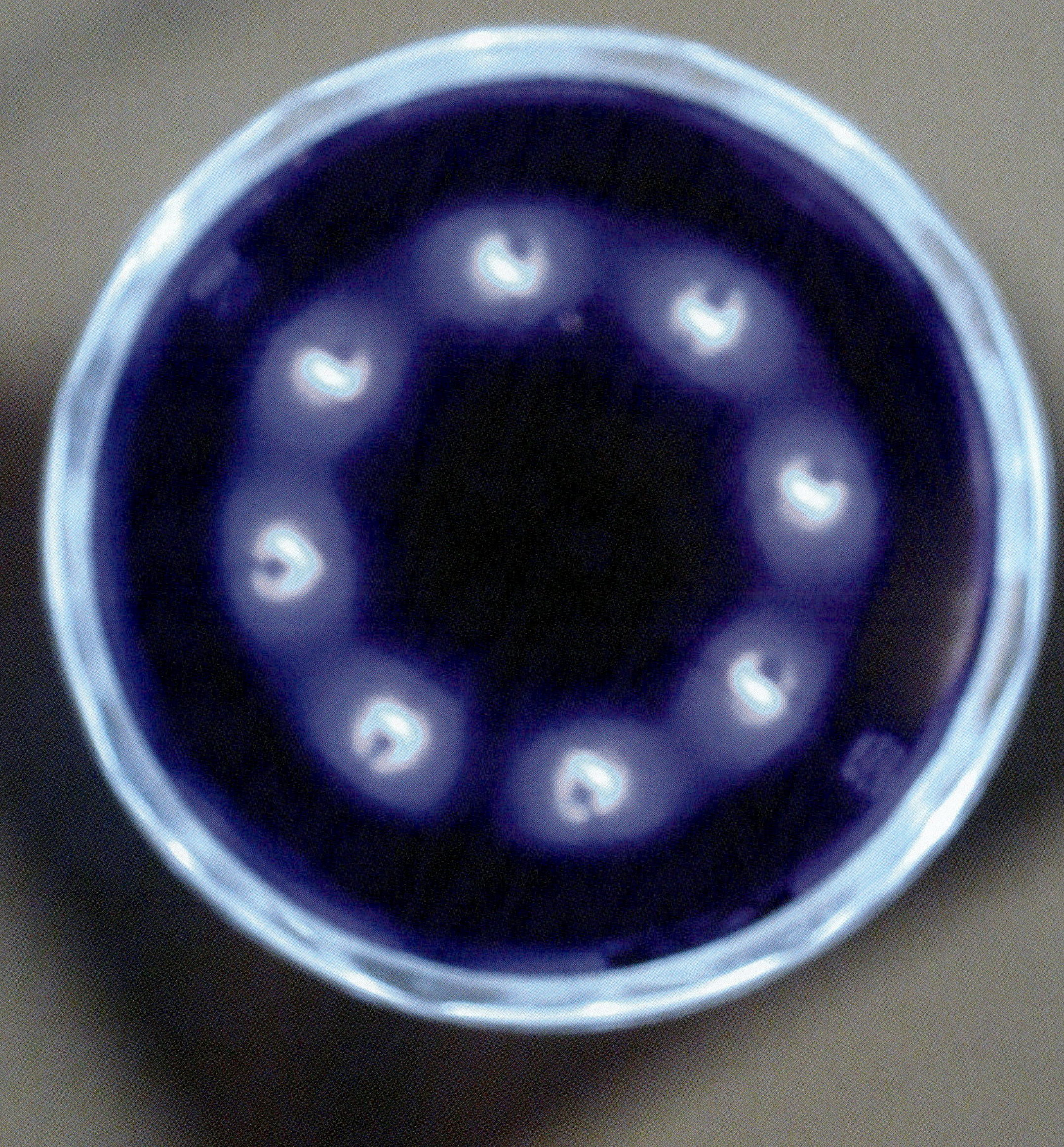

THE OFFICIAL POINT OF VIEW

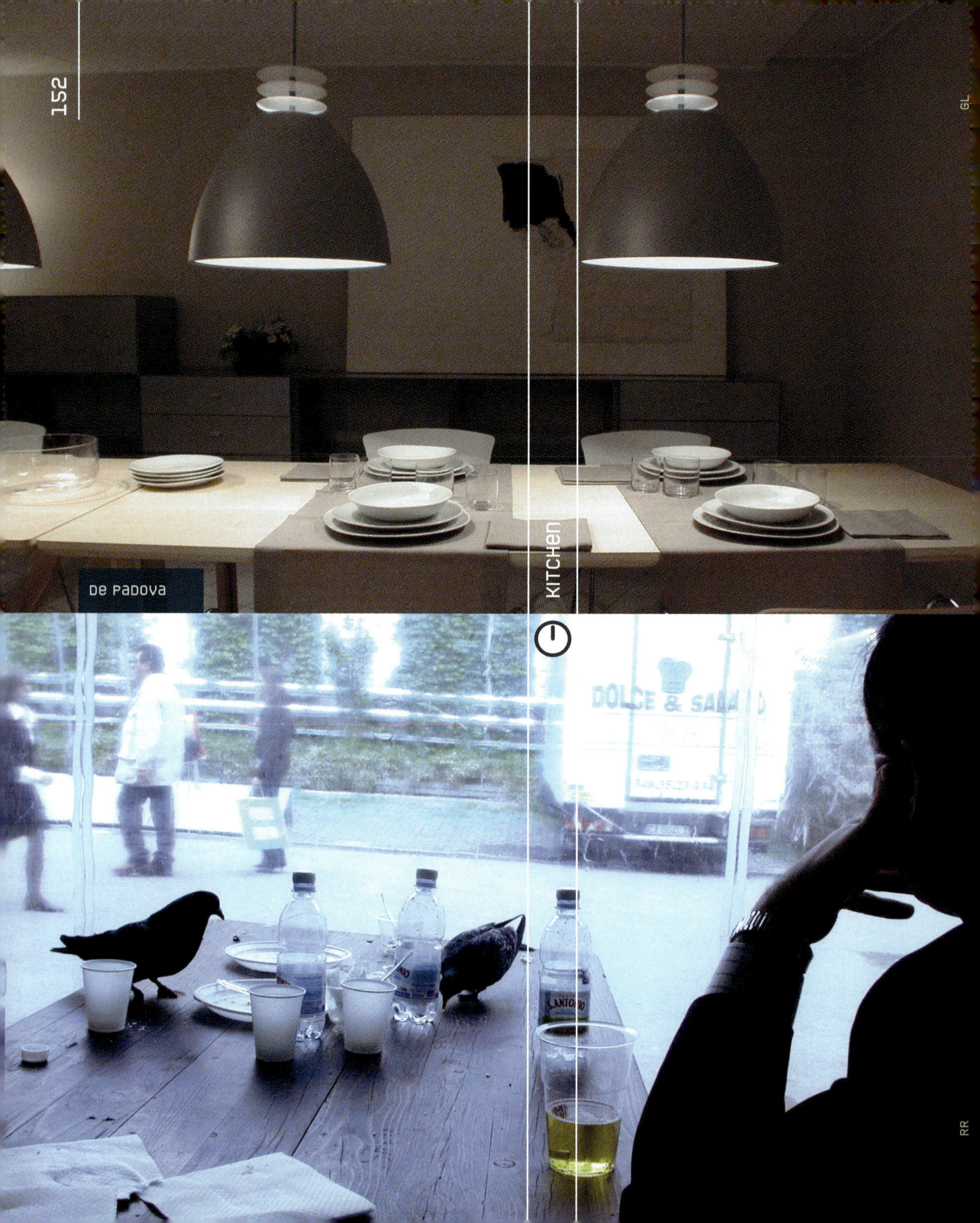
De PaDova
KITCHEN
DOLCE & SAL...
ANTONIO

IED
DIET RULES
THE OFFICIAL POINT OF VIEW

KITCHEN
Francesca Gagliardi
Pandora Design
Binova
ORDINE
ORDER
ORDRE
ORDNUNG
PANDORA DESIGN

GIULIO IACCHETTI-MATTEO RAGNI
"MOSCARDINO" FOR PANDORA
DANIELA DANZI
PANDORA DESIGN
THE OFFICIAL POINT OF VIEW

156
DIEGO TOSELLO
SATELLITE
KITCHEN
GHS

DESIGNERS BLOCK
STEFANO PILOSIO
THE OFFICIAL POINT OF VIEW

158
KITCHEN
CARLO CONTIN
SATELLITE
ZEUS

CAPPELLINI
SAMOA BY ALIANTEDIZIONI
COLOR PROGIECT
INGO MAURER
PANDORA
THE OFFICIAL POINT OF VIEW

"TO me an OBJeCT IS
CHaRaCTeRISeD BY
SuRPRISe, BY maGIC"
DENIS SANTACHIARA - DESIGNER -

DeNIS SaNTaCHIaRa

CONSOLATO BRITANNICO
FIGURA D. CAMERIN
THE OFFICIAL POINT OF VIEW

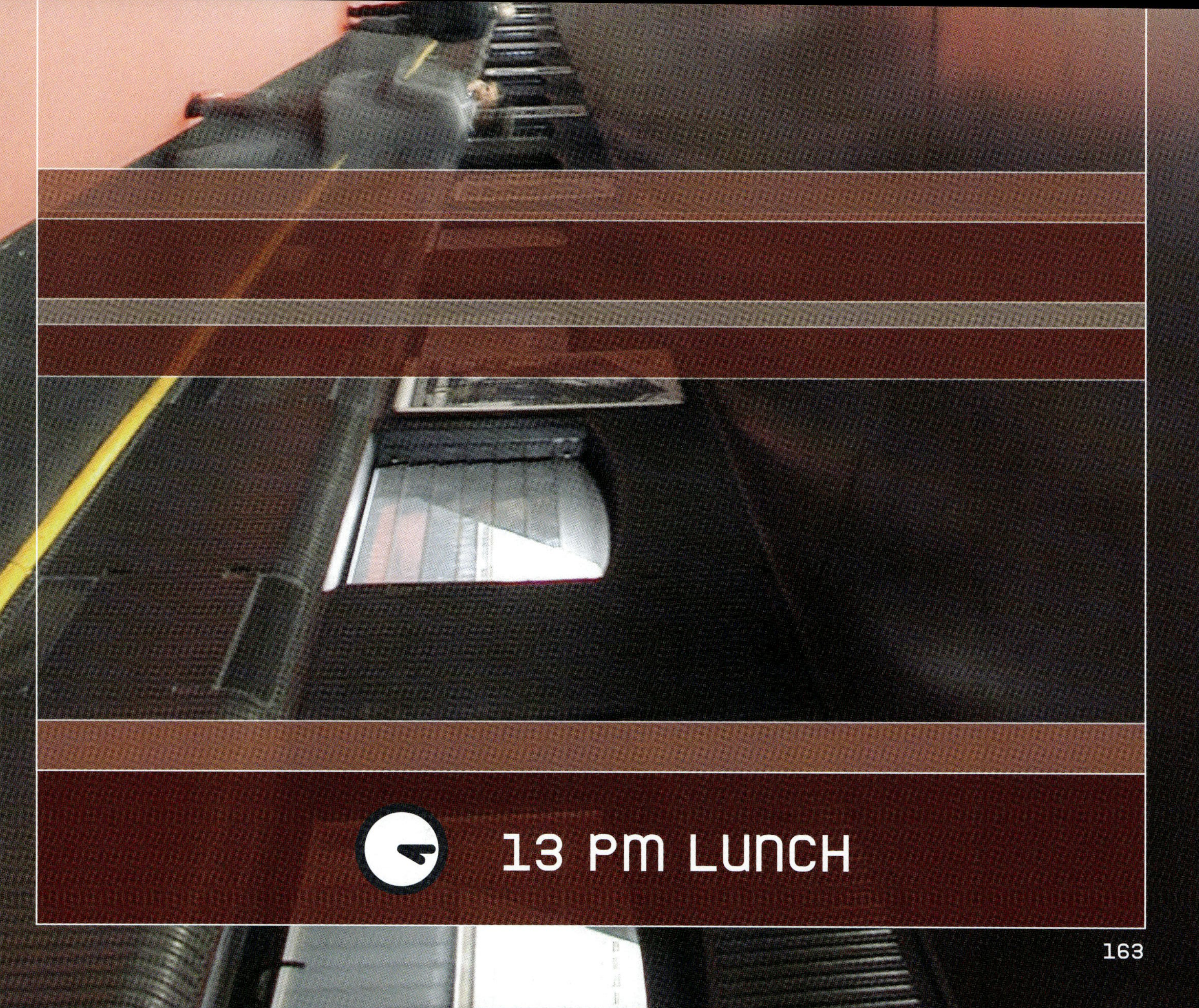

13 PM LUNCH

164
LUNCH
GL
SB
TM
SALAME
Riso alla Marinara

165
THE OFFICIAL POINT OF VIEW

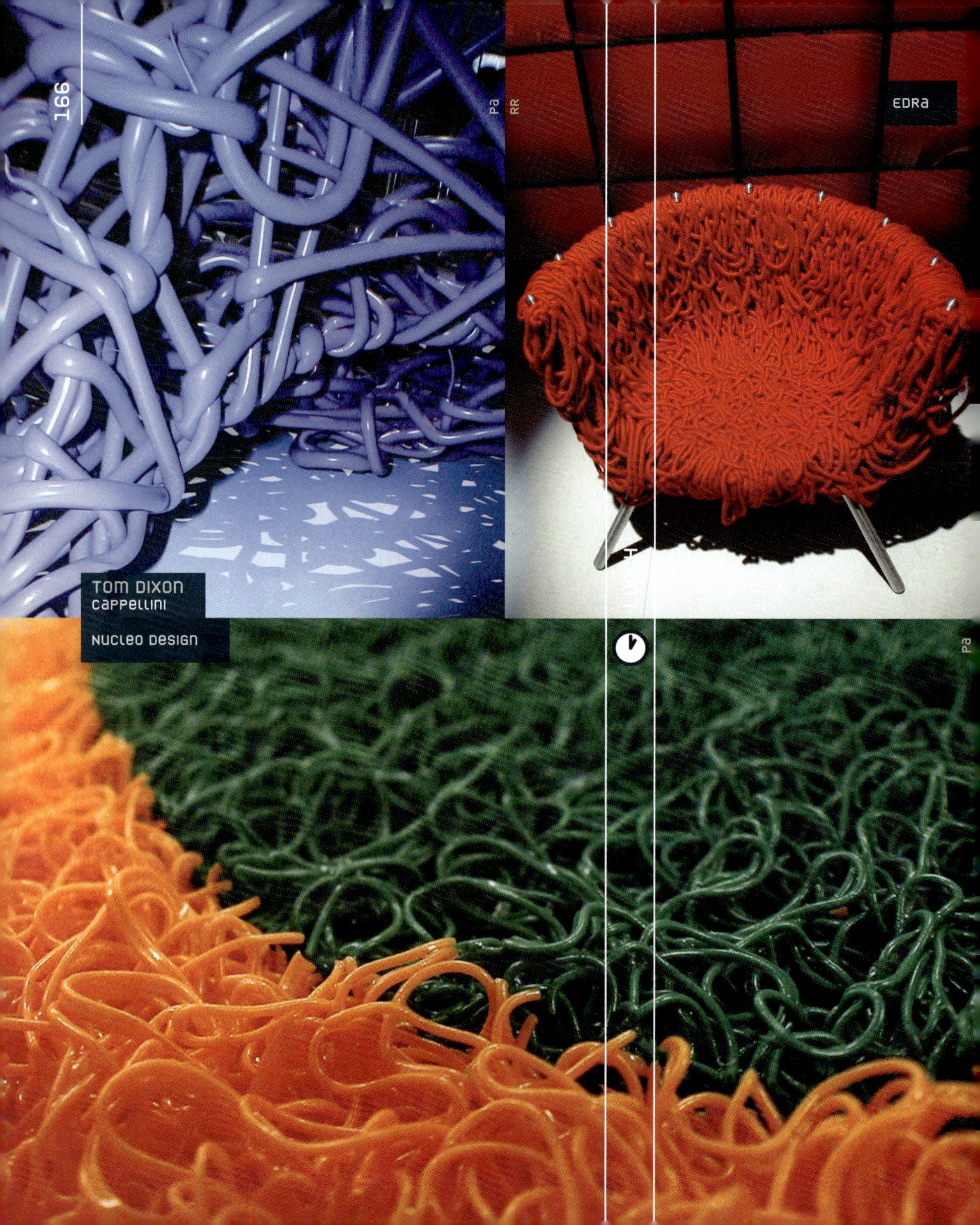

166
Pa
RR
EDRa
TOM DIXON
CAPPELLINI
NUCLEO DESIGN
Pa

"In Design too a sense of humor is
useful; to catch the attention of
the people and to play with them,
even though this is often immoral"
FRANCESCA FRIGINO - QUALITY MANAGER -

168
EKWC
"WETDESIGN"
LUNCH

LORNA LEE LESLIE "WASH BASIN"
FOR EKWC
DESIGN DPAPULI
DILMOS
169
THE OFFICIAL POINT OF VIEW

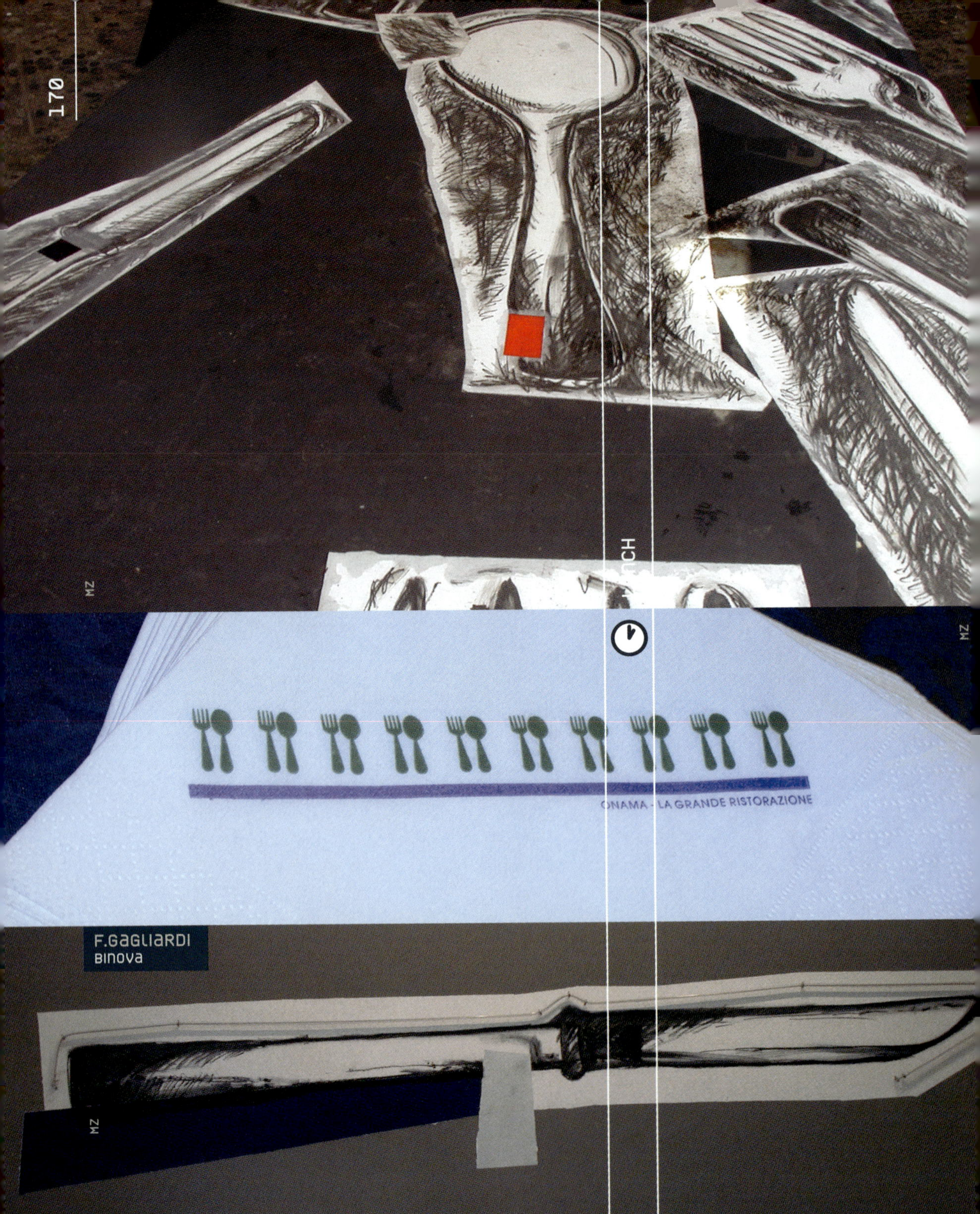
MZ
MZ
ONAMA - LA GRANDE RISTORAZIONE
F.GaGLIaRDI
BInOVa
MZ

DRIaDe

TM

IITTaLa

PC

THE OFFICIAL POINT OF VIEW

LUNCH
Coca Cola
Caffe

173
PIANTA GENERALE
GENERAL PLAN
"IS A SENSE OF HUMOR INDISPENSABLE
FOR A DESIGNER?
TRY ASKING SOTTSASS"
DANIELA DANZI
THE OFFICIAL POINT OF VIEW

GRAND HOTEL SALONE

EACH YEAR COSMIT SPONSORS A MAJOR NON-COMMERCIAL EXHIBIT DEDICATED TO EXPLORING CONTEMPORARY DESIGN AND CULTURAL ISSUES. THE 2002 EXHIBIT ENTITLED, GRANDHOTELSALONE IS THE FIRST OF ITS KIND TO CELEBRATE HOSPITALITY DESIGN WHOSE POPULARITY AND INFLUENCE THESE DAYS RENDERS IT A GLOBAL CULTURAL PHENOMENON.

GRANDHOTELSALONE IS THE BRAINCHILD OF WORLD-RENOWNED INTERIOR DESIGNER ADAM D. TIHANY, WHO HAS MAINTAINED CLOSE TIES WITH THE LEADERS OF THE ITALIAN DESIGN COMMUNITY WHICH HAS INCORPORATED INTO HIS CUSTOM HOSPITALITY DESIGNS WORLDWIDE.

GRANDHOTELSALONE WILL PRESENT A FULLY-FUNCTIONAL "BOUTIQUE HOTEL LOBBY", DESIGNED BY TIHANY, INCLUDING A CONCIERGE DESK, GIFT SHOP, ATRIUM, QUIET AND MEDIA LOUNGES, AND THE GHS RESTAURANT & WINE BAR.
BEYOND THE LOBBY IS THE "HOTEL ROOM OF THE FUTURE", WHERE TIHANY HAS INVITED 10 TOP ARCHITECTS/DESIGNERS WHO WERE GIVEN IDENTICAL PROGRAMS AND GUIDELINES AND ASKED TO REPRESENT A WORLD CAPITAL. EACH OF THESE ROOMS WILL BE BUILT BY LEADING ITALIAN MANUFACTURERS WHO SPECIALIZE IN HOSPITALITY.
COURTESY OF ADAM TIHANY PRESS

17
SILVIO MACCIONI
sue kim
THE OFFICIAL POINT OF VIEW

GRANDHOTELSALONE
RESTAURANT
14 E 15 APRILE 2002

SIRIO MACCIONI
LE CIRQUE 2000
NEW YORK
IN COLLABORATION WITH
SADLER BANQUETING

GRANDHOTELSALONE
RESTAURANT
10 E 11 APRILE 2002

CHEF FABIO PICCHI
RISTORANTE CIBREO
FIRENZE
IN COLLABORATION WITH
SADLER BANQUETING

"A GOOD RESTAURANT IS BASED
ON THE HARMONY OF THREE
ELEMENTS: THE QUALITY OF
ITS FOOD, ITS SERVICE AND ITS
INTERIOR DESIGN. THE LATTER,
ALAS, PLAYS A FUNDAMENTAL
ROLE FOR A SINGLE DAY:
THAT OF THE OPENING. AFTER
THAT THE SUCCESS OF THE
RESTAURANT WILL DEPEND ON
THE QUALITY OF ITS FOOD AND
ITS SERVICE."

ADAM TIHANY

ADAM TIHANY

GRANDHOTELSALONE
RESTAURANT
12 APRILE 2002

THOMAS KELLER
THE FRENCH LAUNDRY
IN COLLABORATION WITH
SADLER BANQUETING

THE OFFICIAL POINT OF VIEW

GRAND HOTEL salone

BLANCHAERT AND SOLBIATI
THE OFFICIAL POINT OF VIEW

GRAND HOTEL SALONE

TOYO ITO - NEW YORK
MANUFACTURER: PRESOTTO INDUSTRIE MOBILI

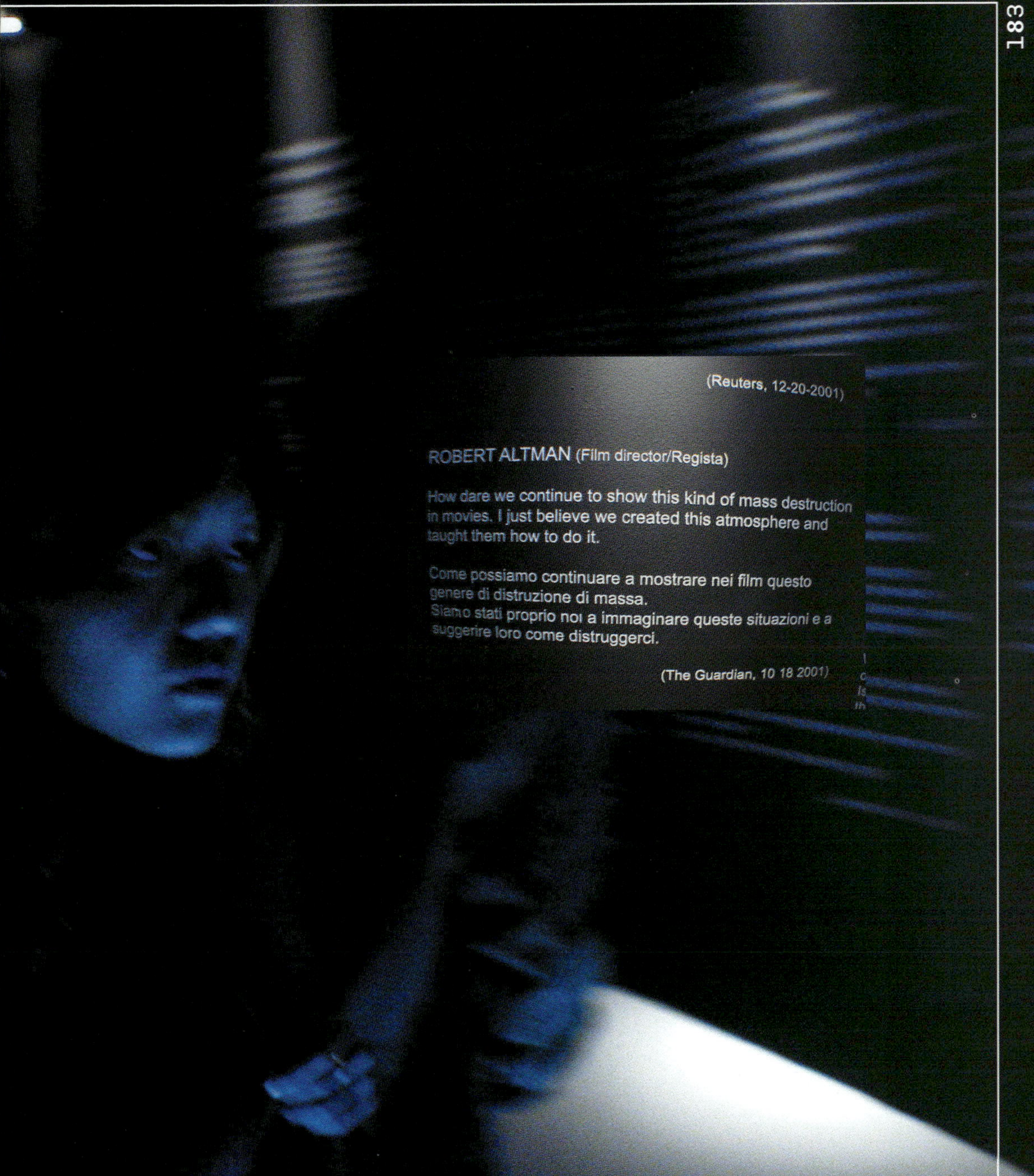
(Reuters, 12-20-2001)

ROBERT ALTMAN (Film director/Regista)

How dare we continue to show this kind of mass destruction
in movies. I just believe we created this atmosphere and
taught them how to do it.

Come possiamo continuare a mostrare nei film questo
genere di distruzione di massa.
Siamo stati proprio noi a immaginare queste situazioni e a
suggerire loro come distruggerci.

(The Guardian, 10 18 2001)

"THE FLOU BEDROOM AIMS TO CONVEY A SENSE OF COSY FAMILIARITY, THAT WARM, FRIENDLY FEELING THAT TRAVELLERS GENERALLY ENJOY ENSCONCED IN THEIR OWN HOME."
VICO MAGISTRETTI

VICO MAGISTRETTI - LONDON
MANUFACTURER: FLOU

ZAHA HADID - SIDNEY
MANUFACTURER: MISURA EMME TIZIANA E GIUSEPPE MASCHERONI

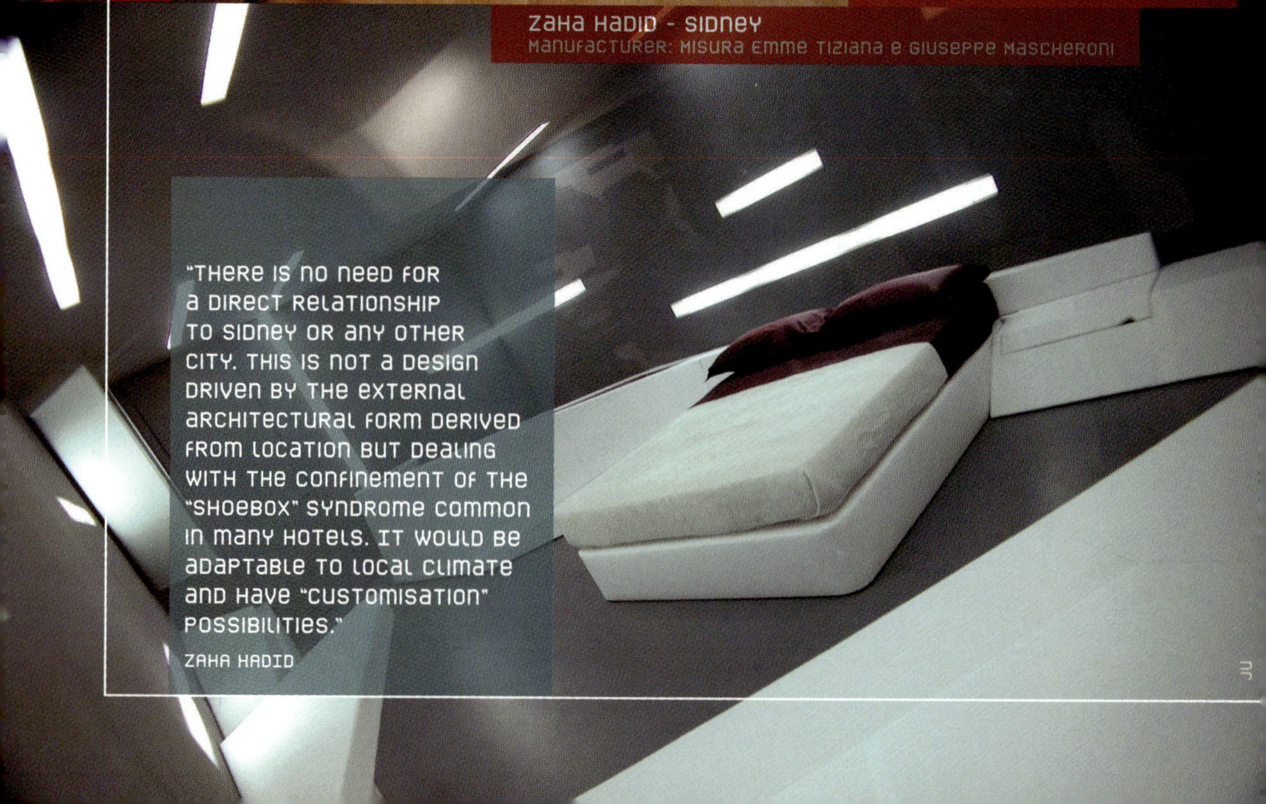

"THERE IS NO NEED FOR A DIRECT RELATIONSHIP TO SIDNEY OR ANY OTHER CITY. THIS IS NOT A DESIGN DRIVEN BY THE EXTERNAL ARCHITECTURAL FORM DERIVED FROM LOCATION BUT DEALING WITH THE CONFINEMENT OF THE "SHOEBOX" SYNDROME COMMON IN MANY HOTELS. IT WOULD BE ADAPTABLE TO LOCAL CLIMATE AND HAVE "CUSTOMISATION" POSSIBILITIES."
ZAHA HADID

185

"MOSCOW, THE CAPITAL OF
A COUNTRY IN TRANSITION.
METAPHYSICAL, SHAPELESS.
A MODEL HOTEL BEDROOM
THAT OUGHT TO REPRESENT
THE PLACE IN WHICH IT IS
LOCATED.
A SPACE THAT SPEAKS
DIRECTLY TO THE SENSES,
AND NOT JUST OF
"COMFORT".
A SHELL WITHIN WHICH
OBJECTS FLOAT IN SPACE,
FORMLESSLY, DEFORMED OR
STILL UNFORMED."
GAETANO PESCE

GAETANO PESCE - MOSCOW
MANUFACTURER: MERITALIA

THE OFFICIAL POINT OF VIEW

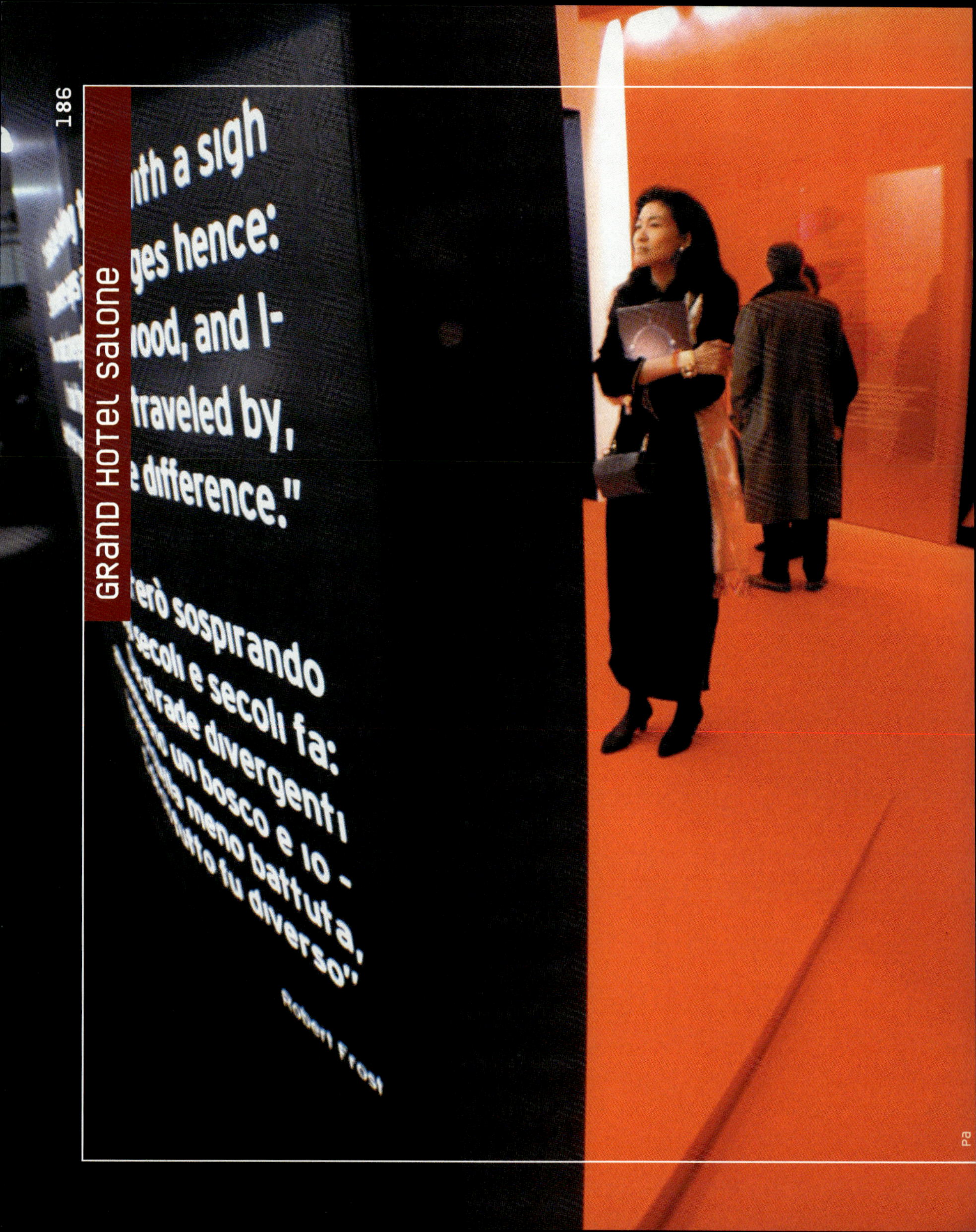

...th a sigh
...ges hence:
...ood, and I-
...traveled by,
...e difference."

...terò sospirando
...secoli e secoli fa:
...strade divergenti
...n un bosco e io -
...la meno battuta,
...tutto fu diverso"

Robert Frost

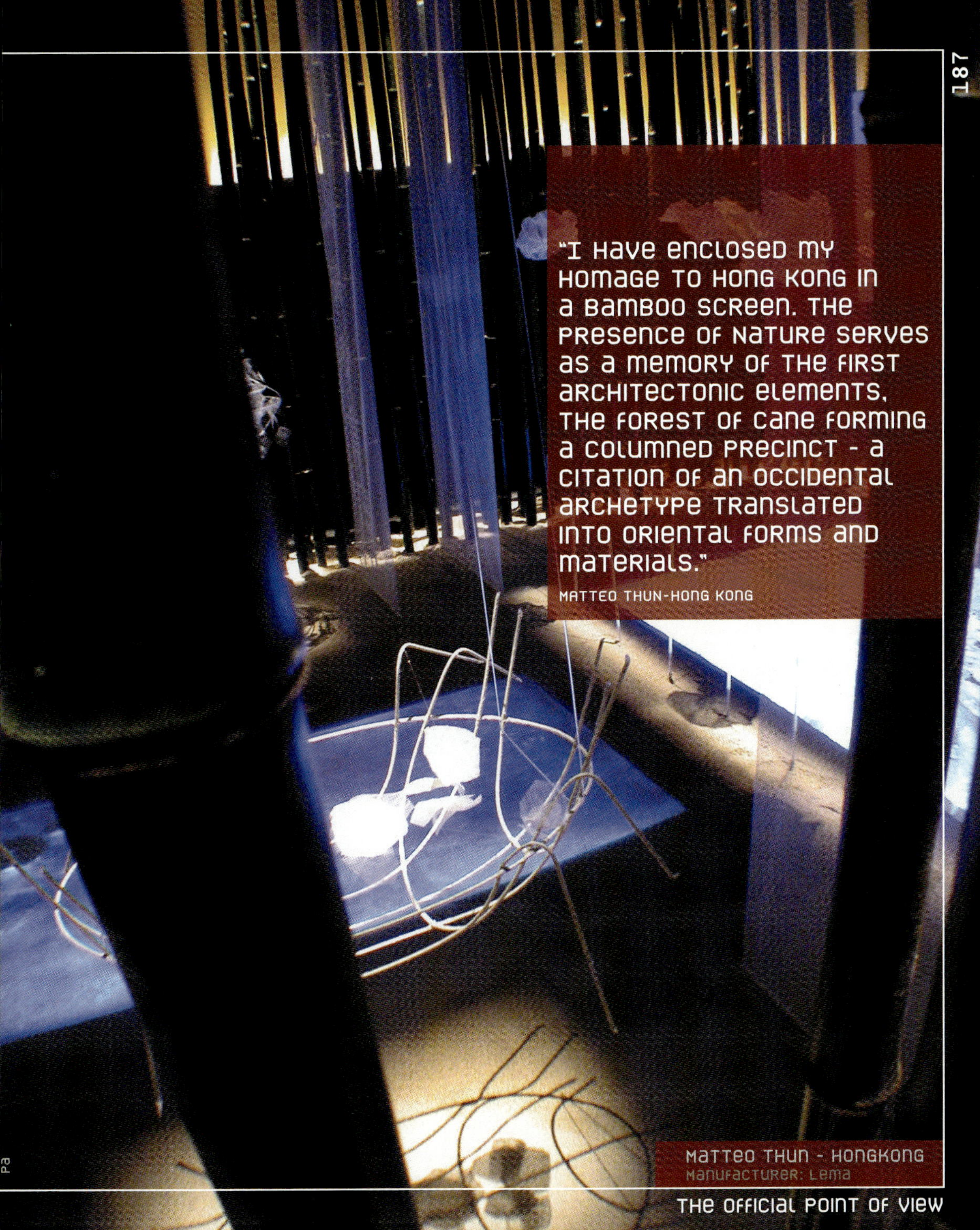

"I Have enclosed my
Homage to Hong Kong in
a bamboo screen. The
Presence of nature serves
as a memory of the first
architectonic elements,
the forest of cane forming
a columned precinct - a
citation of an occidental
archetype translated
into oriental forms and
materials."
MATTEO THUN-HONG KONG

MATTEO THUN - HONGKONG
Manufacturer: Lema

"THE SILK ROAD TRAVELLER HIS LODGINGS ENROUTE WERE CALLED A CARAVANSERAI. HIS JOURNEY WAS DESCRIBED BY ALESSANDRO BARICCO'S SETA."

ARATA ISOSAKI

ARATA ISOZAKI - ROME
MANUFACTURER: B & B ITALIA

RICHARD MEYER - PARIS
MANUFACTURER: POLIFORM

"...INTO A SINGLE "PARISIAN" ROOM? PERHAPS IN BOTH THE CITY AND THE ROOM, THE ELEMENTS ARE CLEAN, CLASSIC AND CLEAR. THE QUALITY OF LIGHT IS DIFFUSED, DISPERSED AND EVER-CHANGING."

RICHARD MEYER

"THE HOTEL ROOM IS NOT A HOME
AWAY FROM HOME, BUT AN EXILE
FROM HOME...
WHAT WOULD PLEASE ME MOST IN
A HOTEL IS NOT SOMEONE ELSE'S
IDEA OF CHIC, ELEGANCE OR STYLE
BUT RATHER COMFORT, CLARITY, AND
EASE OF ACCESS TO INFORMATION,
ENTERTAINMENT AND AMBIENCE...
COMFORT IS MAINLY CENTERED
AROUND THE BED..."

RON ARAD

RON ARAD - MEXICOCITY
MANUFACTURER: CECCOTTI INTERIOR HOTEL DESIGN

THE OFFICIAL POINT OF VIEW

LEGORRETA - BERLIN
MANUFACTURER: FEG INDUSTRIA MOBILI DI ROSA ELLI & C

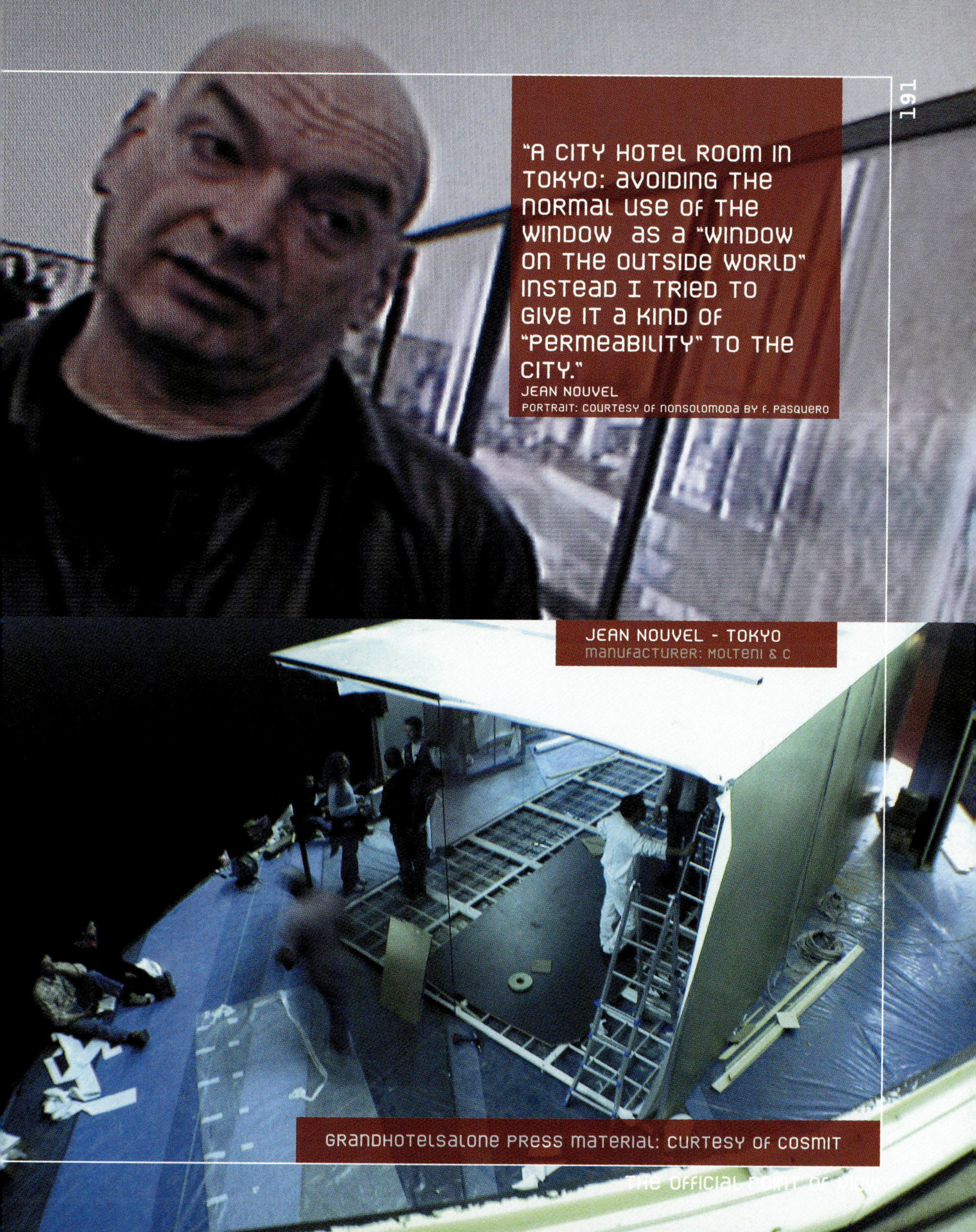
191
"A CITY HOTEL ROOM IN TOKYO: AVOIDING THE NORMAL USE OF THE WINDOW AS A "WINDOW ON THE OUTSIDE WORLD" INSTEAD I TRIED TO GIVE IT A KIND OF "PERMEABILITY" TO THE CITY."
JEAN NOUVEL
PORTRAIT: COURTESY OF NONSOLOMODA BY F. PASQUERO
JEAN NOUVEL - TOKYO
MANUFACTURER: MOLTENI & C
GRANDHOTELSALONE PRESS MATERIAL: CURTESY OF COSMIT
THE OFFICIAL POINT OF VIEW

FI
Pezzotta
VILLA DI SERIO - BG
VOLVO
812
BG 673PC
ADONI
80
100
VOITH
RETARDER
VIDEO
STEREO
80
2002
GL

A MILANO
ELAINI
I
BK·491TE
80
14 PM LIVING

MORENO FERRARI "ABITI NAVIGANTI"
MARANGONI SCHOOL OF FASHION
LIVING
It's raining Cats & Dogs

CODICAR
DUMB

MATTEO THUN "HONG KONG ROOM"
GRANDHOTELSALONE

LIVING

BRAZIL FAZ DESIGN
INSTITUTE BRASILE ITALIA

B&B ITALIA
TEXTILE BOOKSHELVES

NIELS VAN EIJIK
GLASS FIBRE LAMP
THE OFFICIAL POINT OF VIEW

198
AATTACK
FRONT DESK
samuele mazza
INSIDE OUTSIDE
INGEGNOLI
FLOWER SHOP
LIVING

Questo verde
e' curato da
esterni
ESTERNI
THIIS GARDEN IS TAKEN CARE BY...
THE OFFICIAL POINT OF VIEW
RR

200
GL
LIVING
EYES ON WORLDS
GERVASONI
GL
SB

"THE OFFICIAL FIGURES FOR THE MILAN
FURNITURE FAIR ARE GRATIFYING
AND GIVE THE IDEA OF A WELL
CONSOLIDATED FAIR, BUT THE EVENT
SHOULDN'T BE APPRECIATED IN TERMS
OF QUANTITY ALONE AS IT RESULTS
FROM EXCELLENT QUALITY."
LAURA LAZZARONI - COSMIT IMAGE AND COMMUNICATIONS MANAGER
LANDSCAPE FURNITURE
DOVE C/O DOVE
THE OFFICIAL POINT OF VIEW

SB
DeSIGN ACCADeMI eINDHOVeN
"IMPROVVISARe" eXHIBITION

OS
JUHANNA GRAWUNDeR
FOR Le CASe D'ARTe

AATTACK

FRANCK BRAGIGAND FOR DROOG DeSIGN
PAINTeD PLASTIC PLANTS

LIVING

CRISTINA MOROZZI (JOURNALIST)
PANDORA EXHIBITION

SHARP OR SPIKY?

THE OFFICIAL POINT OF VIEW

DUILIO FORTE "ANIMAL HOUSE"
GUIDO FORNARO ANIMAL HO
PALESTRA RAGNO
LIVING
ETTORE SOTTSAS FOR CLIO CALVI E RUDI VOLPI
"FORESTA"

DUILIO FORTE "ANIMAL HOUSE"
THE OFFICIAL POINT OF VIEW

LIVING

THONET
installation

THE OFFICIAL POINT OF VIEW

HALL 02
DOVE C/O DOVE
FAZ
DOVE C/O DOVE
LIVING
PC
TM

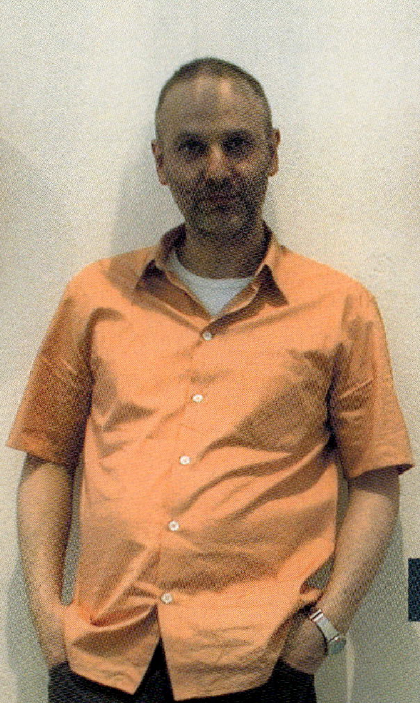

Comune di Milano
passo
carrabile
Aut n. 1113/C001/98

DESIGNERS BLOCK
Dove c/o Dove
THE OFFICIAL POINT OF VIEW

NINA FARKACHE "MARBLEROOM"
HOTEL DROOG

"Rolling Stones" are free objects. The
no left - they have no solid
chekerdjian/gunnardsdottir "rolling stones"
salone satellite
moooi
monkej boys "knitted lamps"
the official point of view

DESIGNER BLOCK

AGENTURA CAROLINA LTD.
salone satellite

LIVING

HALL 02 "PROGRESS..TO DREAM"
THE OFFICIAL POINT OF VIEW

A SHOW OF 50 PROJECTS CREATED BY 50 SIGNIFICANT FIGURES FROM THE DESIGN AND FASHION FIELDS (RON ARAD, ANTONIO BERARDI, MICHELE DE LUCCHI, TOM DIXON, STELLA MCCARTNEY, JEAN NOUVEL, PHILIP TREACY, ETC.) TO CELEBRATE 50 YEARS OF MOROSO'S ACTIVITY, LEADER IN THE PRODUCTION OF UPHOLSTERED PRODUCTS.
"OFF SCALE" HAS BEEN ORGANISED BY PATRIZIA MOROSO WITH THE DIRECT COLLABORATION OF FRANCA SOZZANI, DIRECTOR OF VOGUE ITALY.
A SERIES OF IDEAS IS MADE TO SCALE. TWO OF EACH DESIGN WILL BE PRODUCED: ONE FOR MOROSO TO EXHIBIT IN EACH MAIN CITY, WHILE THE SECOND WILL BE PUT UP FOR AUCTION TO RAISE FUNDS FOR THE CHILD PRIORITY FOUNDATION, ESTABLISHED BY CONDÉ NAST.

"WHAT IS VERY DIFFERENT IN THE WORLD OF FASHION AND OF DESIGN IS THE ROLE OF THE BODY. CLOTHES ARE SENSUALITY AND SEDUCTION. THEY ARE THE PROJECTION OF OUR BODY TOWARDS OTHERS. OBJECTS AND ARCHITECTURE GIVE US PLEASURE AND SATISFACTION COMING TOWARDS US"
ENNIO CAPASA - COSTUME NATIONAL

rt, Victoria design Ron Arad Malm, Fjord design Patricia U
215
PATRICIA URQUIOLA
FJORD
ESSANDRO DELL'ACQUA "ARMCHAIR"
CHRISTOPHE PILLET "RELAX CHAIR"
RENCE WOODGATE "SOFA"
MASSIMO IOSA GHINI "SHELL"
ENNIO CAPASA
COSTUME NATIONAL "CHAISE LONGUE"
MOROSO
MOROSO

15 PM LIVING

2.18
RR
MARTA MARZOTTO
M07 POODLE
M07 POODLE
MY GOAL IS TO HAVE PEOPLE
COME TO ME AND SAY
"THANKS FOR YOUR DESIGN,
IT CHANGED MY LIFE"
ANNE-LAURE GIMENEZ - ARCHITECT
LIVING
MIRIAM VAN DER LEBBE

THE OFFICIAL POINT OF VIEW
RICCARDO RINETTI
LUCIANA "MAESTRA DI COLORE"
SWAROVSKI EXHIBITION
THE OFFICIAL POINT OF VIEW

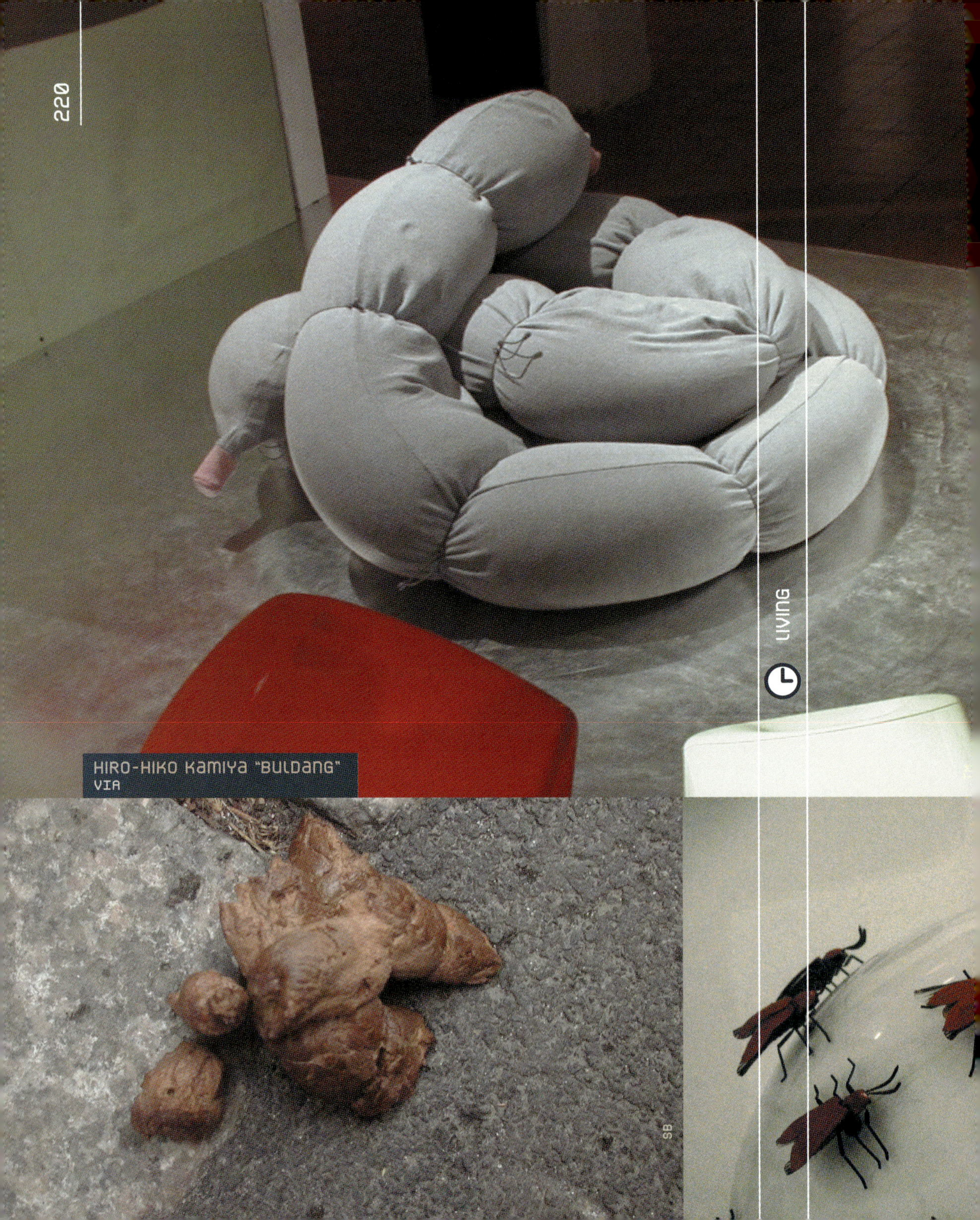

HIRO-HIKO KAMIYA "BULDANG"
VIA

"Design must reflect one's values, self respect, communication, effectiveness"

MARNIX OOSTERWELD - DESIGNER

222
Pa
RON ARAD FOR MOROSO
VIA
FAZ
moooi
LIVING
SB
CB

WUNDERKAMMER STUDIO
FIGURA P
THE OFFICIAL POINT OF VIEW

DROOG DESIGN

PC
Pa
IPD
RR
RR
LUBBE-EIJK
installation spazioconsolo
THE OFFICIAL POINT OF VIEW

LIVING

COR UNUM
CHI HA PAURA?

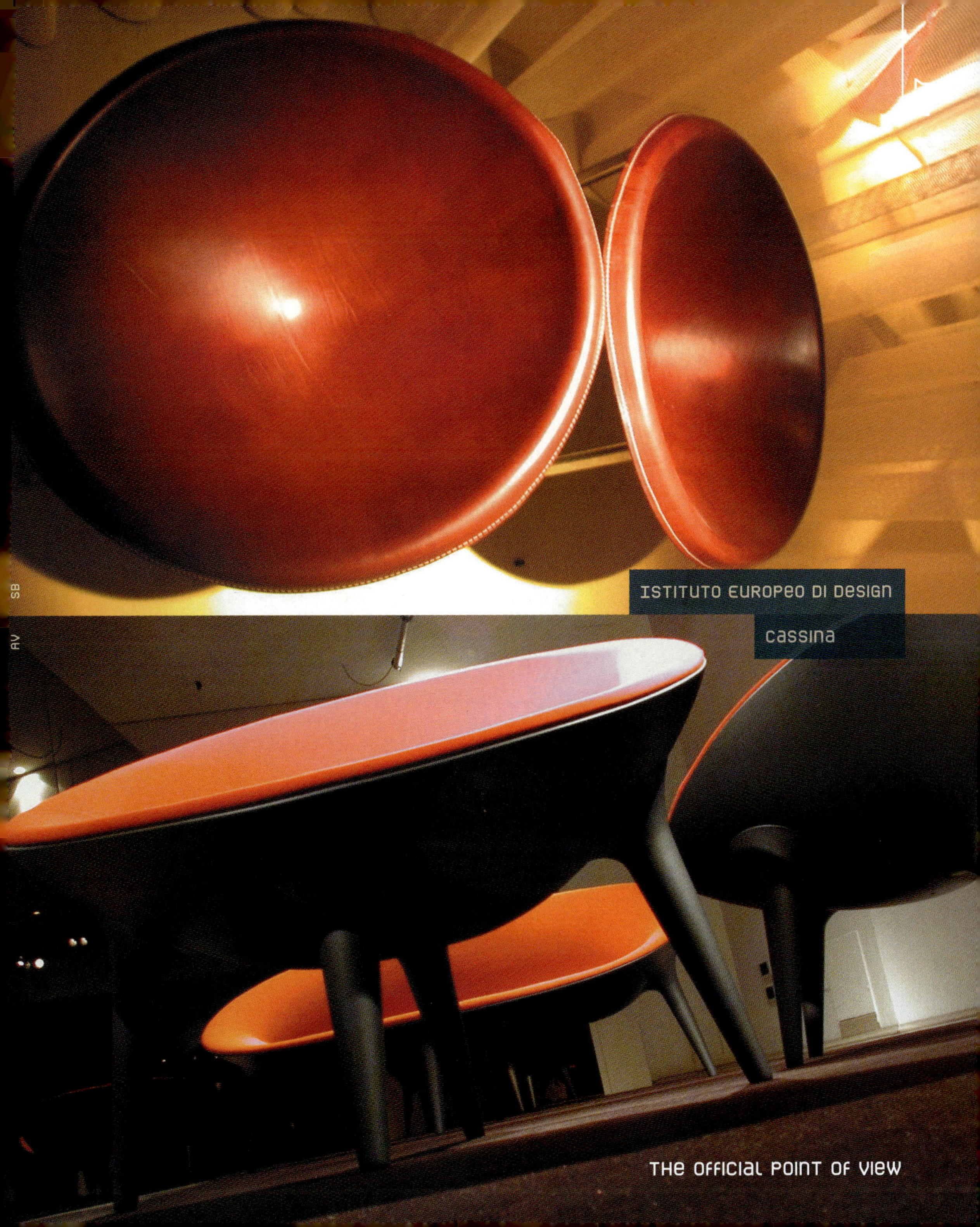

ISTITUTO EUROPEO DI DESIGN
CASSINA
THE OFFICIAL POINT OF VIEW

FOGGINI
LIVING
PC
PC
SOLARIUM
SUN PARADISE
SB

229
"RELIGION
IS ONE OF THE MOST
SOPHISTICATED APPLICATIONS
OF DESIGN IN HISTORY.
IT IS ALSO ONE
OF THE MOST DANGEROUS"
JOZEPH FORAKIS
SALONE SATELLITE
THE OFFICIAL POINT OF VIEW

"A LARGE PART OF THE HISTORY OF ITALIAN DESIGN IS BASED ON THE DNA OF THE COUNTRY'S FURNITURE INDUSTRY. THERE WAS NO REAL MARKETING OR PLANS BEHIND WHAT APPEARS TO BE THE GLOBAL PROJECT OF THE ITALIAN FURNITURE INDUSTRY. IT WAS THE DNA TOGETHER WITH THE WILLINGNESS TO TAKE THE RISK AND A DOUBLE SOUL WHICH ALLOWED THE PRODUCTION OF BOTH THE OBJECTS REQUIRED BY THE MARKET AND OTHERS MEANT TO CONVEY JUST IMAGE OR CREATIVITY AND POSSIBLY NEVER PRODUCED"

LAURA LAZZARONI

COSMIT IMAGE AND COMMUNICATIONS MANAGER

MARCO ZANIN - SOTTSASS ASSOCIATES

0c 70m 100y 0k
0c 10m 100y 0k
0c 70m 90y 0k
0c 70m 90y 0k
0c 70m 90y 0k
0c 70m 90y 0k
0c 70m 90 0k
0c 70m 90y 0k
0c 70m 9
0c 100m 70y 0k
0c 100m 70y 0k
0c 100m 70y 0k
0c 100m 70y 0k
PC
231
COLOR PROJECT
STUDIO SALVATI FOR ATELIER ZAV
SB
THE OFFICIAL POINT OF VIEW

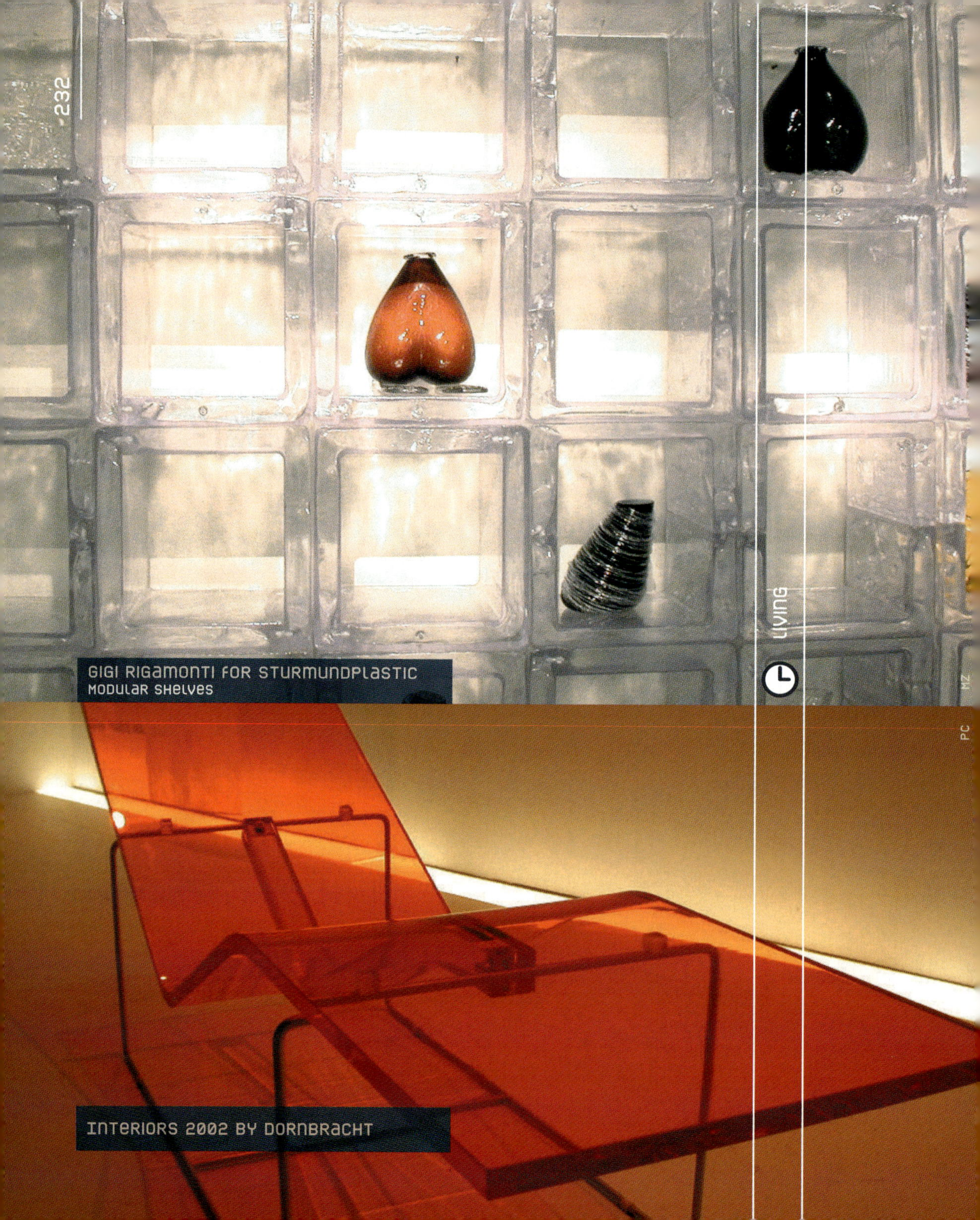
LIVING
GIGI RIGAMONTI FOR STURMUNDPLASTIC
MODULAR SHELVES
INTERIORS 2002 BY DORNBRACHT
PC
MZ

ENNEMLAGHI LTD.
design Village.it
THE OFFICIAL POINT OF VIEW

234
SB
DESINGERSBLOCK
STURM UND PLASTIK
LIVING
MZ

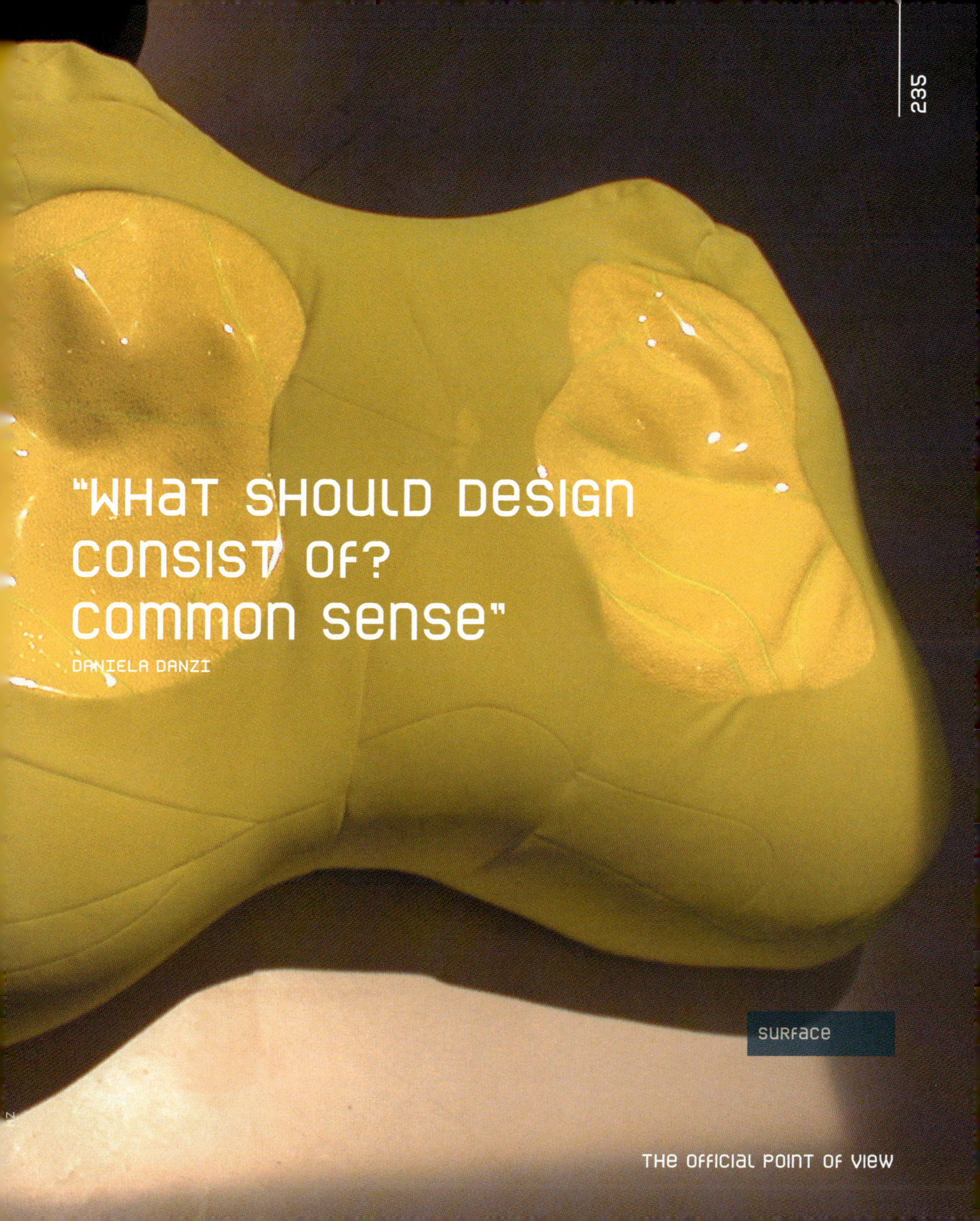

"WHAT SHOULD DESIGN
CONSIST OF?
COMMON SENSE"
DANIELA DANZI

THE OFFICIAL POINT OF VIEW

LIVING
GL
TM

ROSENTHAL SHOP
COLOR PROJECT
THE OFFICIAL POINT OF VIEW

ZANOTTA
MDF
KARTELL

Feeling Blue?

LIVING
WUNDERKAMMER STUDIO
aattak

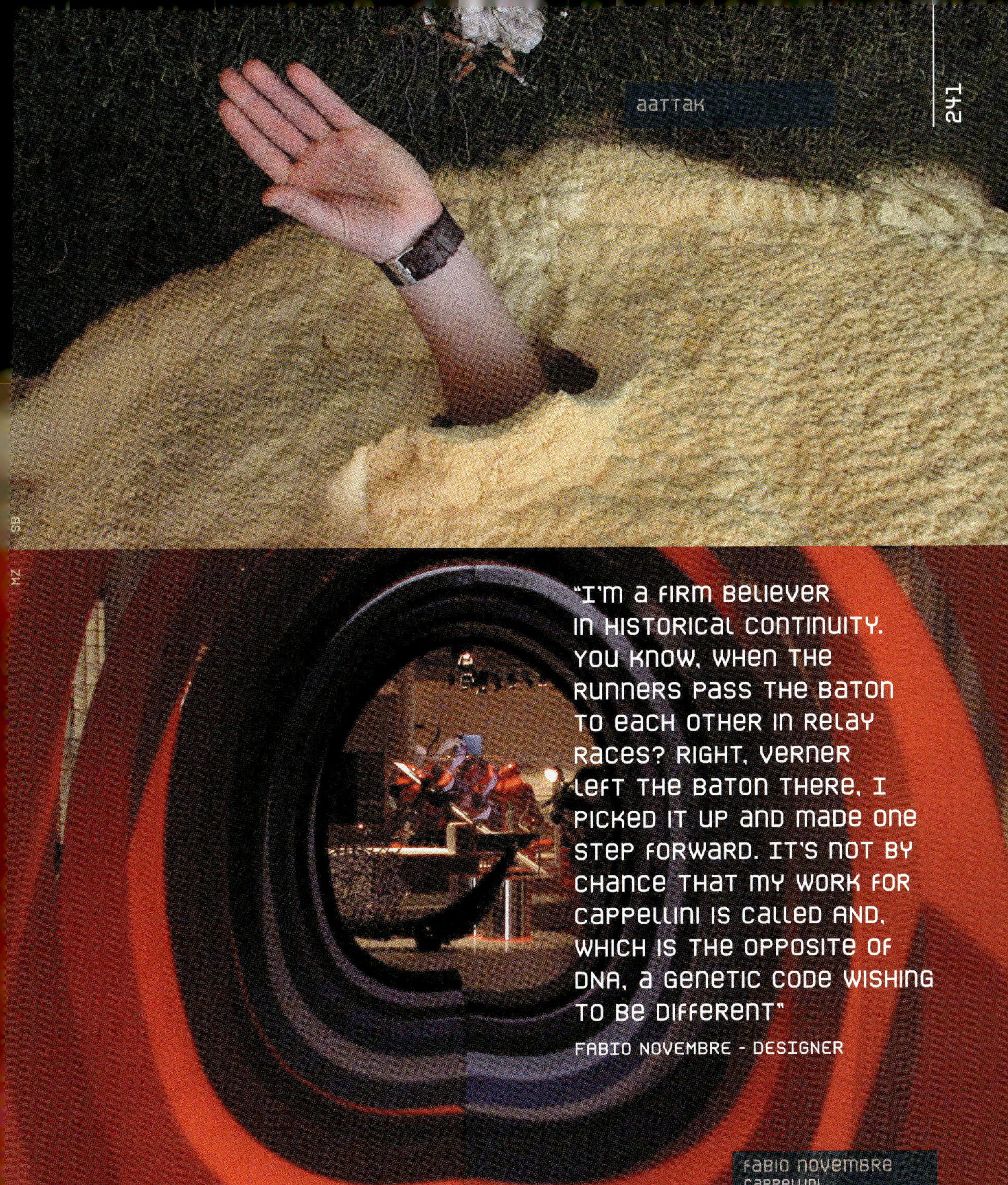

"I'M A FIRM BELIEVER
IN HISTORICAL CONTINUITY.
YOU KNOW, WHEN THE
RUNNERS PASS THE BATON
TO EACH OTHER IN RELAY
RACES? RIGHT, VERNER
LEFT THE BATON THERE, I
PICKED IT UP AND MADE ONE
STEP FORWARD. IT'S NOT BY
CHANCE THAT MY WORK FOR
CAPPELLINI IS CALLED AND,
WHICH IS THE OPPOSITE OF
DNA, A GENETIC CODE WISHING
TO BE DIFFERENT"

FABIO NOVEMBRE - DESIGNER

FABIO NOVEMBRE
CAPPELLINI

THE OFFICIAL POINT OF VIEW

242
MZ
FOLDING CHAIRS
YON RACEK/KEVIN RACEK -STEW-
LIVING

"MY OBSESSION IS WITH MINIMALISM AND CURVES;
THEY MIRROR MY PERSONALITY WHICH IS CLEAN
AND NEAT YET ALSO CURVILINEAR"
ERICA ELLENA   ARCHITECT

FIRE HOSE

HALL 02

THE OFFICIAL POINT OF VIEW

PAUL SMITH FOR CAPPELLINI
LIVING
SB
PC

THE COMPLEX OF FIRMS CHARACTERISING
THE ITALIAN FURNITURE INDUSTRY TODAY
IS THE RESULT OF A GREAT CULTURE
OF CRAFTSMANSHIP. EVERY YEAR NEW
PROVOCATIVE IDEAS SEE THE LIGHT
THANKS TO THAT GREAT TRADITION IN
CRAFTSMANSHIP, WHICH IS STILL ALIVE
TODAY IN THE ITALIAN PRODUCTION GIVING
IT EXTRAORDINARY AGILITY AND INNOVATIVE
DRIVE
MANLIO ARMELLINI - CEO COSMIT
BERTOLINI ARTE
THE OFFICIAL POINT OF VIEW

DOMUS ACADEMY
LIVING

247
CORSO COMO 10
SHOP
cavalli
THE OFFICIAL POINT OF VIEW

salonesatellite

FOR YOUNG DESIGNERS WHO HAVE SOMETHING TO SAY. FOR COMPANIES THAT AREN'T AFRAID TO TAKE RISKS. FOR EVERYONE WHO WANTS TO SEE WHICH WAY THE DESIGN WINDS ARE BLOWING. FOR EVERYONE WHO KNOWS US AND EVERYONE WHO DOESN'T KNOW US. SALONESATELLITE CONTINUES ITS EXCITING ORBIT AROUND THE WORLD OF FURNITURE DESIGN. (COURTESY COSMIT)

KEISUKE FUJIWARA

ome winners of awards with Marva Griffin Wilshire, curator of Salone Satellite
THE OFFICIAL POINT OF VIEW

salonesatellite

MZ

PC

BIANCHINI ROZENBERG

MASTRO DESIGN

MARC KRUSIN

KAZUHIRO YAMANAKA

251
A.K.I.S.
KaY THOSS
D+P
Käss und Heck
THE OFFICIAL POINT OF VIEW

salonesatellite

EVA SHCHILDT DESIGN    SATOCO TAKASHI

FRÉDÉRIC SCHAUMBURG

FORM SWISS PLUS -DESIGNTEAM
Gallana BARTHOLDI -HÖRR

KEISUKE FUJWARA BÜRO FÜR FORM

254
salonesatellite
drove spun lamp
DROVE
M.N.O.
GL
Pa
CLARISSA DORETTE LESSMAN
CDLDESIGN
QUINZE & MILAN
RR
Pa
RESERVED

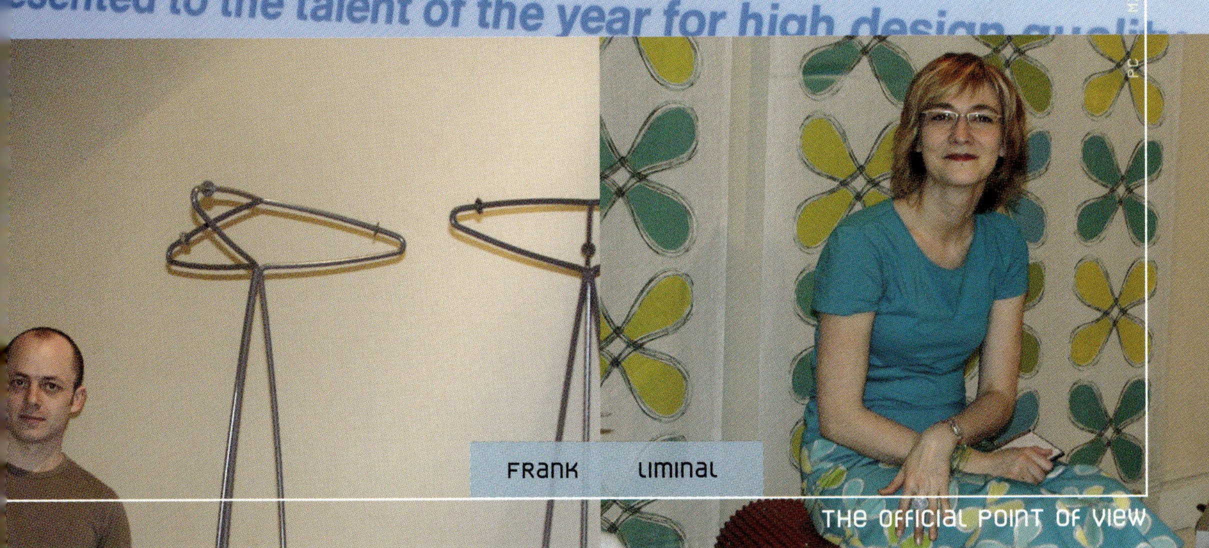

design report award 2002

the award for young international designers

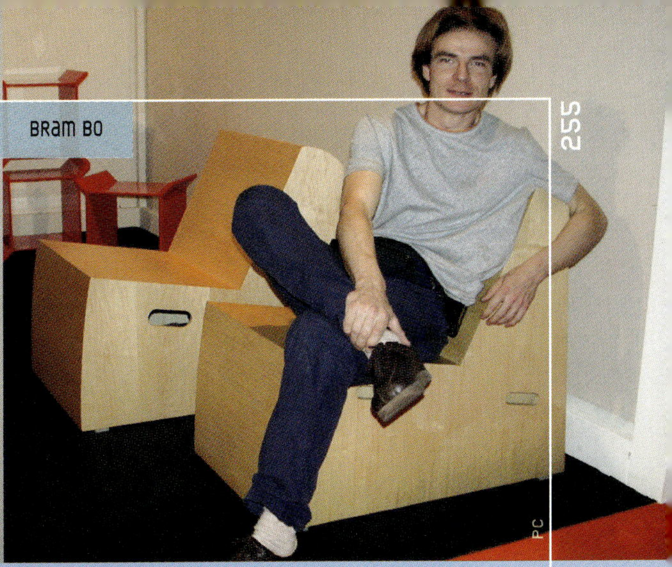

presented to the talent of the year for high design quality

salonesatellite
RISD
BE ALL THAT YOU CAN BE.
Barcelona+
HIROSHI TSUNODA
single
loredana longo design
norway says
LOREDANA LONGO
TORE BORGENSEN
NORWAY SAYS

ELBAZ/LIFEFORM
D-NISH
HIROKI TAKADA
ANTENNA.02
JACOPO DE CARLO
OPEN SPACES
NORWAY SAYS
THE OFFICIAL POINT OF VIEW
PC

salonesatellite
EHRIL AZZIMONTI
JORDI PIGEM
KNOCHDESIGN
AZZIMONTI /PIGEM
DREIPUNKT
KNOCH
DESIGN
HFD

LORBUS
POLLINE2
Kai RICHTER
CHARLES O. JOB DESIGN
259
report
design report
of view

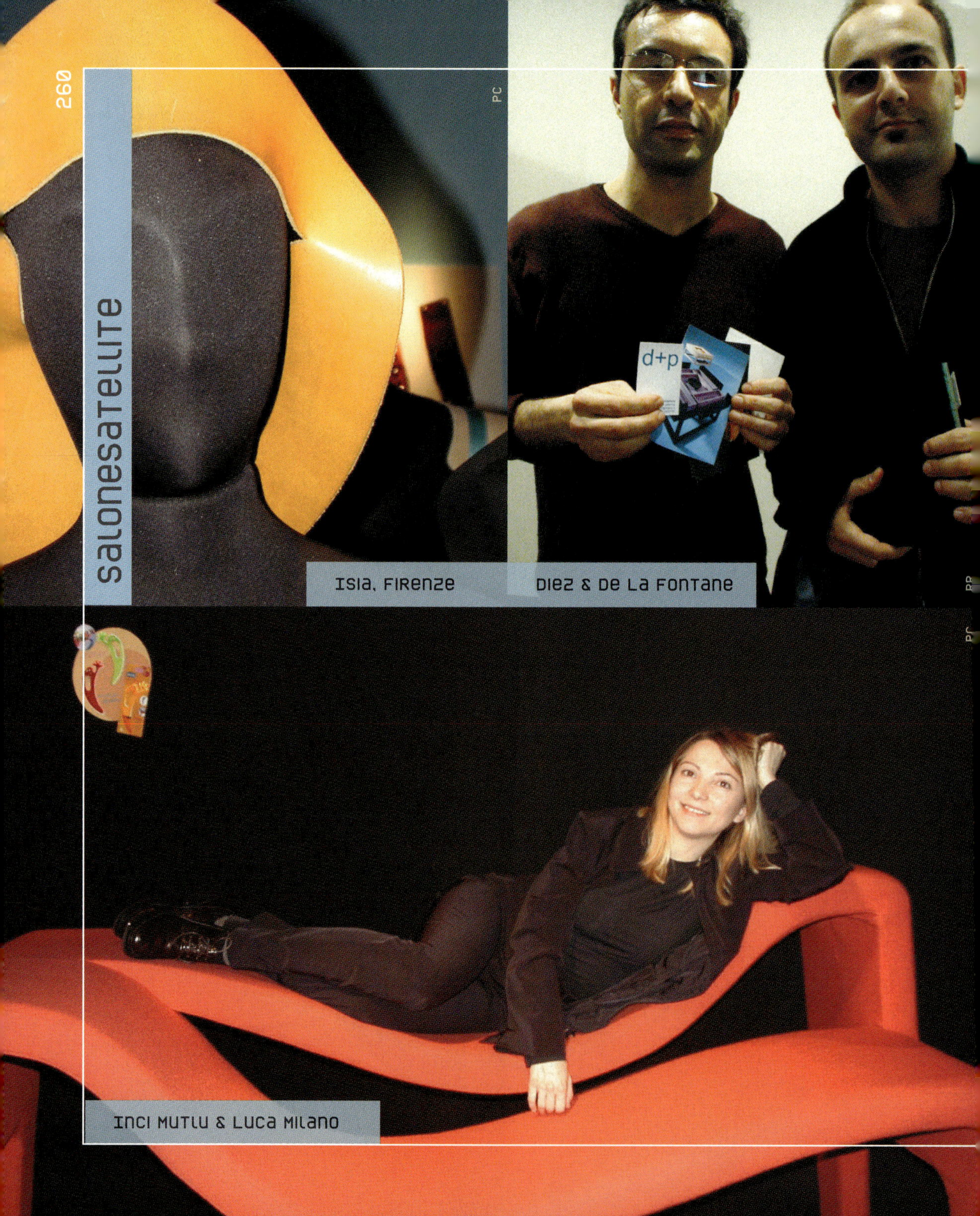

260
salonesatellite
PC
d+p
PP
PC
ISIa, FIReNze
DIez & De La FONTANe
INCI MUTLU & LUCa MILaNO

BÜRO FÜR FORM
DROVE
PC
FASHION FORCE
THE OFFICIAL POINT OF VIEW

263
16 PM PLAYGROUND
THE OFFICIAL POINT OF VIEW

NEGOZIO DI MOBILI
P.C.
ALBERTO SALVATI
PLAYGROUND

265
DOMUS ACADEMY
PANDORA   DRIADE
PC
PC
THE OFFICIAL POINT OF VIEW

ETRO
PLAYGROUND
Pa
SB

THE OFFICIAL POINT OF VIEW

268
APT. 5 DESIGN
PLAYGROUND
MZ
PC

THE OFFICIAL POINT OF VIEW

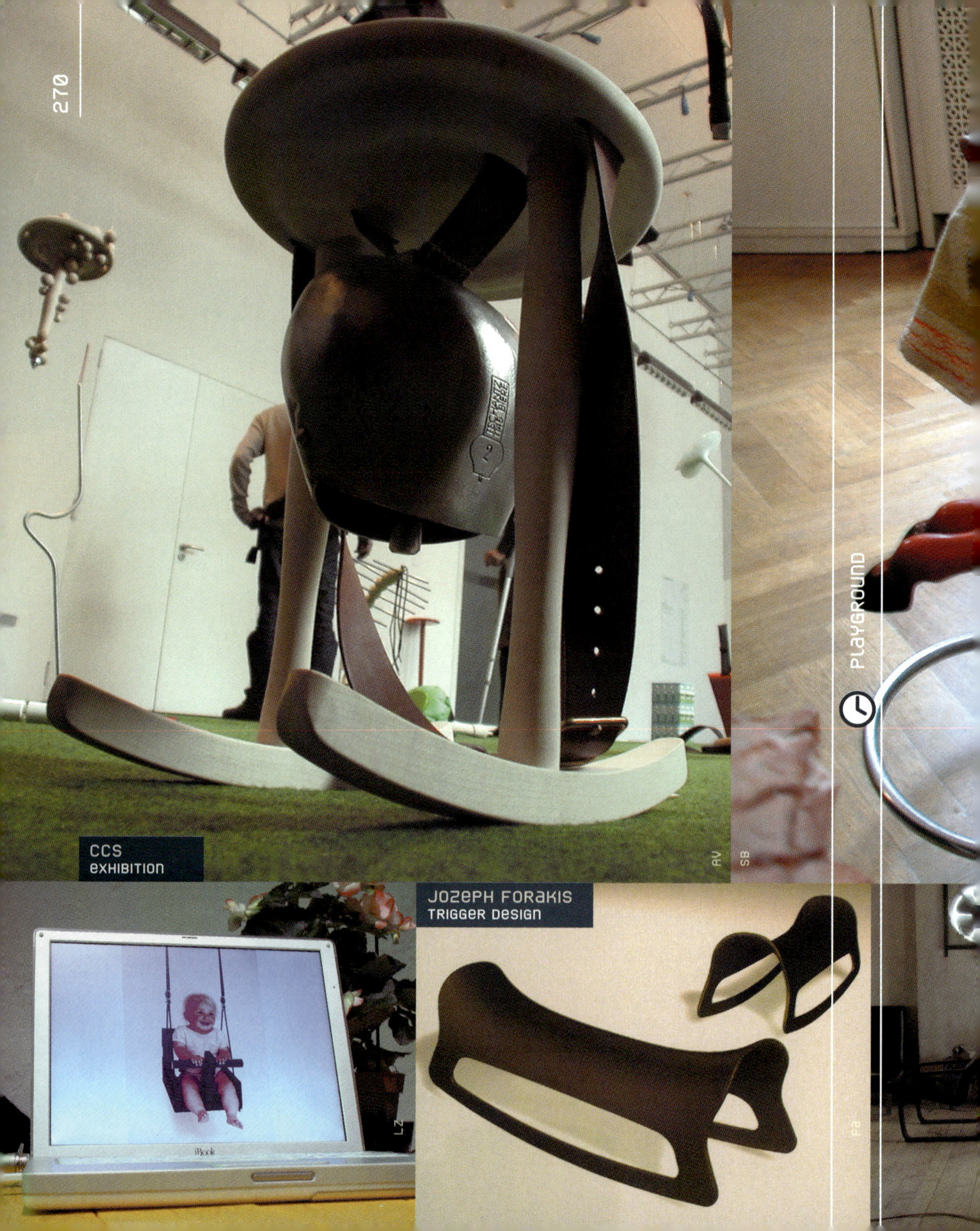
CCS
exhibition
AV
SB
PLAYGROUND
JOZEPH FORAKIS
TRIGGER DESIGN
iBook
LZ
P2

"DESIGN CAN TEACH US, AS WE MUST
TEACH ONE ANOTHER, INTELLIGENCE,
TOLERANCE, COMPASSION, HUMOR,
HARMONY, SENSITIVITY AND SENSUALITY"
JOZEPH FORAKIS
DESIGN ACADEMY EINDHOVEN
"IMPROVVISARE" EXHIBITION
MARCO SOUZA SANTOS FOR MOROSO
"OFF SCALE" EXHIBITION
THE OFFICIAL POINT OF VIEW

DENIS SANTACHIARA FOR DOMODINAMICA
DIEZ & DE LA FONTAINE
SATELLITE
THE OFFICIAL POINT OF VIEW

PC
KATHLEEN WALSH "SLIP KNOT SOFA"
SURFACE TAG TEAM 2002
body's perfect
nobody's per
SB
PLAYGROUND
JU

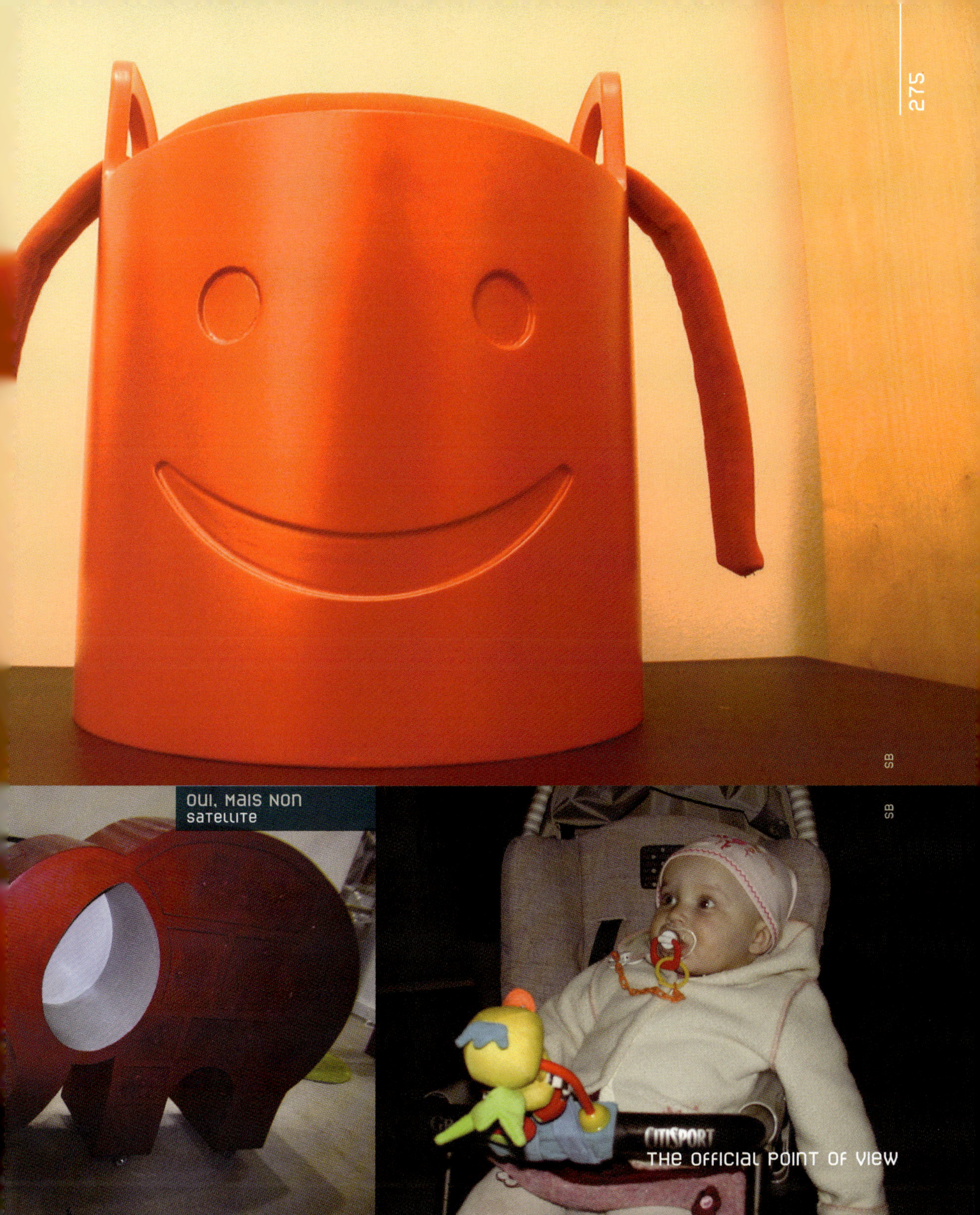
SB
SB
OUI, MAIS NON
SATELLITE
CITISPORT
THE OFFICIAL POINT OF VIEW

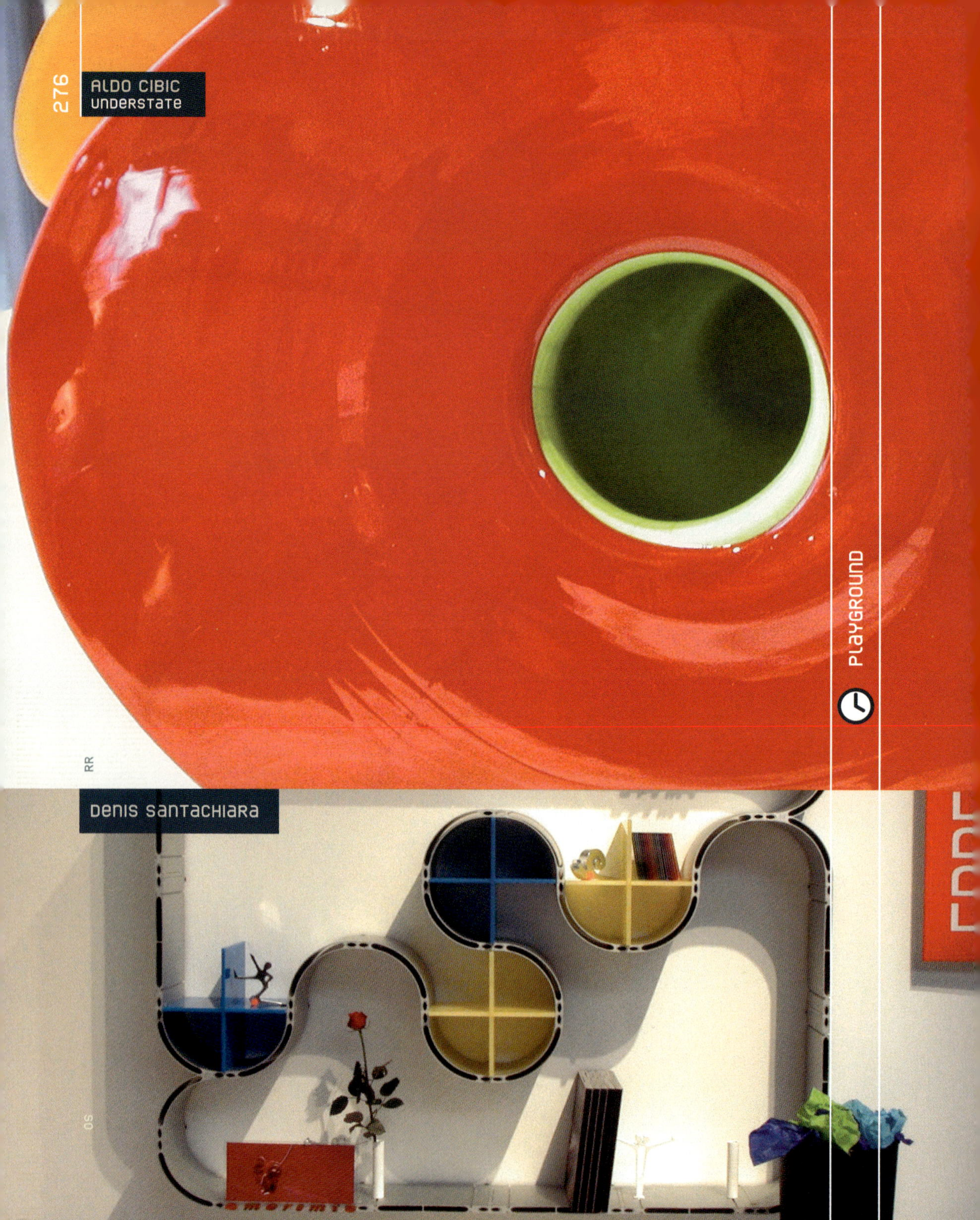

denis santachiara

THE OFFICIAL POINT OF VIEW

278
PLAYGROUND
OLMO & BRANDO
Pa
RR
RR
ALIAS

"EVERY TIME A DRAW A CIRCLE
I IMMEDIATELY WANT
TO GET OUT OF IT"
R. BUCKMINSTER FULLER

MARCO FARINELLA
FOR FIBER CLASS

HIJIRI SAKISAKA
FOR FIBER CLASS

DAVIDE MERCATALI
FOR FIBER CLASS

THE OFFICIAL POINT OF VIEW

RR

17 PM MARKET

AUPING-MORNATA
"S.L.A.K." SUITS
MARKET

83
FASHION FORCE
SATELLITE
"LIKE FASHION,
DESIGN HAS A HIGH MORTALITY RATE
AND THIS MAKES IT RICH IN PATHOS"
ACHILLE BONITO OLIVA - ART CRITIC
THE OFFICIAL POINT OF VIEW

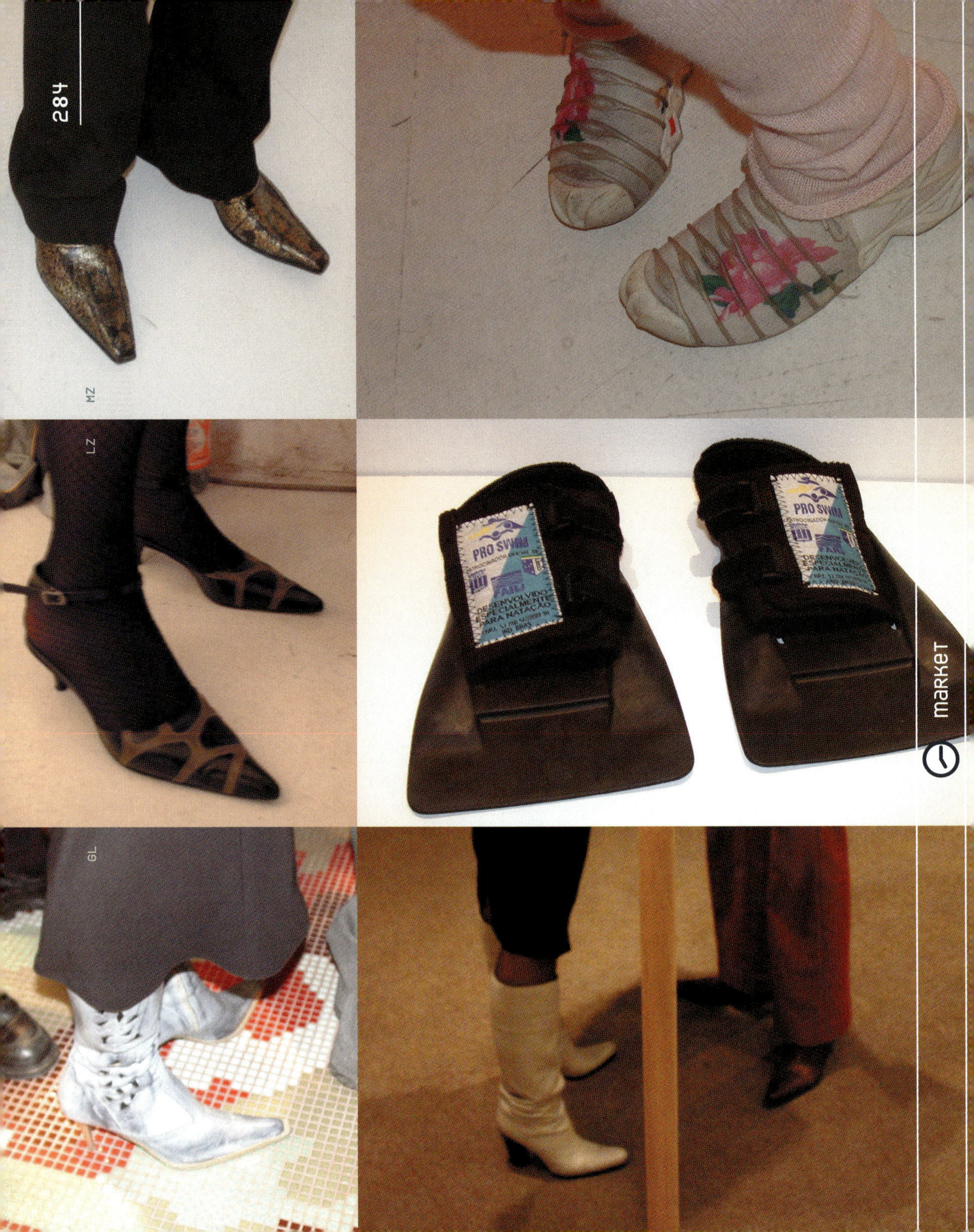

284
MZ
LZ
GL
market
PRO SWIM

285
"SHOES ARE
MY OBSESSION:
I'M LIVING IN QUEST
OF THE SHOES
OF MY DREAMS"
CLAUDIA FIGNANI X WUNDERKAMMER STUDIO
THE OFFICIAL POINT OF VIEW

STYLE
www.pubsiemme.it
art design group
17
dorr

david joyce
THE OFFICIAL POINT OF VIEW

MANDARINA DUCK

market

289
FRAGILE
estela
estela
EMERGENCY
Arancia
THE OFFICIAL POINT OF VIEW

BAGGIO
LIZARAZU
3
TOTTI
MARADONA
castoris

DEFEN
BROOKLYN
driade
design report
Gestaltung erleben   www.design-report.de 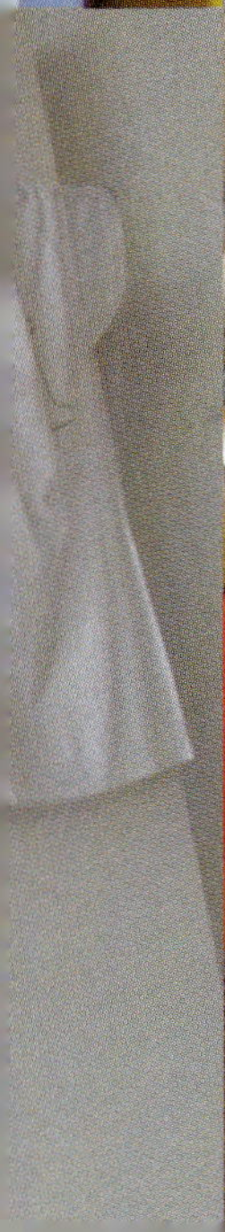
ABITARE 
A
ABITARE
A
GIROTONDO
PER L
AMO
THE OFFICIAL POINT OF VIEW

market

hidden
febal
iittala
FINAZZA
THE OFFICIAL POINT OF VIEW

emergency

SOS DESIGN WAS A CONTRIBUTION BY THE WORLD OF
DESIGN TO AN IMPORTANT HUMANITARIAN PROJECT.
THE AIM WAS TO COLLECT FUNDS FOR EMERGENCY, THE
ITALIAN HUMANITARIAN ORGANISATION FOR THE CARE
AND REHABILITATION OF THE CIVIL VICTIMS OF WAR AND
LAND-MINES. SOS DESIGN ORGANISED AN EXHIBITION OF
DESIGNER OBJECTS FOR SALE AT SOLIDARITY PRICES.
THE PROCEEDS OF THE SALE WERE ENTIRELY DONATED
TO EMERGENCY.
MANY DESIGN COMPANIES, DESIGNERS AND ART SCHOOLS,
ALMOST 200 PEOPLE IN ALL, WERE INVOLVED IN THE
PROJECT, TURNING IT INTO A TRUE HOMMAGE BY THE
WORLD OF DESIGN TO HUMANITARIAN ACTIVITIES.

ORDO
ETTO
QUANTO COSTA?
ORIZZONTALE
TENERE ORIZZONTALE TRANSPORTIEREN UND LAGERN
LEGEND TRANSPORT AND STORE FLAT
FRAGILE
QUANTO COSTA?
QUANTO COSTA?
QUANTO COSTA?
SOS DESIGN EMERGENCY
NO PROFIT
€2
EAU DE
FLEUR D'ORANGE
PER IL BAGNO
VENDUTO
PAGATO
MARCARINI
THE OFFICIAL POINT OF VIEW

TOTÒ
POLIZIA
18 pm GALLERY

YON RACEK/KEVIN RACEK -STEW-
SPAZIO ROMEO GIGLI

GALLERY
DILMOS
THE OFFICIAL POINT OF VIEW

Raffaele Celentano for Ingo Maurer
"Campari Light"

THE OFFICIAL POINT OF VIEW

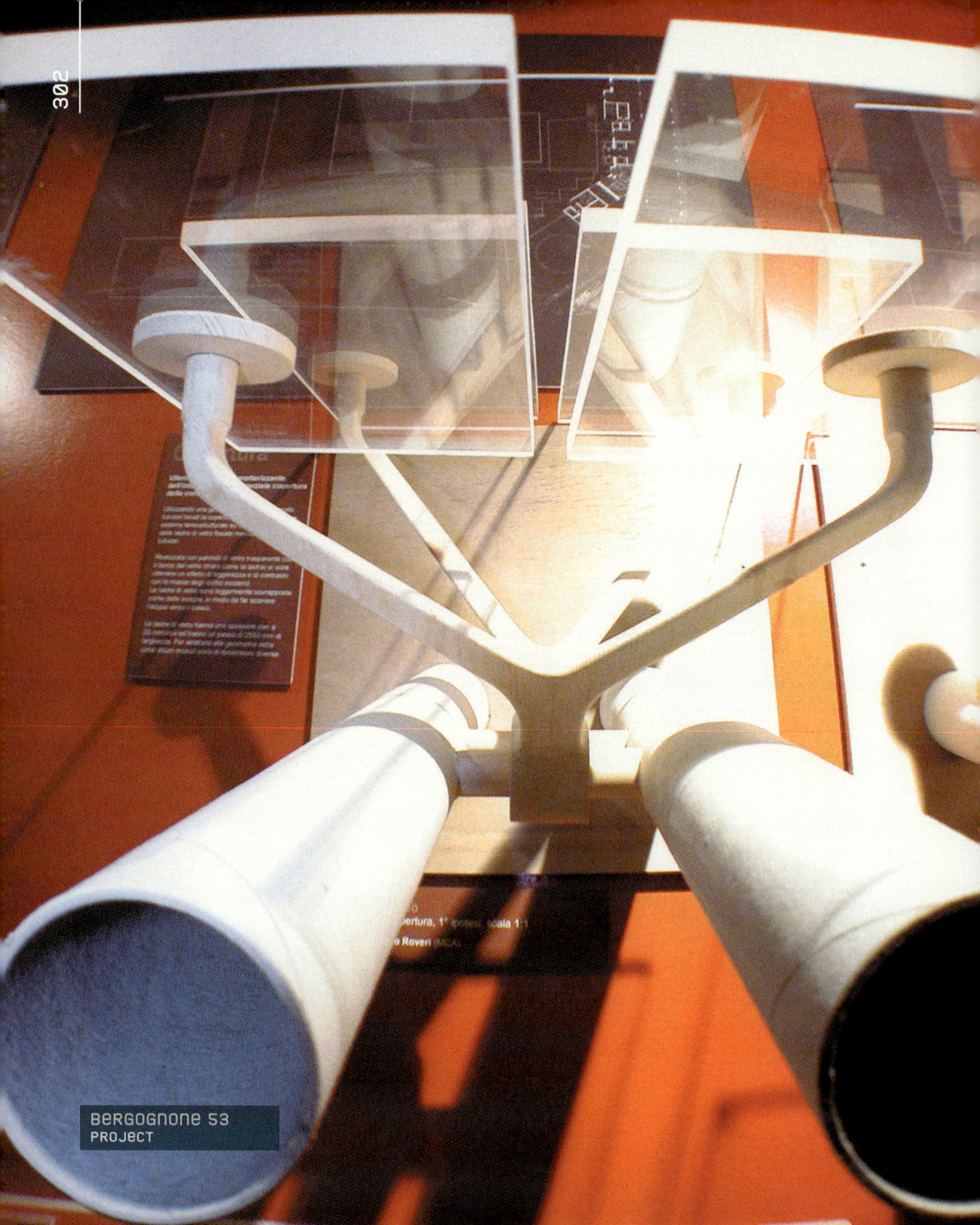
BERGOGNONE 53
PROJECT

ZAHA HADID FOR GRANDHOTELSALONE
"SYDNEY ROOM"
www.edra
EDRA
THE OFFICIAL POINT OF VIEW

CBI
SOFT TRANSPORT by cbi
niels van eijk

GALLERY
POLICE EVENTS
"IN ORDER TO KNOW IF DESIGN IS
GLOBAL OR NO-GLOBAL, WE FIRST
NEED TO KNOW WHO DESIGNS
FIRE EXTINGUISHERS AND WHO
DESIGNS GUNS"
FILIPPO MAZZARELLA - JOURNALIST AND FILMCRITIC
THE OFFICIAL POINT OF VIEW

MIRIAM VAN DER LUBBE FOR SPAZIO CONSOLO
Fucile d'assalto M70AB2 – Ex-Jugoslavia, Arsenale di Kragujevac

307
GALLERY
CAR DECORATION FOR KRIZIA
THE OFFICIAL POINT OF VIEW

GERALD PLOEGSTRE
SPAZIO CONSOLO

PRESIDENT
A UNIQUE CLITORAL STIMULATOR
EAGLE VIBRATOR
WITH COMFORT HARNESS
YOU'LL
REALLY
LOVE THIS
BEAUTIFULLY
SCULPTURED
VIBRATOR!
MADE OF
DURABLE
NONTOXIC
MATERIAL AND
A COMFORTABLE
MULTI-SPEED
VIBRATOR
CONTROLS
GALLERY
THE OFFICIAL POINT OF VIEW

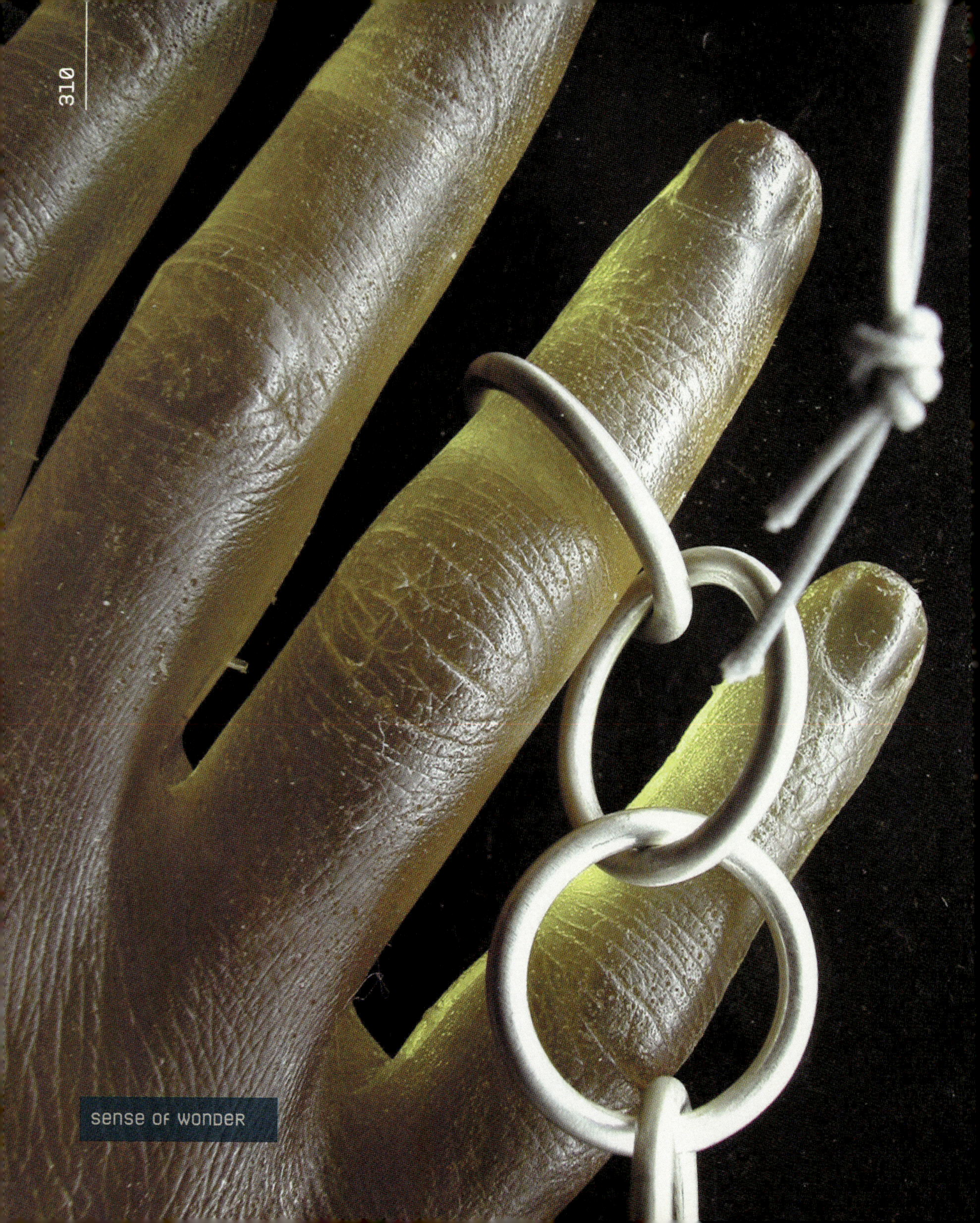
sense of wonder

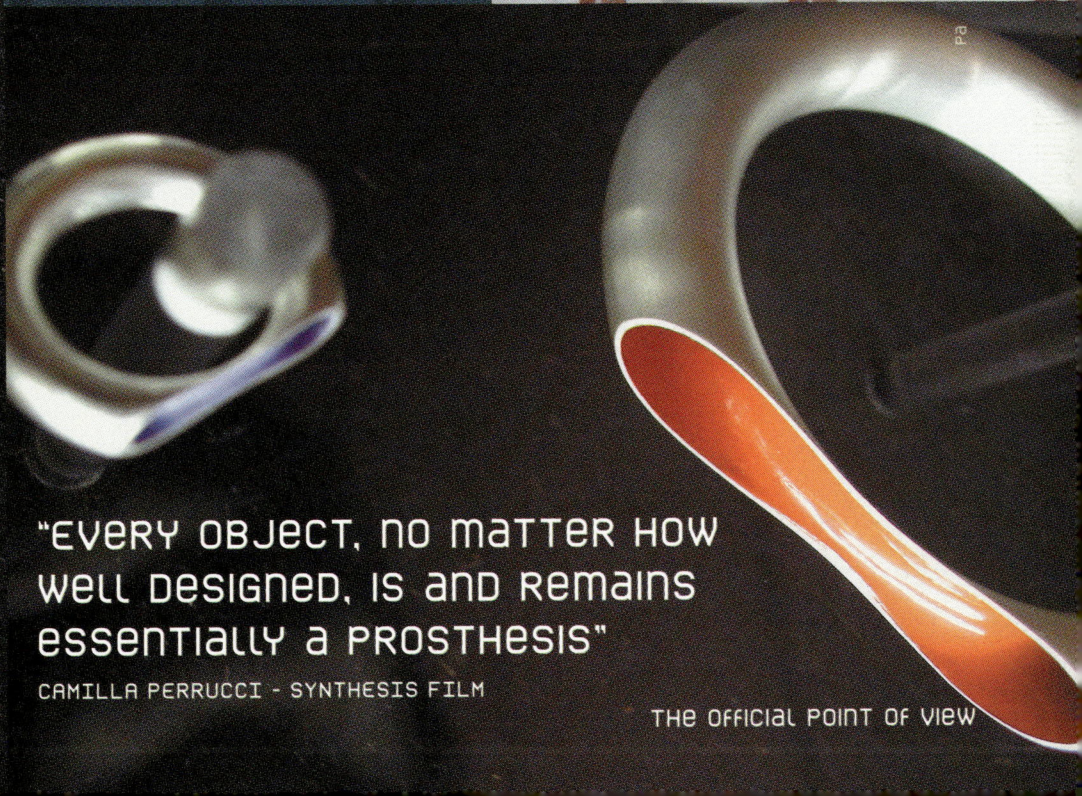

"EVERY OBJECT, NO MATTER HOW
WELL DESIGNED, IS AND REMAINS
ESSENTIALLY A PROSTHESIS"
CAMILLA PERRUCCI - SYNTHESIS FILM

THE OFFICIAL POINT OF VIEW

GALLERY

"A FEW YEARS AGO THEY SAID THAT THE INTERNET WOULD BE THE TOMB OF COMMERCIAL FAIRS. ON THE CONTRARY THE TREND OF VISITORS HAS BEEN CONSTANTLY GROWING SINCE THEN AND THE ACTUAL FAIR IS THE PLACE TO VISIT IF YOU WANT TO BE WHERE IT'S AT"
LAURA LAZZARONI, COSMIT IMAGE AND COMMUNICATIONS MANAGER
MASSIMILIANO E DORIANA FUKSAS FOR INTERNI
"THE HABITATION CAPSULE"

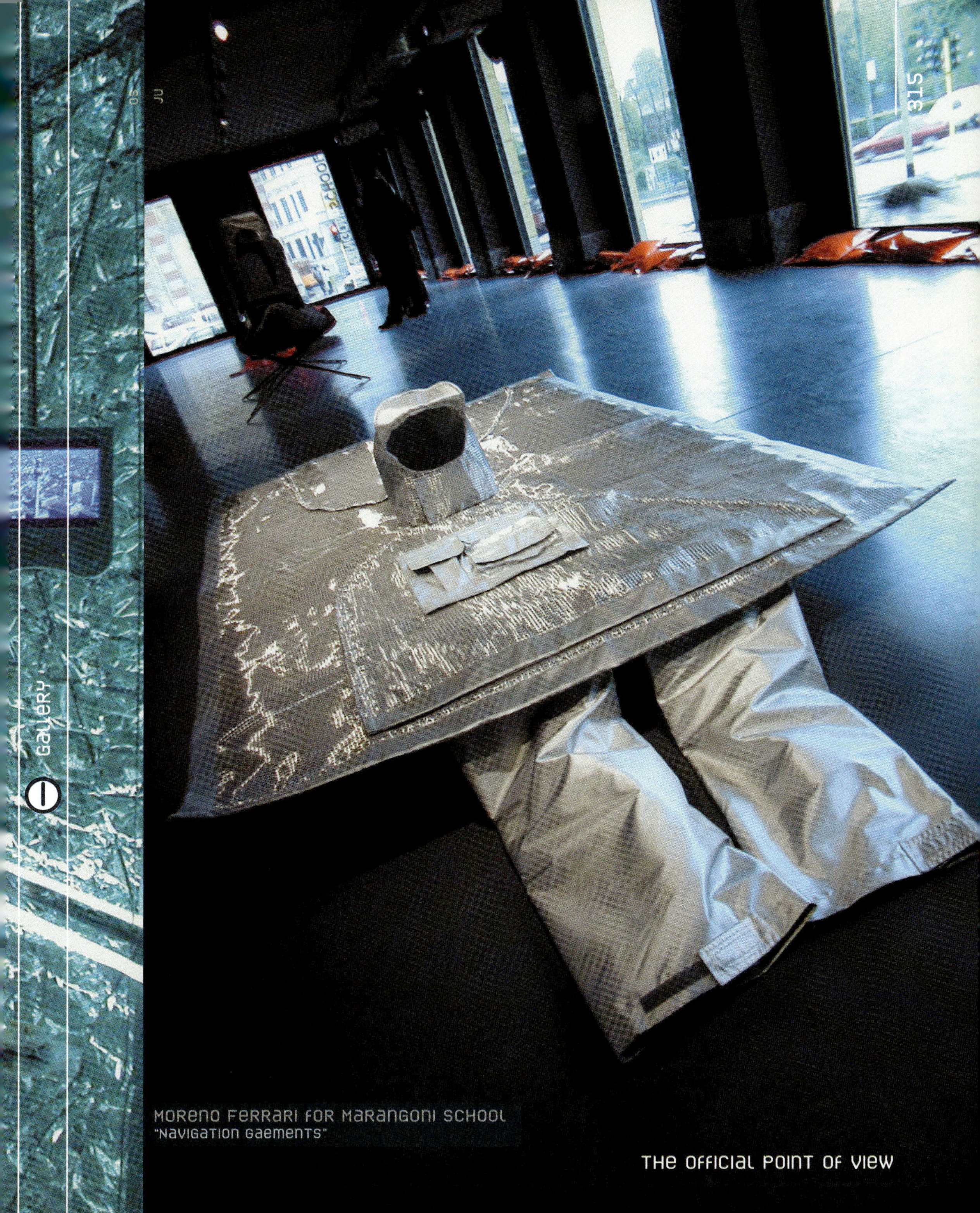

MORENO FERRARI FOR MARANGONI SCHOOL
"NAVIGATION GAEMENTS"

THE OFFICIAL POINT OF VIEW

19 PM GALLERY

KRIS RUHS FOR SOZZANI GALLERY
MONICA ARMANI

DILMOS
GALLERY
"IT IS ALMOST A
CONTRADDICTION THAT A
COMMERCIAL EXHIBITION
COULD BECOME A CULTURAL
EVENT. IT MIGHT BE A
UNIQUE INSTANCE;
AT LEAST NO OTHER CASE
SPRINGS TO MIND"
LAURA LAZZARONI
COSMIT IMAGE AND COMMUNICATIONS MANAGER
THE OFFICIAL POINT OF VIEW

"THE RELIGION WHICH MOST RESEMBLES DESIGN IS THE PURITAN PROTESTANT RELIGION. IT IS CAPITALISM ITSELF WHICH WAS BORN IN THE PROTESTANT SOCIETY WHERE 'DOING WELL' IS SEEN AS A CONDITION OF GRACE, GRANTING ACCESS TO PARADISE. BEING LINKED TO FUNCTIONALITY, DESIGN IS A CREATION OF THE PROTESTANT SOCIETY WHICH GENERATED IT TOGETHER WITH THE INDUSTRIAL REVOLUTION."

ACHILLE BONITO OLIVA - ART CRITIC

GALLERY
Hela Jongerius for Swarowsky
"Cristal"
THE OFFICIAL POINT OF VIEW

SUONARE

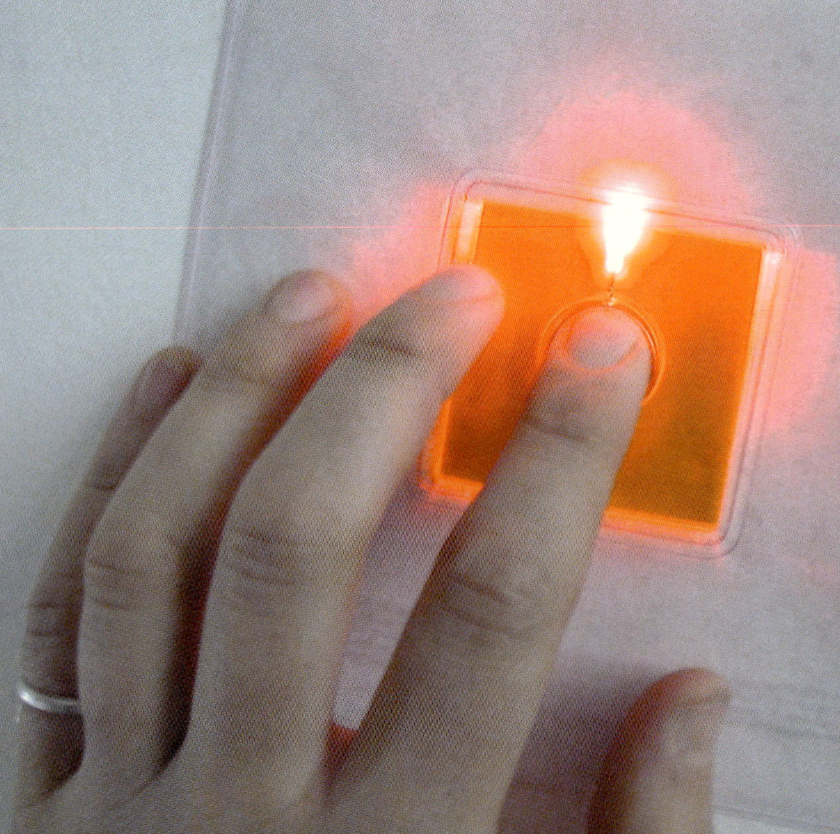

PURTINERIA

A. GARDELA
G. PALETTA
R
SABATINO
TETO
RIDOLFO OREFICI
CINGOLI
DUI
LACORTE

3

GALLERY

← 1° Piano

4

THE OFFICIAL POINT OF VIEW

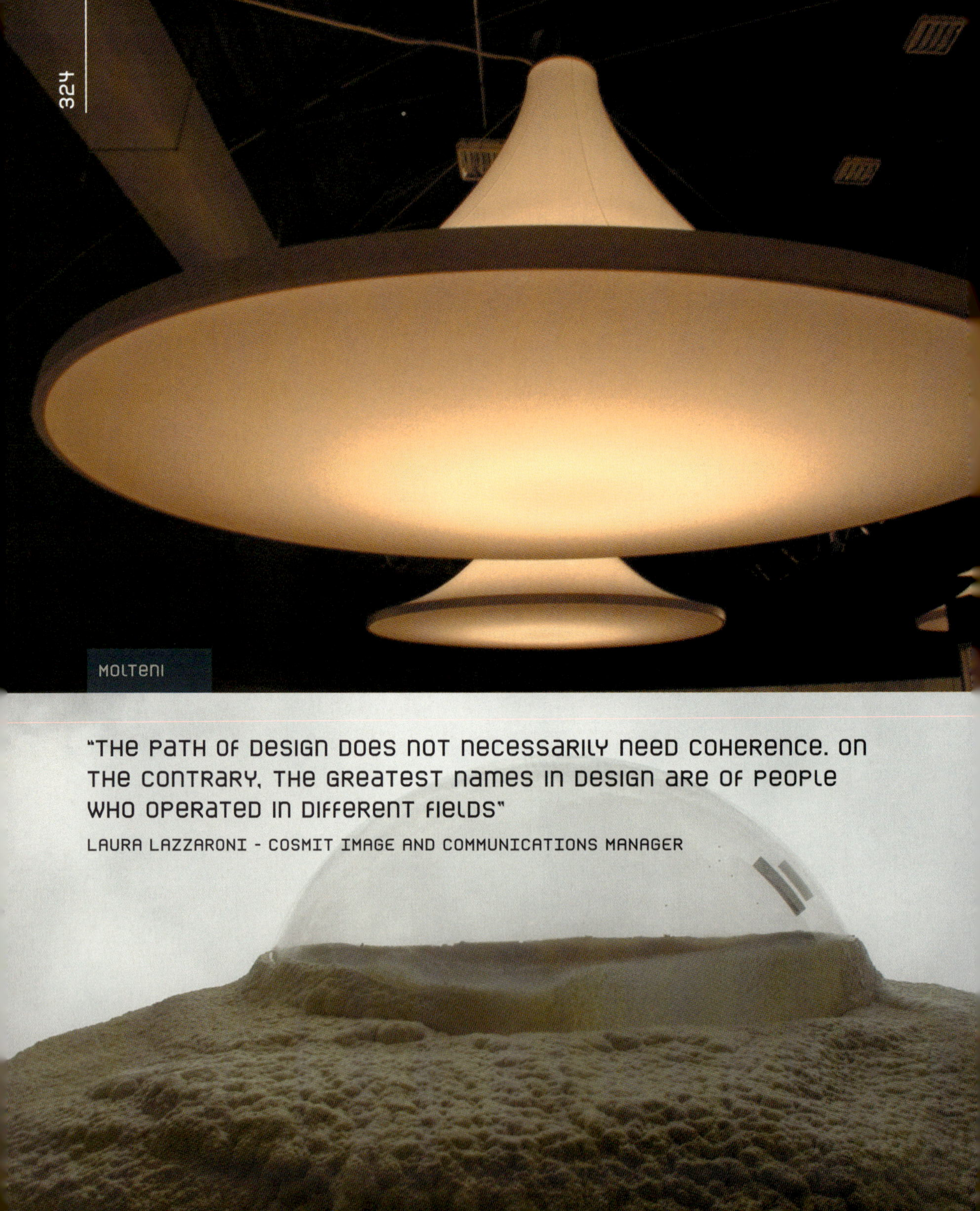

"THE PATH OF DESIGN DOES NOT NECESSARILY NEED COHERENCE. ON THE CONTRARY, THE GREATEST NAMES IN DESIGN ARE OF PEOPLE WHO OPERATED IN DIFFERENT FIELDS"

LAURA LAZZARONI - COSMIT IMAGE AND COMMUNICATIONS MANAGER

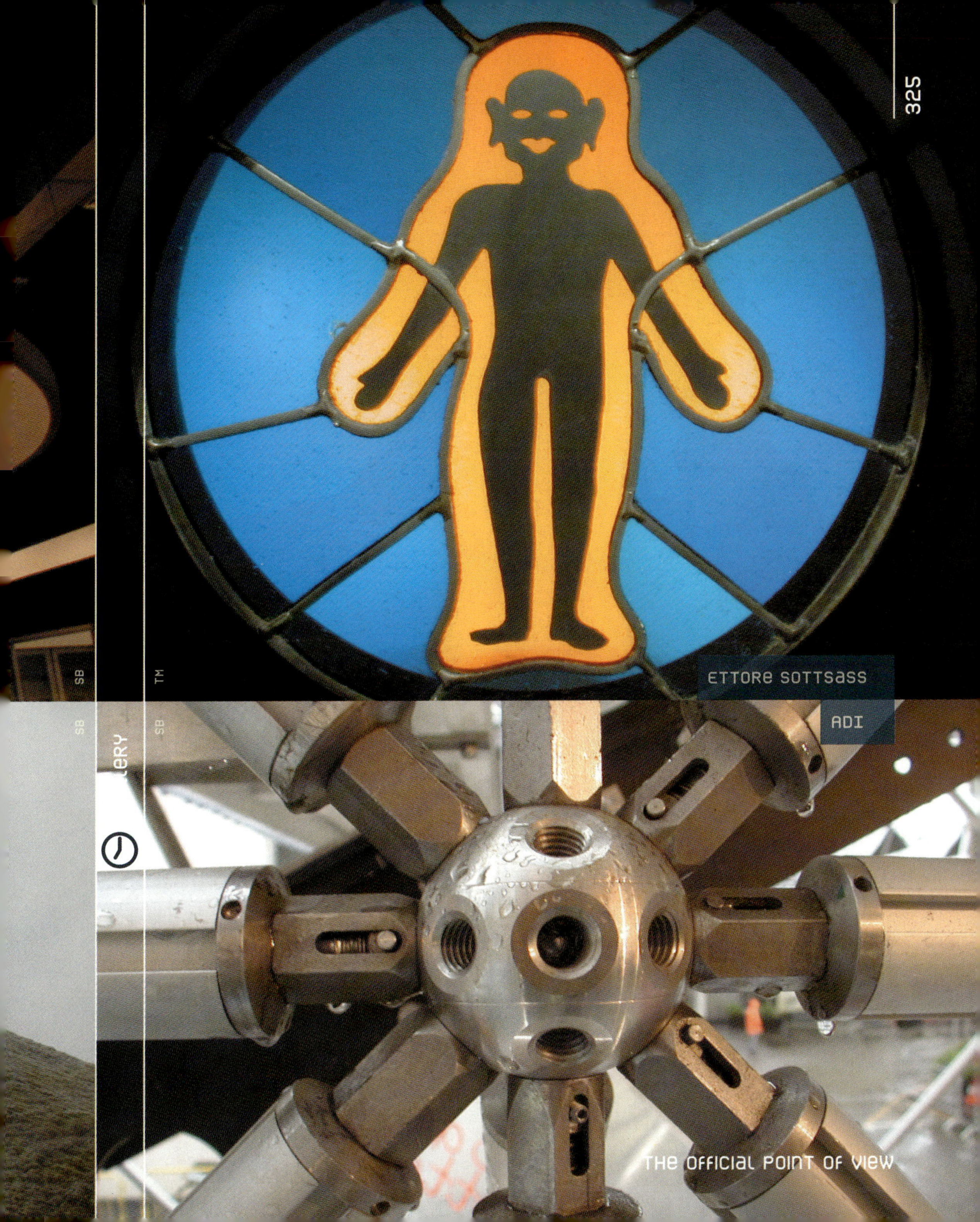
ETTORE SOTTSASS
ADI
THE OFFICIAL POINT OF VIEW

NIKE
PlaySwiss
SONY
C.C.S
SHIT DESIGN

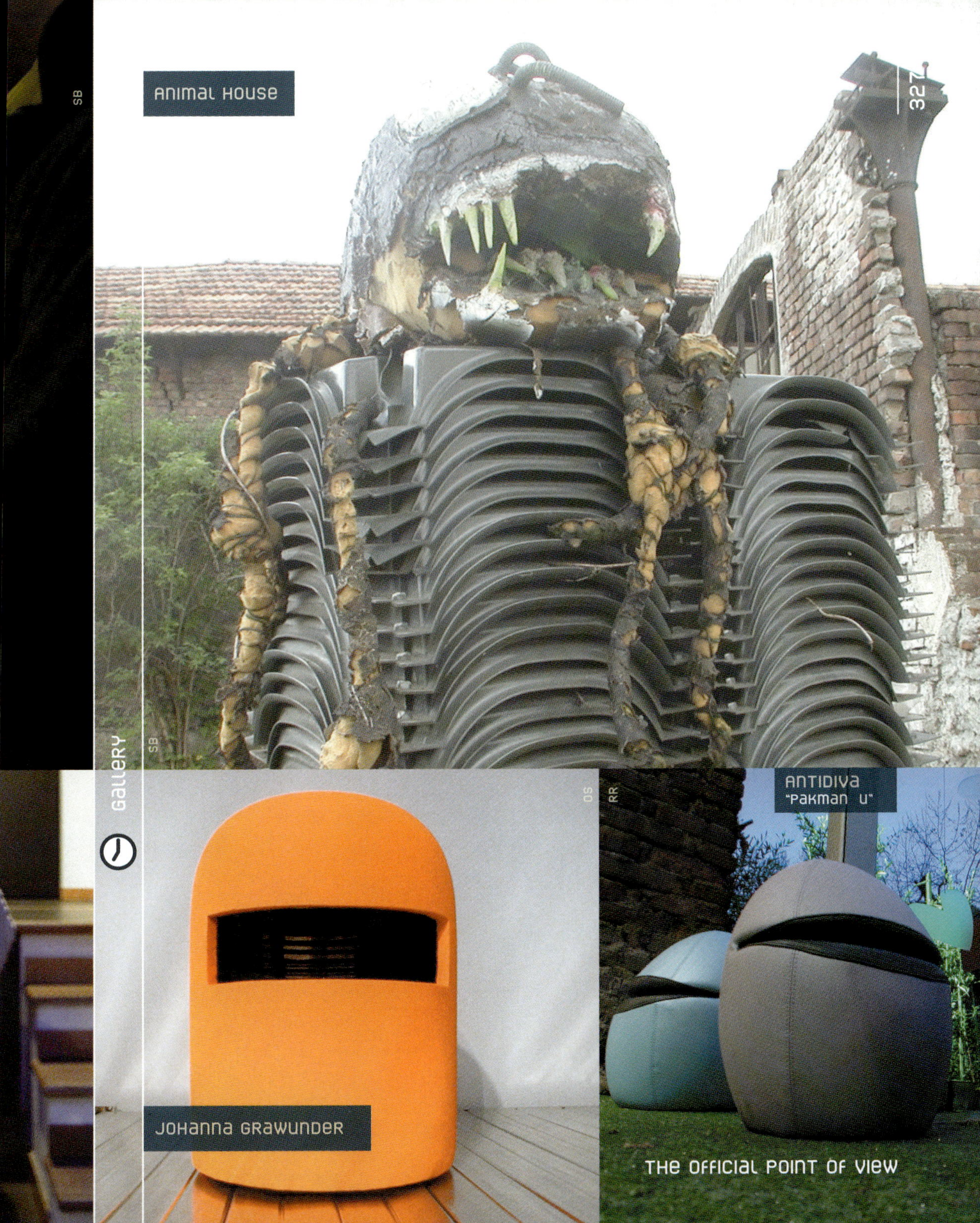
ANIMAL HOUSE

SB
GALLERY
SB
OS
RR
ANTIDIVA
"PAKMAN U"
JOHANNA GRAWUNDER
THE OFFICIAL POINT OF VIEW

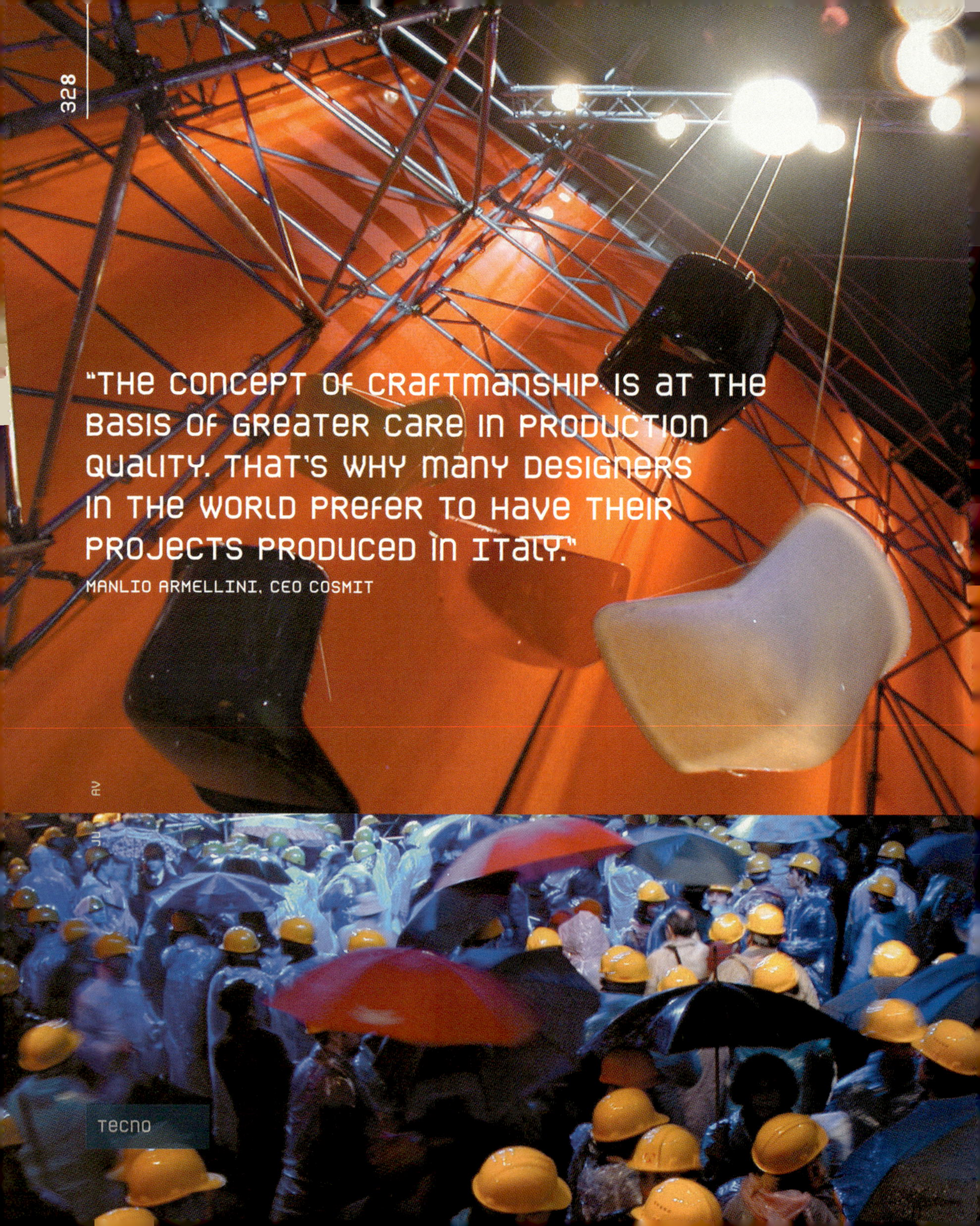
328
"THE CONCEPT OF CRAFTMANSHIP IS AT THE
BASIS OF GREATER CARE IN PRODUCTION
QUALITY. THAT'S WHY MANY DESIGNERS
IN THE WORLD PREFER TO HAVE THEIR
PROJECTS PRODUCED IN ITALY."
MANLIO ARMELLINI, CEO COSMIT
TECNO

CHANEL
SMERA
GALLERY
THE OFFICIAL POINT OF VIEW

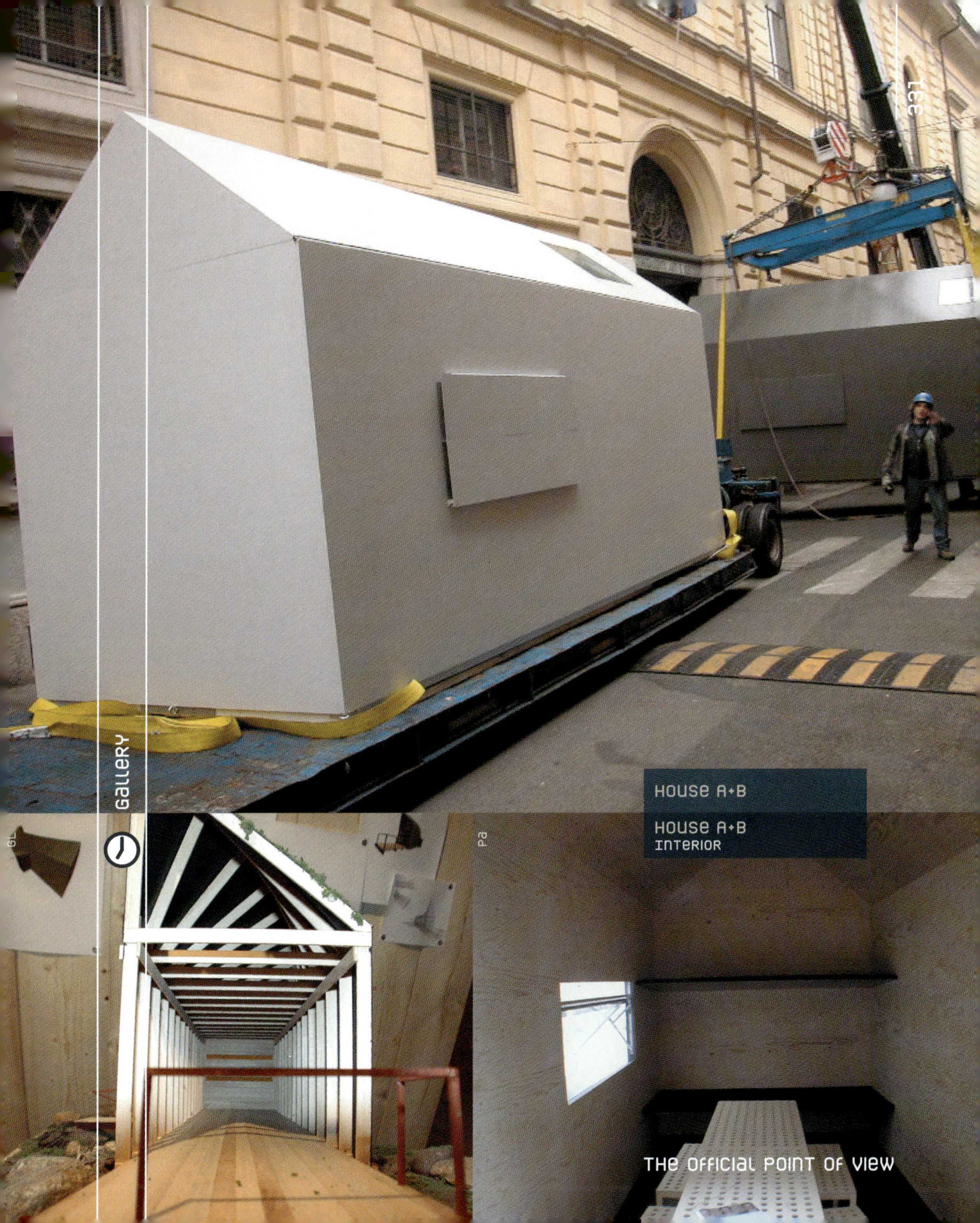
331
GALLERY
HOUSE A+B
HOUSE A+B
INTERIOR
THE OFFICIAL POINT OF VIEW

GRAZIA NERI
KARTELL

THE OFFICIAL POINT OF VIEW

L'anverre
SB
Car
Car
Ca
Ca

GALLERY
THE OFFICIAL POINT OF VIEW

THE 10° EDITION OF DROOG DESIGN IN MILAN MEETS EVERYDAY CULTURE.THE PRESNTATIONS ARE DOMINATED BY THE INTEGRATION OF THE NEW AND THE EXIISTING,THE SPECIAL AND THE COMMON,THE UGLY AND THE BEUTIFUL,PERFECTION AND IMPERFECTION, ILLUSION AND REALITY. FOR FIVE DAYS DROOG DESIGN PUTS UP AN EXISTING ONE-STAR HOTEL.AT FIRST SIGHT EVERYTHING IS WHAT IT USED TO BE.NO REAL CHANGES HAVE BEEN MADE IN THE HOTEL'S INTERIOR BUT IN EACH ROOM SOMETHING HAS BEN ADDED BY THE PARTICIPATING DESIGNERS.

MAUReeN MOOReN/DANIel VAN DeR VelDëN "PASSPORT"
HecTOR SeRRANO
"CLOTHeS HANGeR LAMP"
HAN KONING/LOUISe MANIeTTe/TARMO PIIRMeTS/JeT VeRVeS
-0,028 cal ↑
-0,024 cal ↑
THe OFFICIAL POINT OF VIeW

HOTEL DROOG REAL LIFE REVISITED
CHRIS KABEL "STICKY LAMPS"
CYNTHIA HATHAWAY
"DIGITAL COOCOO CLOCKS"
ALBERGO 18 COMMERCIO

PRELASCIA QUI LE TUE SCARPE
take out your shoes
PAOLO ULIAN "MAT WALK"
EGBERT-JAN LAM "RIETVELD FOLDING CHAIR"
THE OFFICIAL POINT OF VIEW

TET REUVER "PORTABLE BATH"

EMMY BLOK "CHANGE YOUR VIEW"

AV

JOOST GROOTENS " BULLET PROOF SLEEPIG BAG"

MATIJS KORPERSHOEK "BLANCO JIGSAW"

TUB
BE

20 pm Restaurant

BauBau's
Boffi installation

AV
MZ
345
CAP CAP CAP CAP
cappellini
RESTAURANT
THE OFFICIAL POINT OF VIEW

KUNDALINI

RESTAURANT
THE OFFICIAL POINT OF VIEW

ALDO CIBIC
"WORKSHOP NEW STORIES NEW DESIGN"

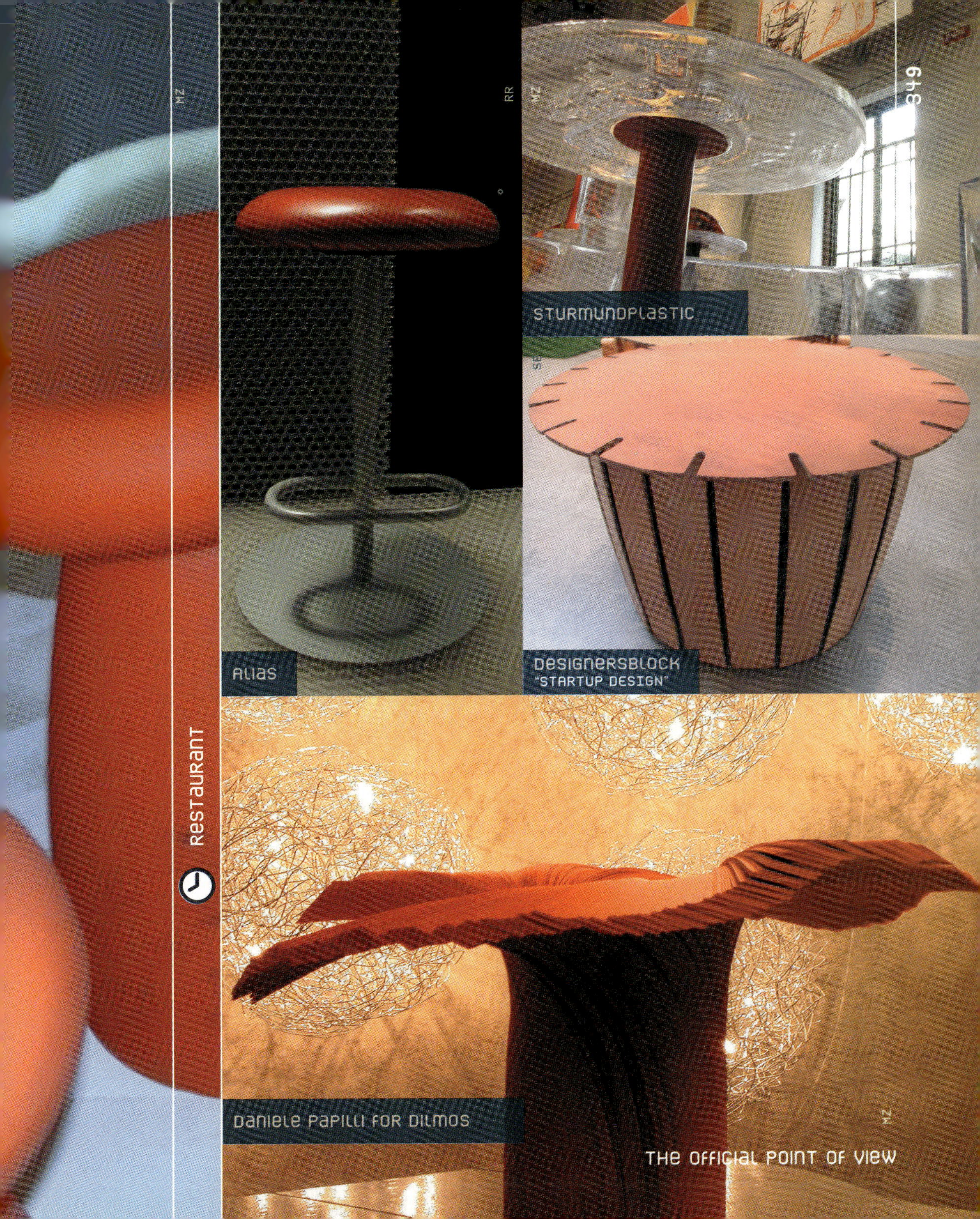
348
RESTAURANT
ALIAS
STURMUNDPLASTIC
DESIGNERSBLOCK
"STARTUP DESIGN"
DANIELE PAPILLI FOR DILMOS
THE OFFICIAL POINT OF VIEW

STEFANO GALLIZIOLI FOR CORO

351
SB
SO
RESTAURANT
EDIZIONE STRAORDINARIA
THE OFFICIAL POINT OF VIEW

352
satellite

353
Restaurant
AIR FRANCE
FRAGILE
THE OFFICIAL POINT OF VIEW

cappellini

miele
droog design

"THE PROBLEM WITH DESIGN
IS THAT IT IS NOT 'GLOBAL'
ANYMORE. THE GOOD THING IN
DESIGN WAS THAT IT HAD TO BE
AFFORDABLE TO EVERYONE, BUT
PRICES TODAY AREN'T.
THE CONCEPT AT THE BASIS
OF DESIGN IS THAT OF LINKING
AN OBJECT WHICH IS ALMOST
A WORK OF ART TO THE
PROCESSES OF LARGE INDUSTRIAL
PRODUCTION. PRICES THEN
SHOULD BE LOW TO ALLOW
EVERYONE TO OWN BEAUTIFUL
OBJECTS. IT IS NOT SO"

ANTONELLA MIANTE - ARCHITECT

RESTAURANT

CAPPELLINI

THE OFFICIAL POINT OF VIEW

RISTORANTE "QUATTROCENTO"

pa
SB
Mila SHöN
zeus
MZ
RESTAURANT
Luca Pacchioni
RISTORANTE QUATTROCENTO
THE OFFICIAL POINT

21 PM BATHROOM

FABIO NOVEMBRE FOR BISAZZA

BATHROOM
SANDRO CHIA
ARTIST
THE OFFICIAL POINT OF VIEW
GL
PA
JU

"DESIGN IS EPIPHANY. IT IS IMPOSSIBLE TO EXPLAIN. DESIGN IS LIKE RIDLEY SCOTT WHO DIRECTED BLADE RUNNER AND NEVER REPEATS HIMSELF. CREATION IS THE CONCENTRATION OF 'BEING' IN A SINGLE INSTANT"

FABIO NOVEMBRE - DESIGNER

FABIO NOVEMBRE FOR BISAZZA

MATIJS KORPERSHOEK FOR HOTEL DROOG
"BLANCO JIGSAW"
393
BATHROOM
THE OFFICIAL POINT OF VIEW

GAETANO PESCE "MOSCOW"
GRAND HOTEL SALONE

FORMULA
SBIANCANTE
Vim
clorex
IGIENE
SICURA
100%
CAPPELLINI
BATHROOM
THE OFFICIAL POINT OF VIEW

MY MIRROR
GL

HECTOR SERRANO "CLOTHES HANGER LAMP"
HOTEL DROOG

HAN KONING/LOISE MANIETTE
TARMO PIIRMETS/JET VERVEST
HOTEL DROOG

BATHROOM

THE OFFICIAL POINT OF VIEW

DONATA PARUCCINI
VIRTUAL DESIGN

369
SB
MZ
BRASIL FAZ
BATHROOM
MY BASIN
THE OFFICIAL POINT OF VIEW

PERSONAL GARDEN

MUTLU/MILANO
salone satellite

WHIRLPOOL
371
BATHROOM
THE OFFICIAL POINT OF VIEW

372
BOFFI
GL
SB
BAGNO ALESSI

BATHROOM
AV
ASTRID KLEIN & MARK DYTHAM FOR INTERNI
"THE SOFT BATH"
THE OFFICIAL POINT OF VIEW

MZ
MZ
GL
BATHROOM
AV
THE OFFICIAL POINT OF VIEW

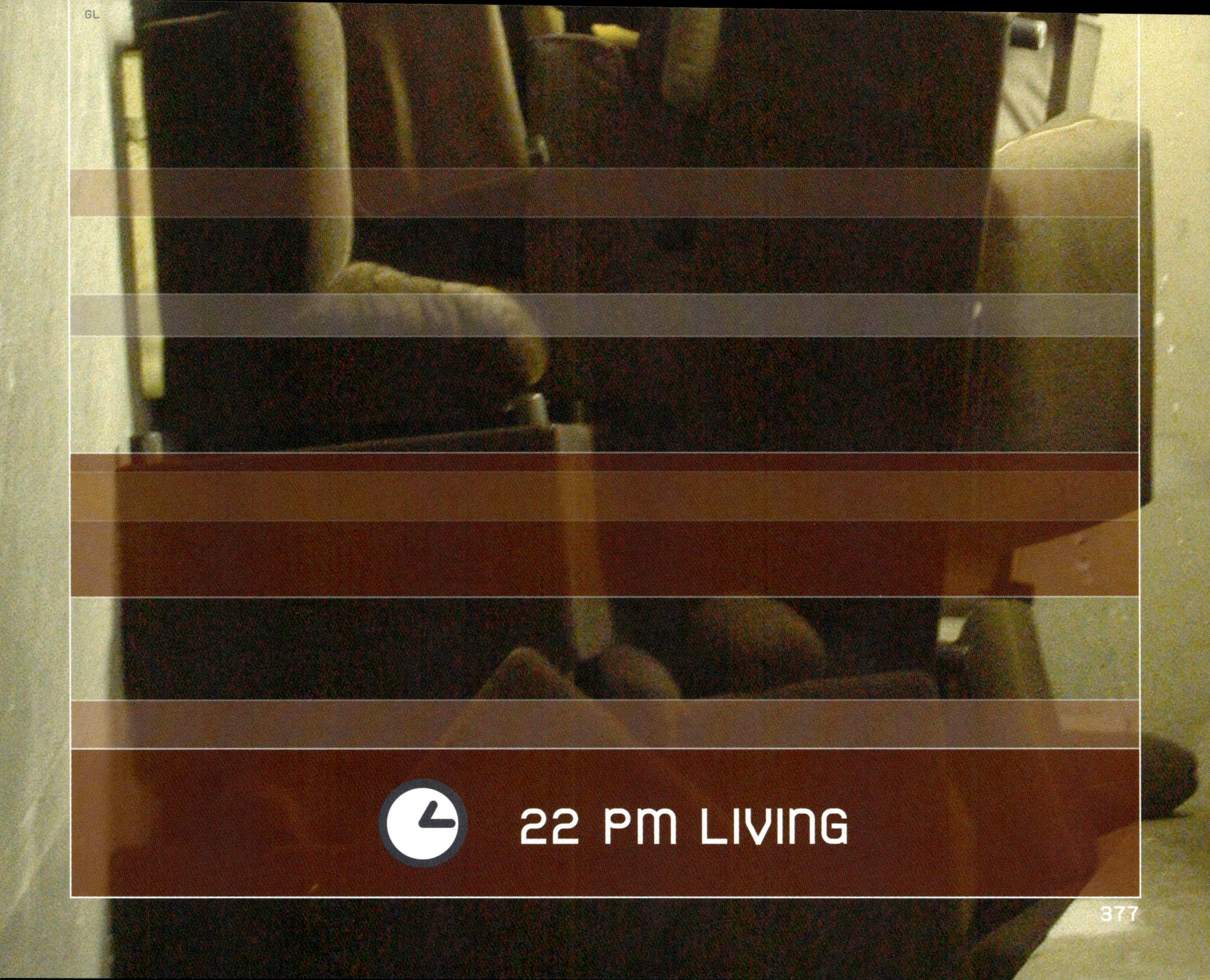
22 PM LIVING
GL
377

JERSZY SEYMOUR
"MUFF DADDY" PROJECT + COVO + INFLATE

379
SNOWCRASH LAMP
ZETA_LAB FREEZER
LIVING
AV
LZ
THE OFFICIAL POINT OF VIEW

"JUST LIKE a BEAUTIFUL WOMAN, DESIGN IS BEAUTIFUL IN RELATION TO THE PHYSIOLOGY OF TIME. I DON'T MEAN TO SAY THAT ITS BEAUTY FADES WITH THE YEARS, BUT THE PASSING OF TIME STIMULATES IN MAN NEW DESIRES FOR DIFFERENT OBJECTS"

ACHILLE BONITO OLIVA - ART CRITIC

MASSIMO IOSA GHINI

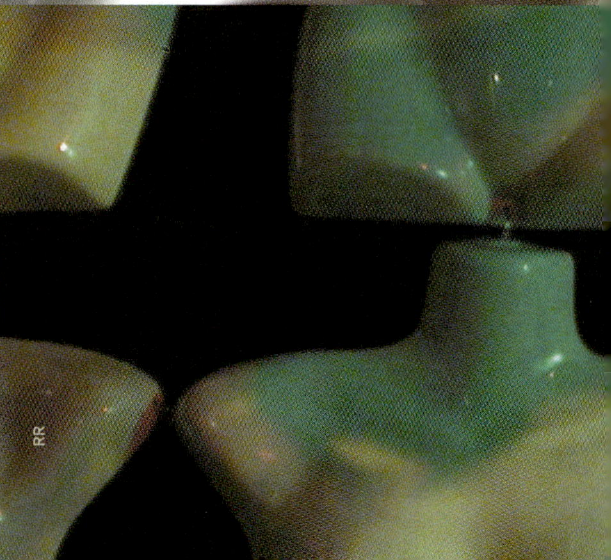

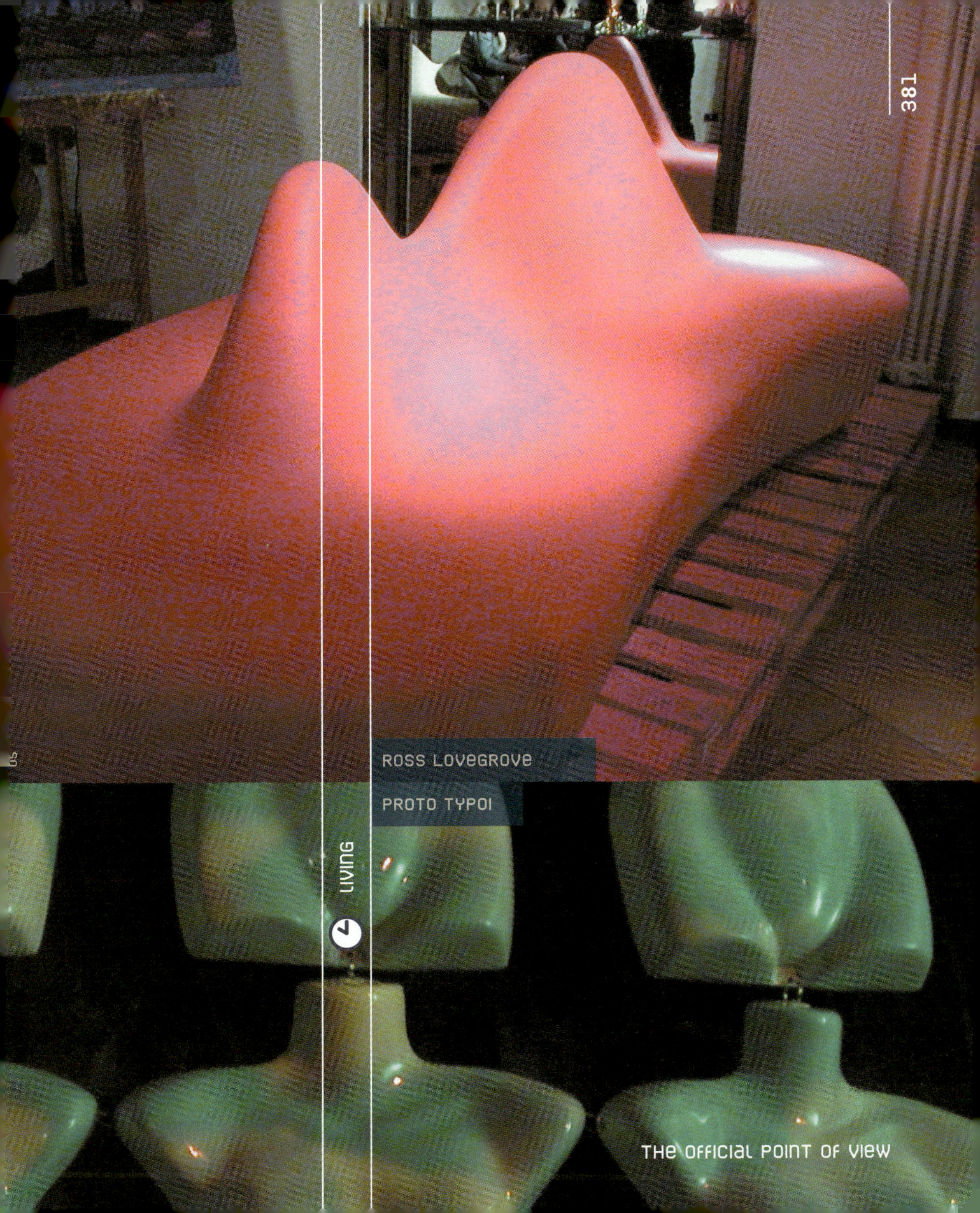
381
ROSS LOVEGROVE
PROTO TYPOI
LIVING
THE OFFICIAL POINT OF VIEW

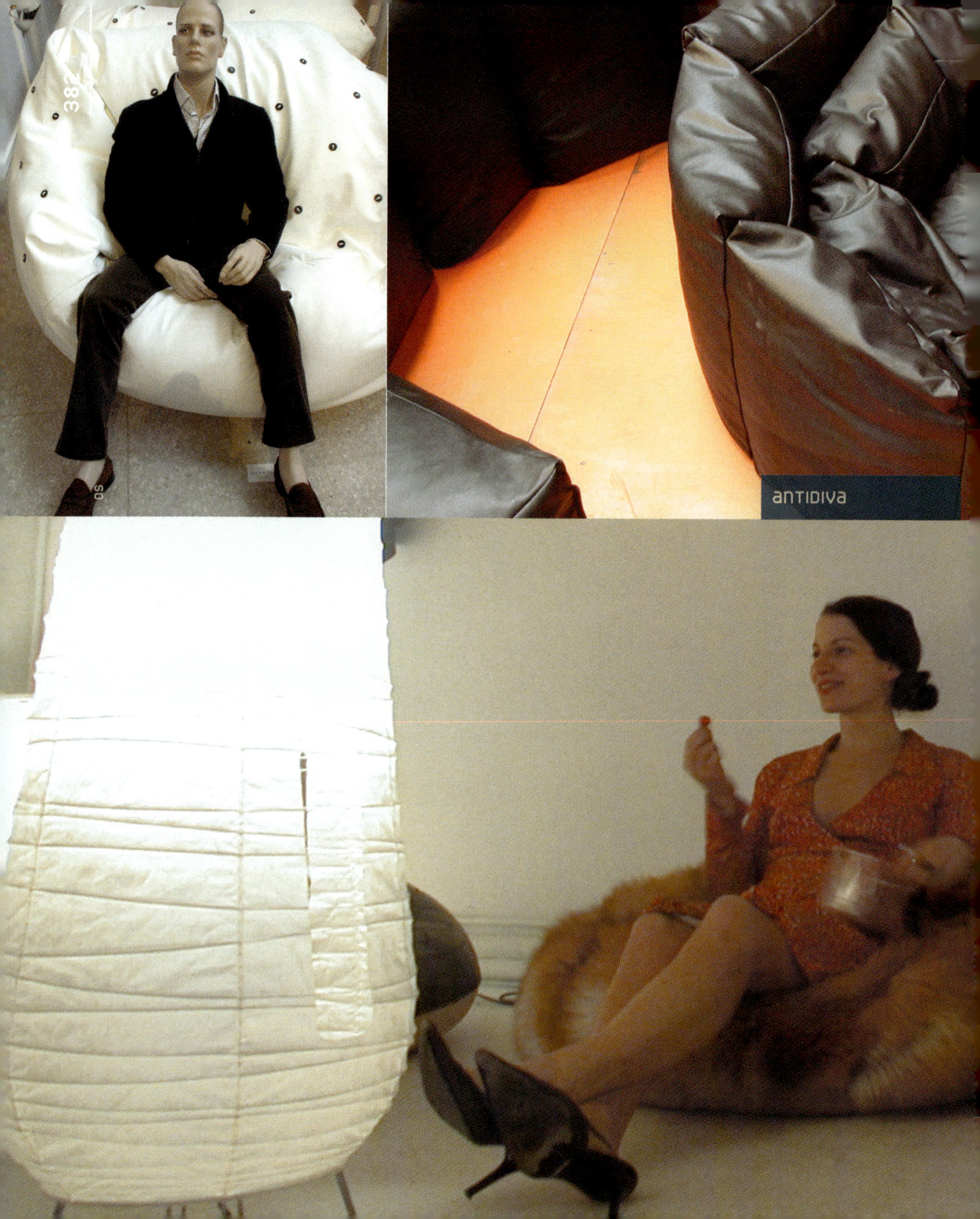
382
antidiva

383
LIVING
THE OFFICIAL POINT OF VIEW

384
Design is the
EDRa
DRiaDe

FOURTH WORLD

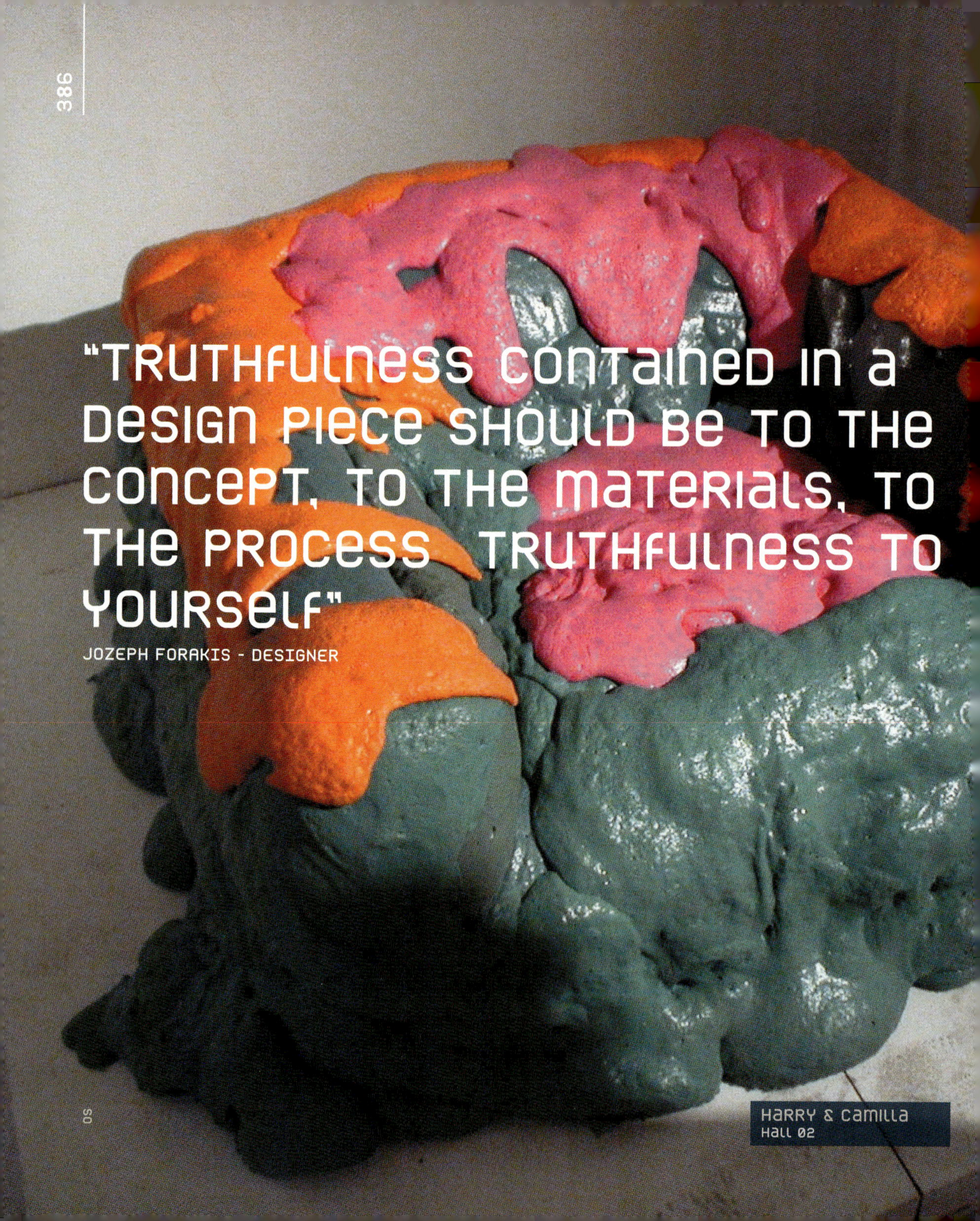

"TRUTHFULNESS CONTAINED IN A DESIGN PIECE SHOULD BE TO THE CONCEPT, TO THE MATERIALS, TO THE PROCESS TRUTHFULNESS TO YOURSELF"

JOZEPH FORAKIS - DESIGNER

387
HARRY
MZ
SB
MZ
LIVING
THE OFFICIAL POINT OF VIEW

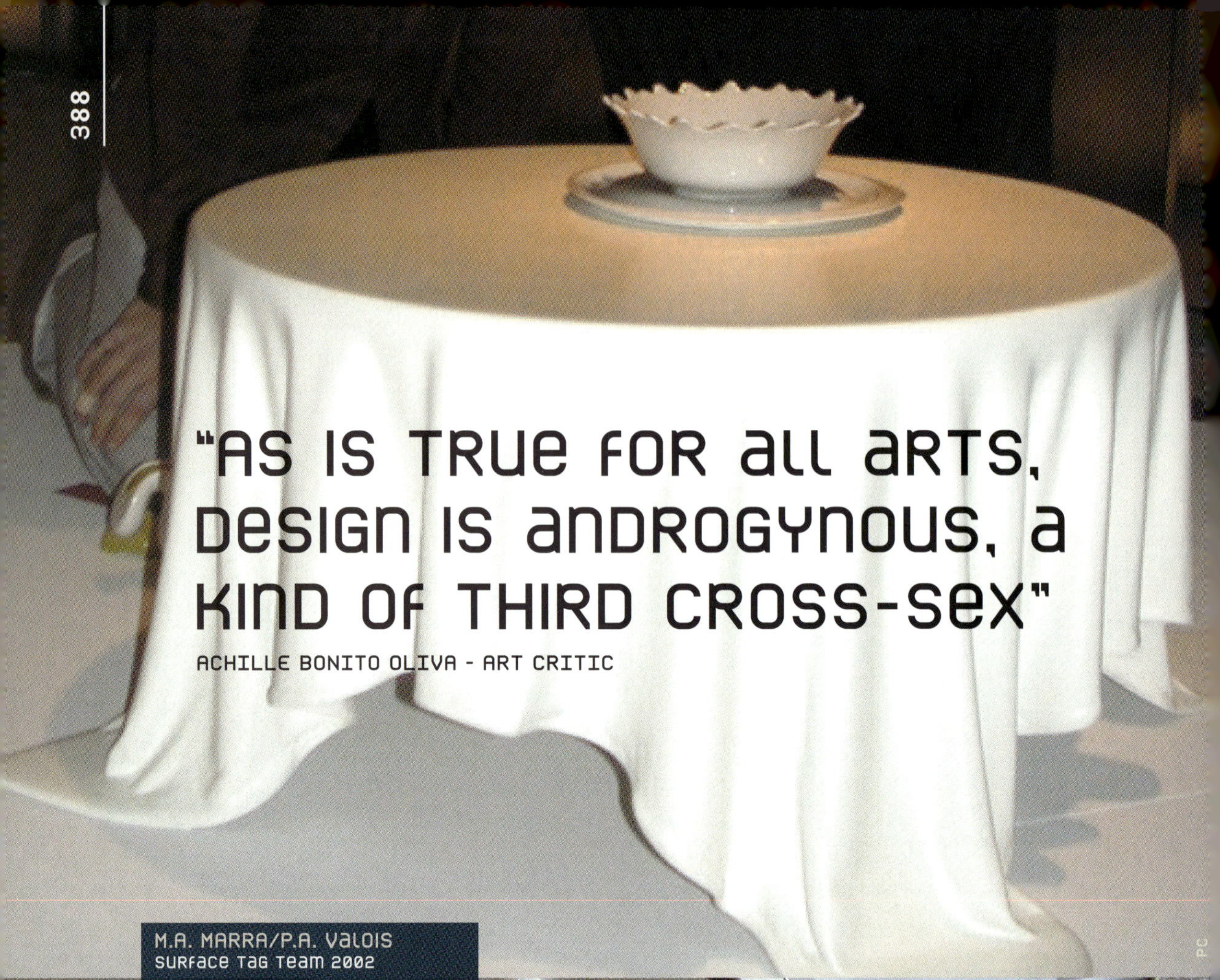

"AS IS TRUE FOR ALL ARTS, DESIGN IS ANDROGYNOUS, A KIND OF THIRD CROSS-SEX"

ACHILLE BONITO OLIVA - ART CRITIC

M.A. MARRA/P.A. VALOIS
SURFACE TAG TEAM 2002

EYES ON WORLD

389
LIVING
THE OFFICIAL POINT OF VIEW

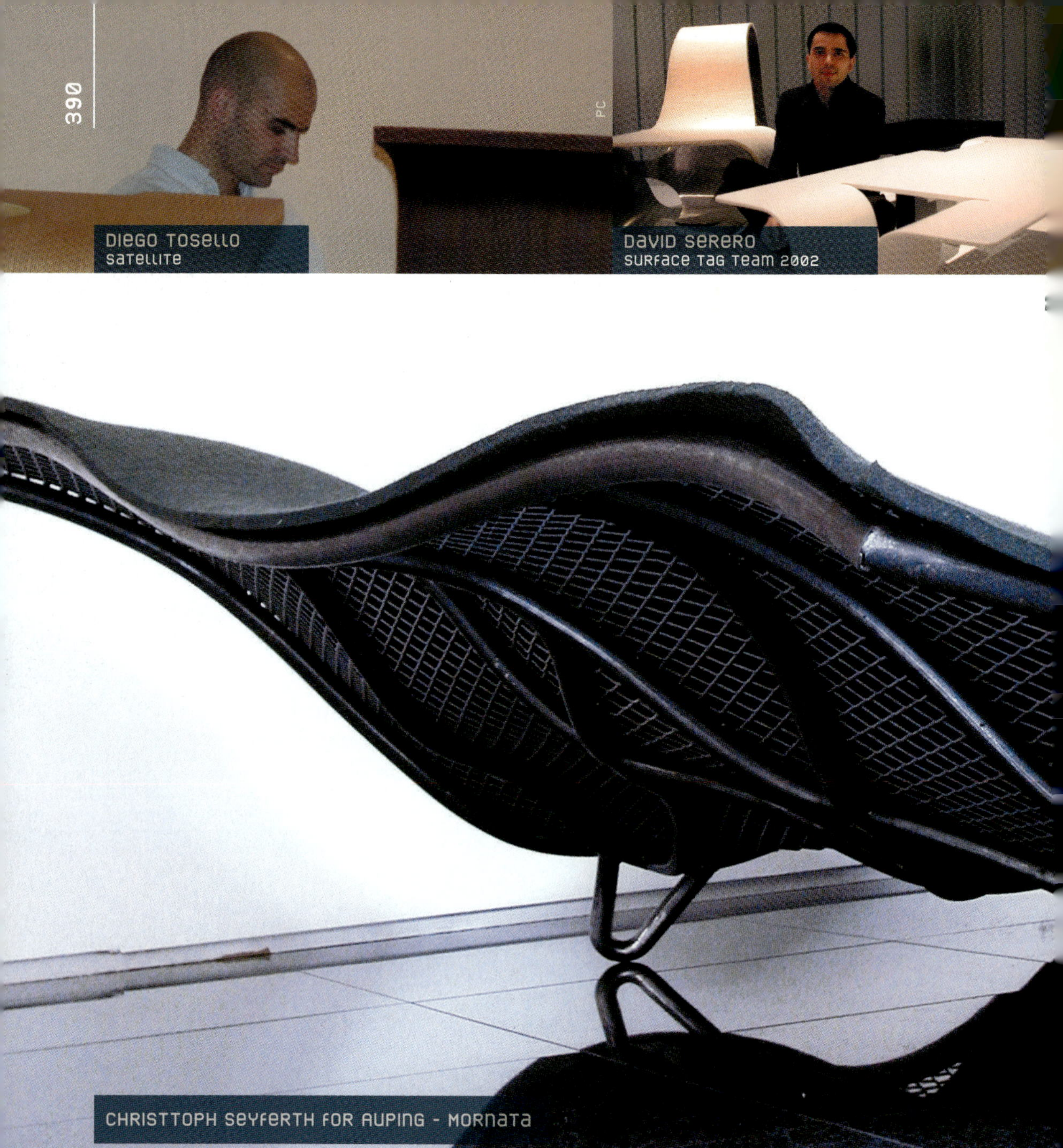
DIeGO TOSELLO
SaTELLITE
DaVID SEReRO
SURFace TaG Team 2002
CHRISTTOPH SEYFERTH FOR AUPING - MORNATA

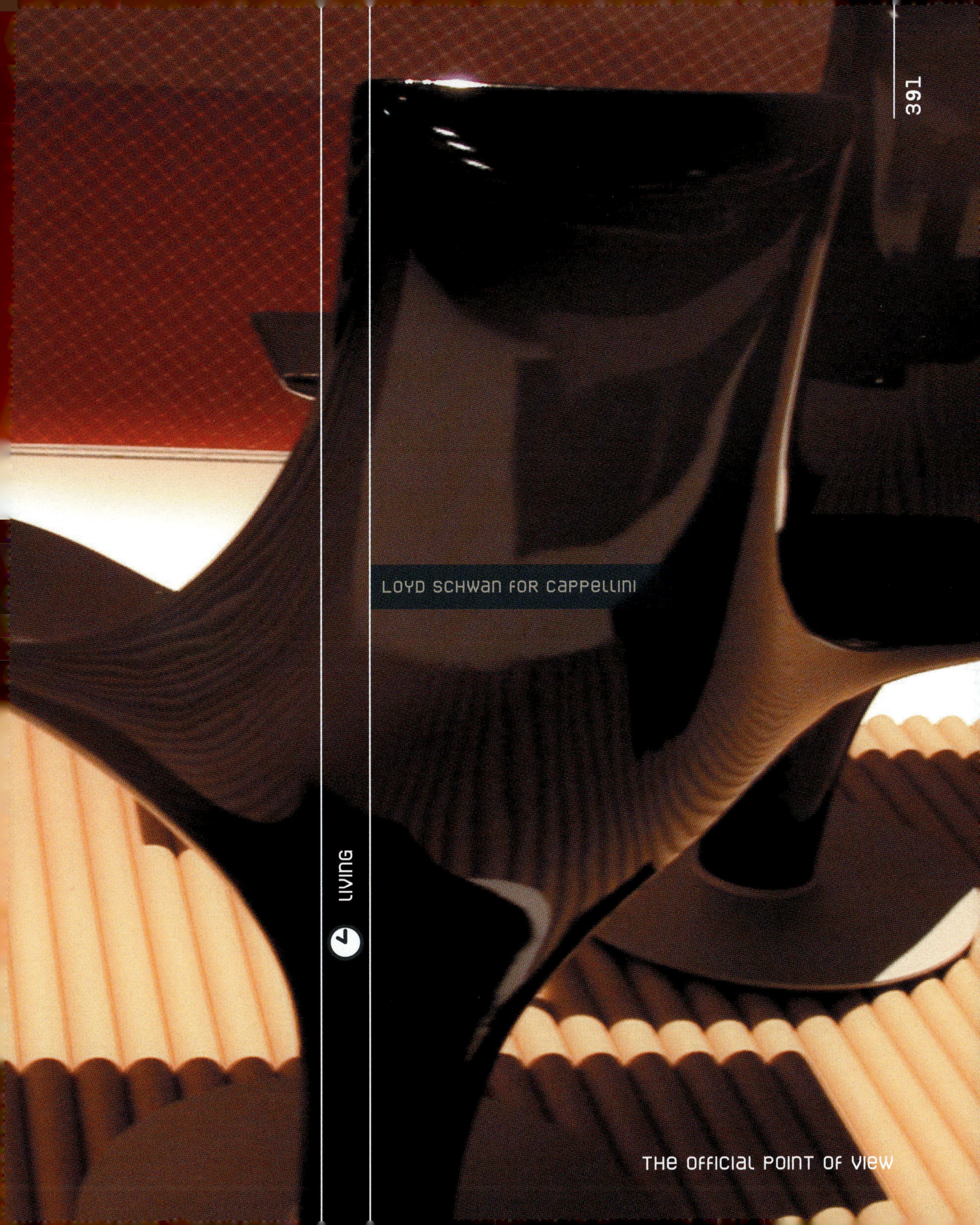
LOYD SCHWAN FOR CAPPELLINI
LIVING
THE OFFICIAL POINT OF VIEW

"DESIGN MUST CONTAIN THE TRUTH OF PRACTICALITY"
CLAUDIA - ILLUSTRATOR

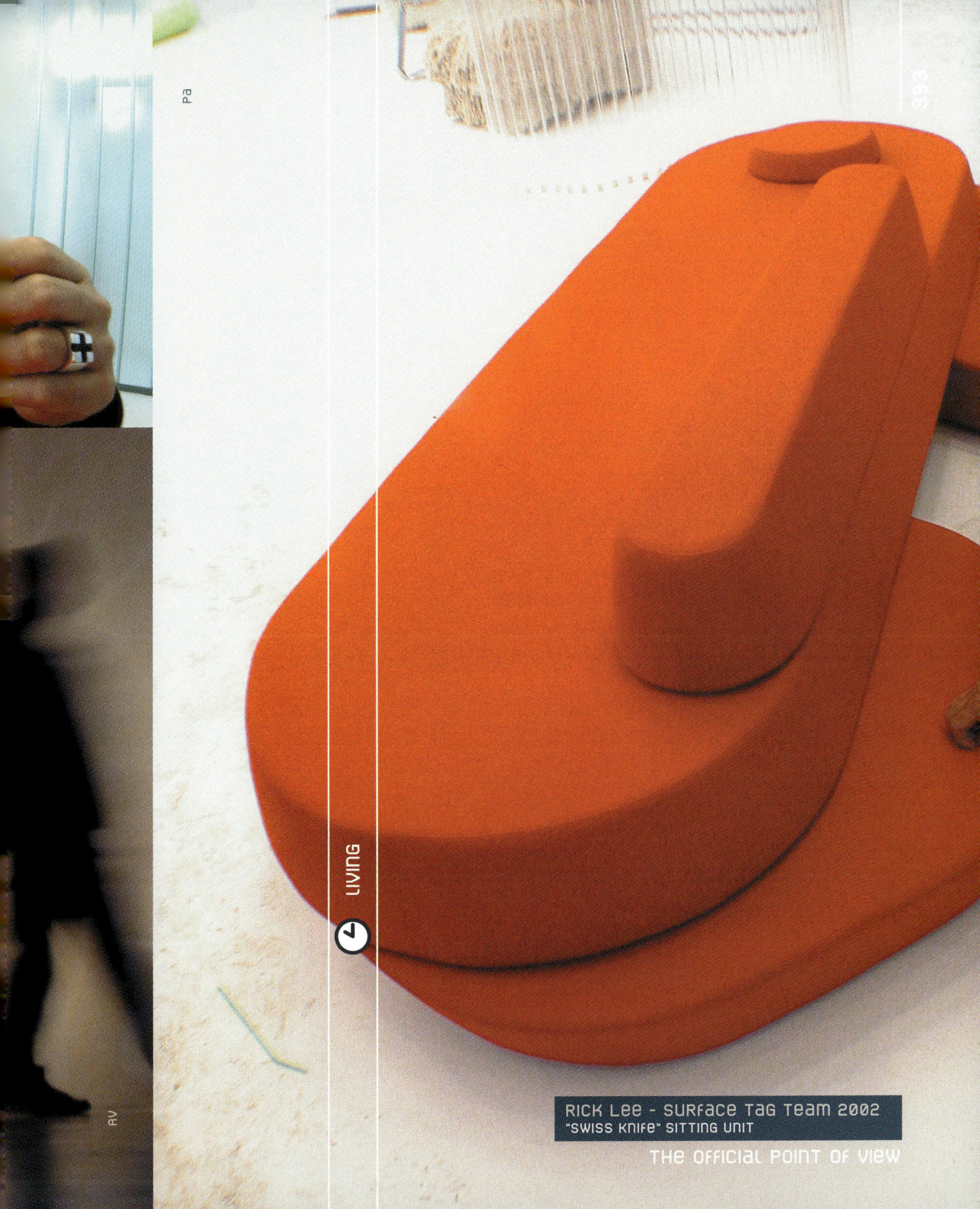

Pa
393
LIVING
AV
RICK LEE - SURFACE TAG TEAM 2002
"SWISS KNIFE" SITTING UNIT
THE OFFICIAL POINT OF VIEW

SB
RR
MZ
DILMOS
RR

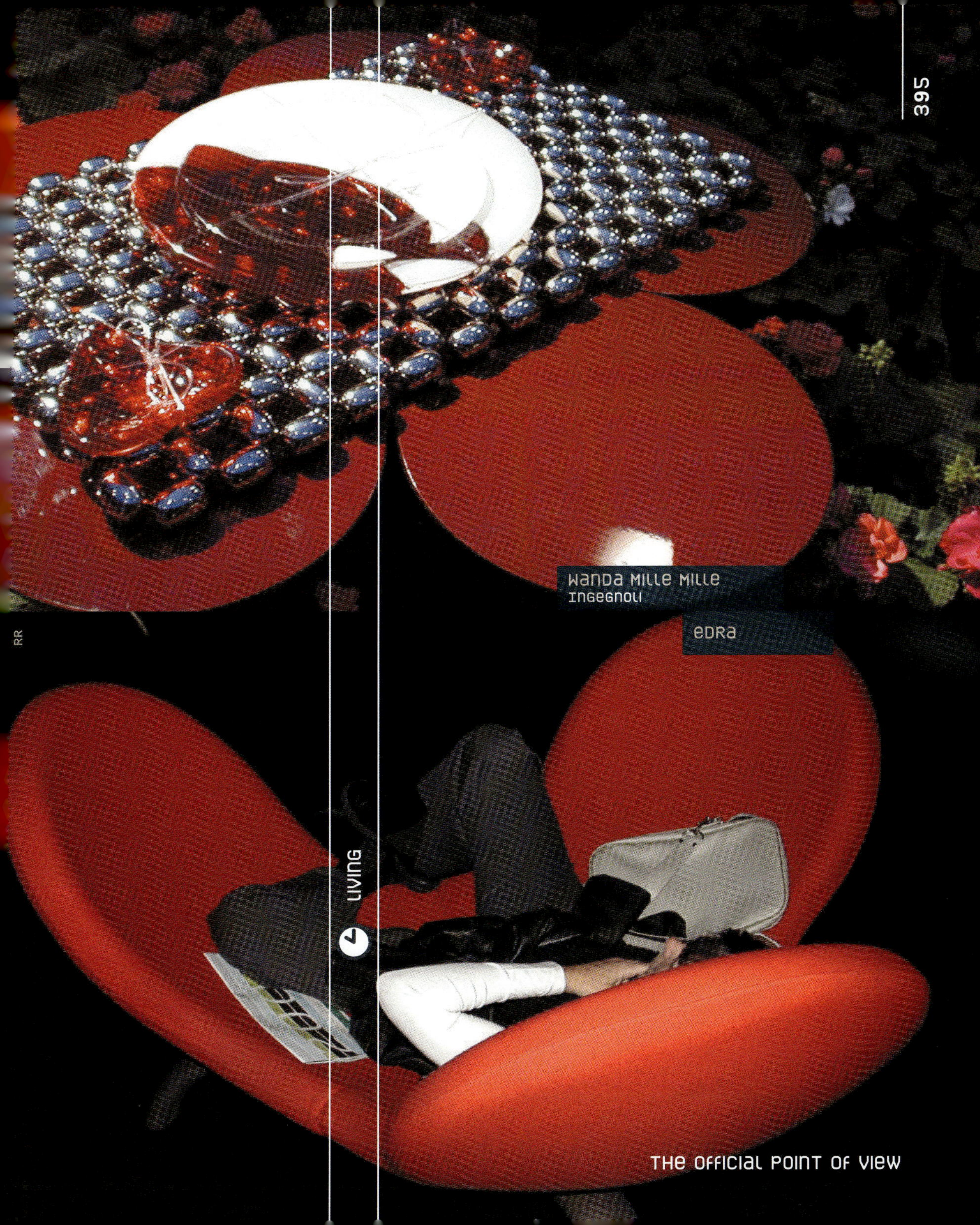

WANDA MILLE MILLE
INGEGNOLI
EDRA
LIVING
THE OFFICIAL POINT OF VIEW
RR
395

WANDA MILLE MILLE
INGEGNOLI

397
LIVING
EDRA
LILI LA TIGRESSE
RR
SO
SB
THE OFFICIAL POINT OF VIEW

walls talk

CARSTEN GERHARDS/ANDREAS GLÜCKER FOR B&B ITALIA

OLIVER THEYSKENS FOR MOROSO

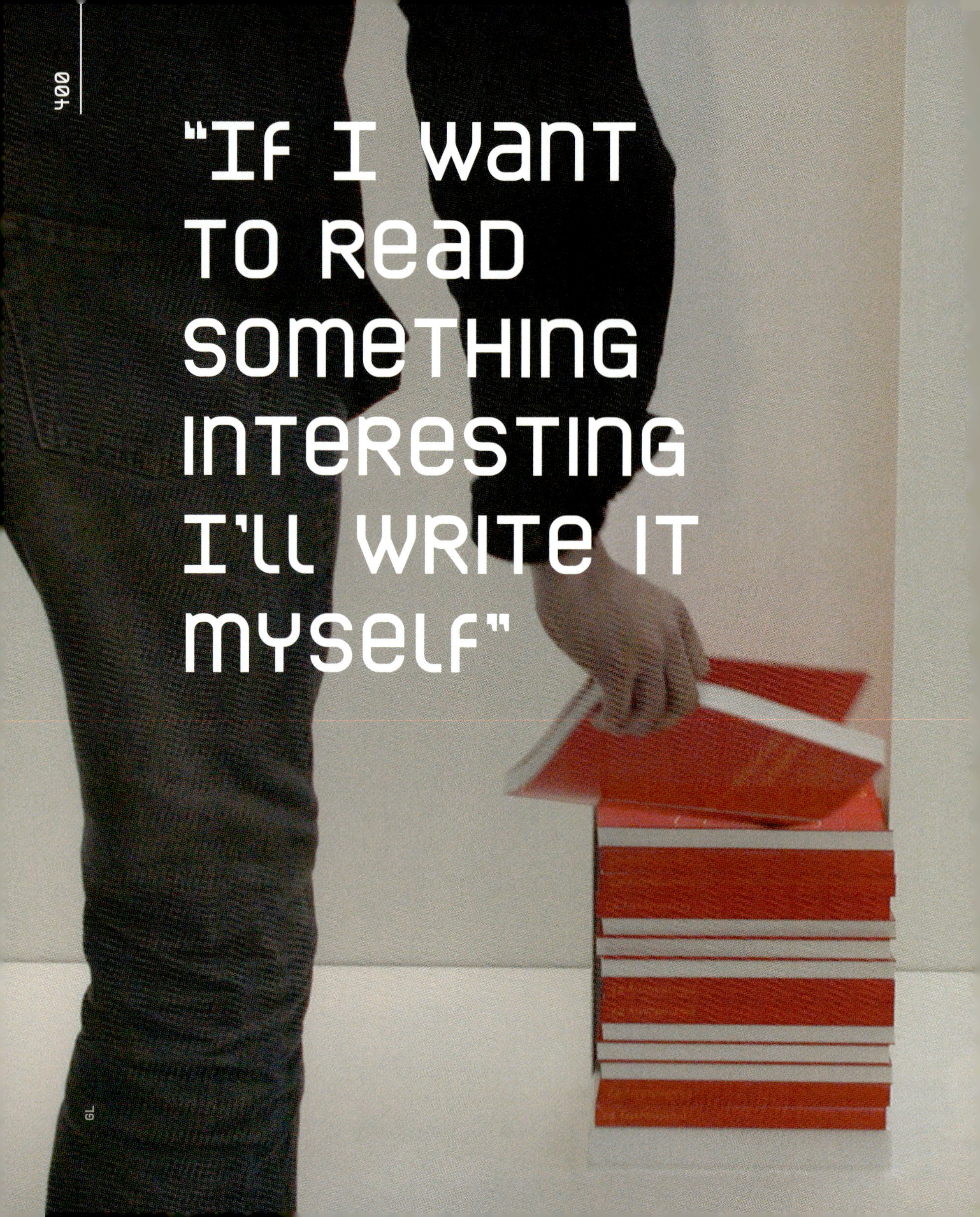

"If I want
to read
something
interesting
I'll write it
myself"

MILAN
FUORISALONE
APR 9-15
20 02
INTERNI
MILANO
FUORISALONE
9-15
MER1
IL BAGNO ALESSI
anteprima
Salone
SOS DESIGN-EMERGENCY
mooo!
1000
1000!
grandhotelsalone
esterni
spazio pubblico in festa
19 aprile 2002
Salone
dell'Arredo Urbano
Milan International
Urban
prima edizione/first edition
LIVING
I CATALOGHI
SONO
TERMINATI
THE OFFICIAL POINT OF VIEW

esterni

THE FIRST EXHIBITION OF STREET AND URBAN
FURNITURE HELD IN THE CITY OF MILAN PRESENTS A
PROVOCATIVE COLLECTION OF OBJECTS, SERVICES AND
IDEAS FOR OPEN-AIR PUBLIC SPACES.
FIFTEEN DIFFERENT CONCEPTS FOR PUBLIC SPACE
CONCEIVED AS CONTAINING EVERYONE AND RESPONDING
TO ALL CULTURES AND THEIR NEEDS.

30 m

the temporary use of this umbrella is to host
other citizens - www.esterni.org
everyone's
umbrella
esterni
THE OFFICIAL POINT OF VIEW

23 PM LIVING

"DESIGN REFLECTS YOUR MIND"

MINNA PASANEN, FINLAND

PHILIPPE STARCK

De PaDova
DaviD DesiGn
FranCo RaGGI For FontaarTe
LIVING
THe offiCIaL POInT Of view

408
SARAH SONG
SURFACE TAG TEAM 2002

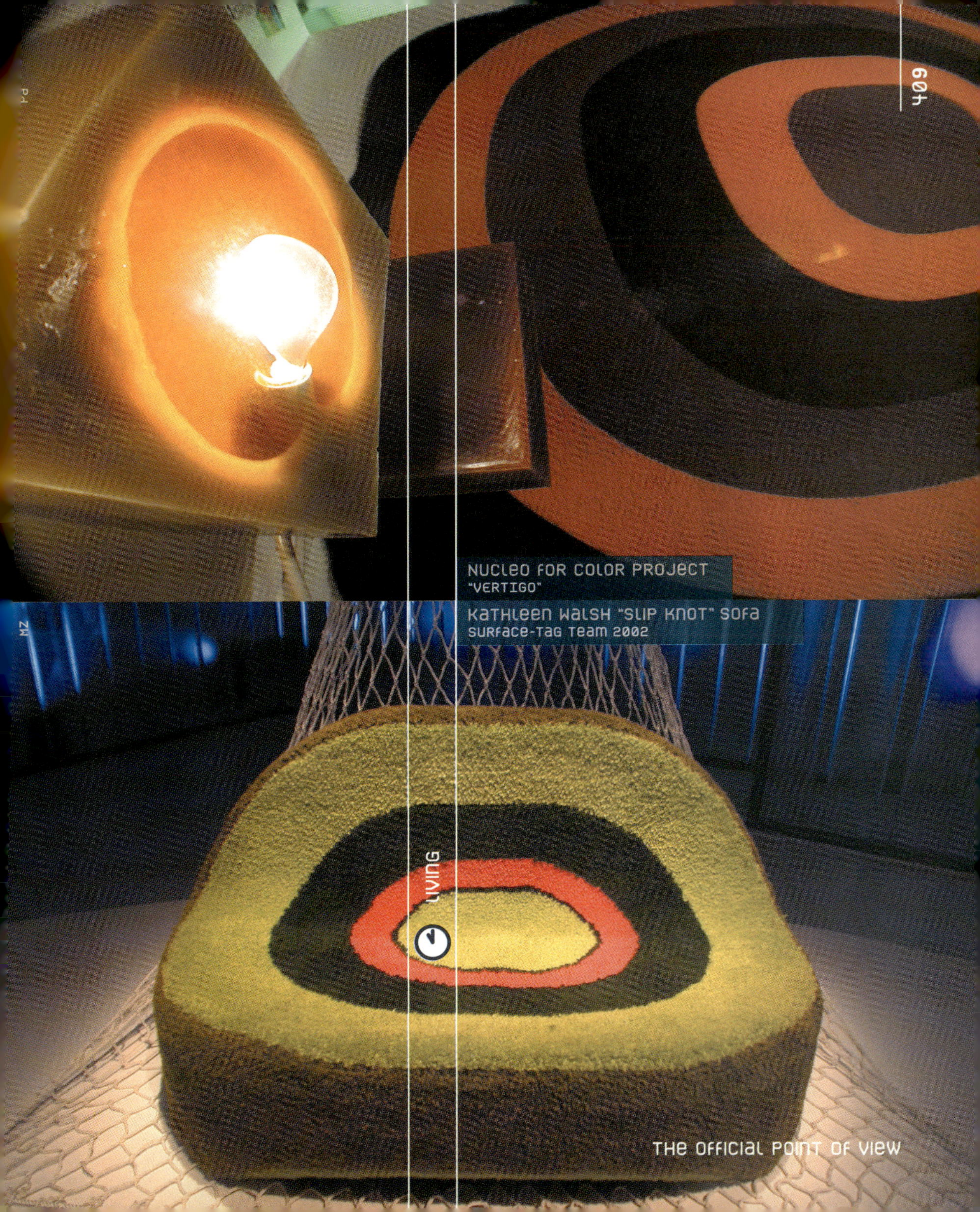
NUCLEO FOR COLOR PROJECT
"VERTIGO"

KATHLEEN WALSH "SLIP KNOT" SOFA
SURFACE-TAG TEAM 2002

LIVING

THE OFFICIAL POINT OF VIEW

MARGY
ANTIIVA

BRAZIL FAZ DESIGN
DRIADE
LIVING
THE OFFICIAL POINT OF VIEW

412
CAMEL
MZ
TM
PC
DRIADE

413
DRIADE
LIVING
THE OFFICIAL POINT OF VIEW

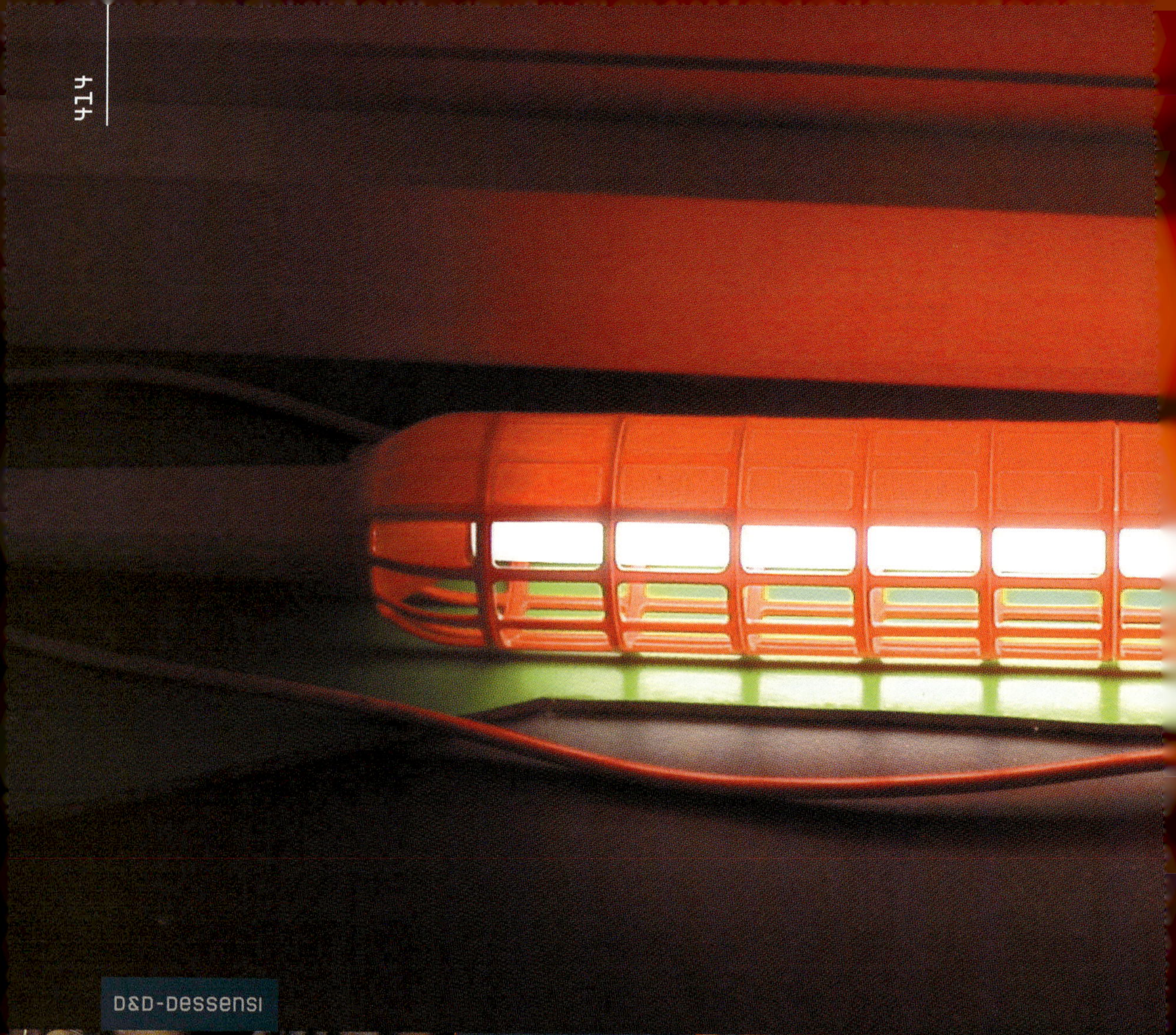

D&D-DESSENSI

BRASIL FAZ DESIGN

PATRICK NORGUET
"RAINBOW CHAIR"

TM
MZ
OS
LIVING
MARKS BENESH
THE OFFICIAL POINT OF VIEW

AGGI MASSIMO
HARD COUNTRY
VITRA DESIGN MUSEUM
SCULPTURAL DESIGN

SB
pa
417
sachio hihara
satellite
"MY OBSESSION IN DESIGN
IS MAKING MONEY"
CORETTA VAN WIJK - DESIGNER
MZ
PC
MZ
LIVING
valTORTA LUCIANO & CO.
THE OFFICIAL POINT OF VIEW

TM
PC
GL
GL
charles o. job design
satellite

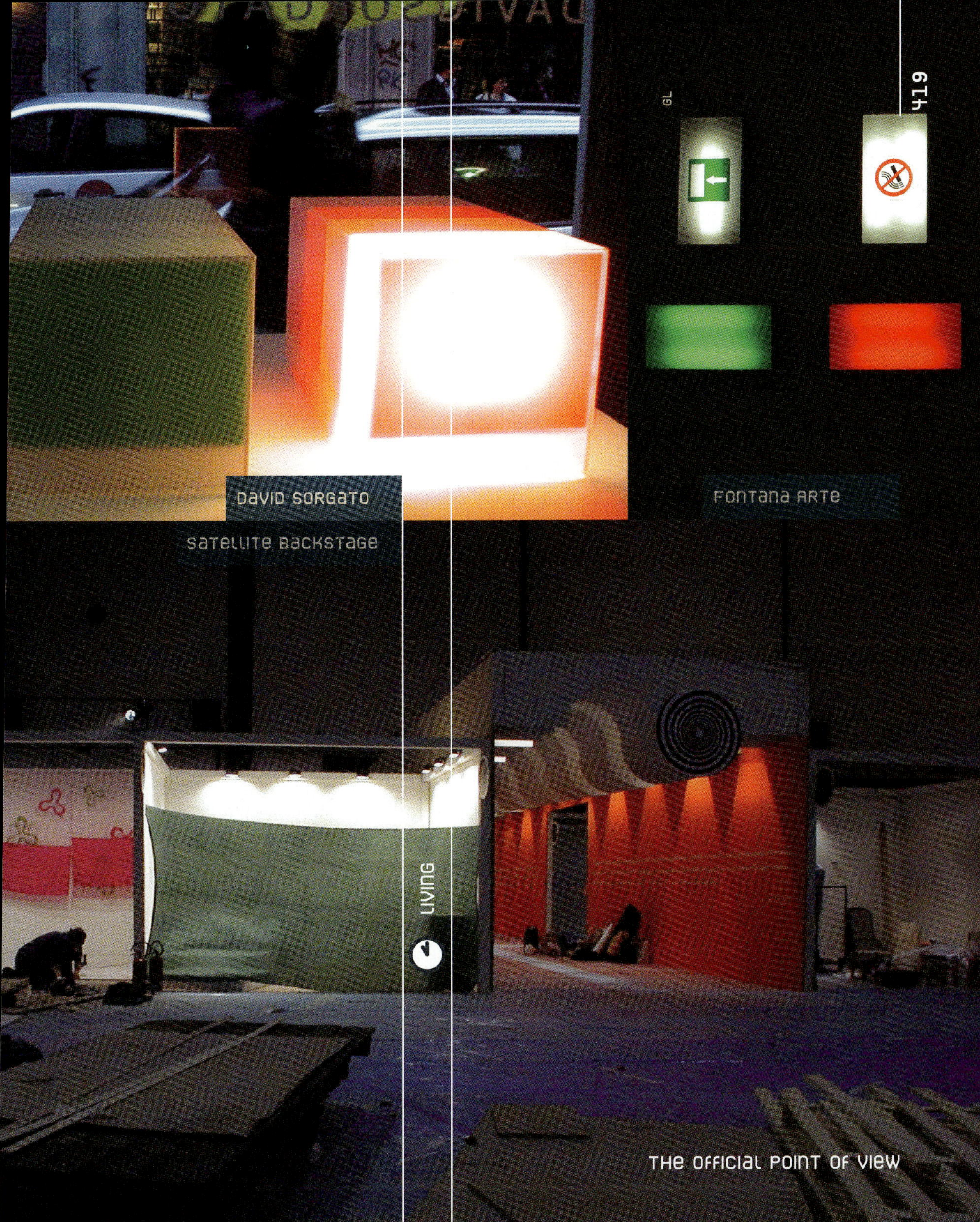
GL
419
DAVID SORGATO
SATELLITE BACKSTAGE
FONTANA ARTE
LIVING
THE OFFICIAL POINT OF VIEW

COMPLE

Mal di schiena!
MATERASSO DA MASSA... ...ATSU JETFOR
LIVING
THE OFFICIAL POINT OF VIEW

422
DJ. scanner at satellite
Hidden
GL
RR
PC

Davide Bertocchi
Luisa Delle Piane Gallery

"Design is a metaphor, often misused"

LEON VAN GERWEN- HIDDEN

LIVING

424
RR
KunDaLini

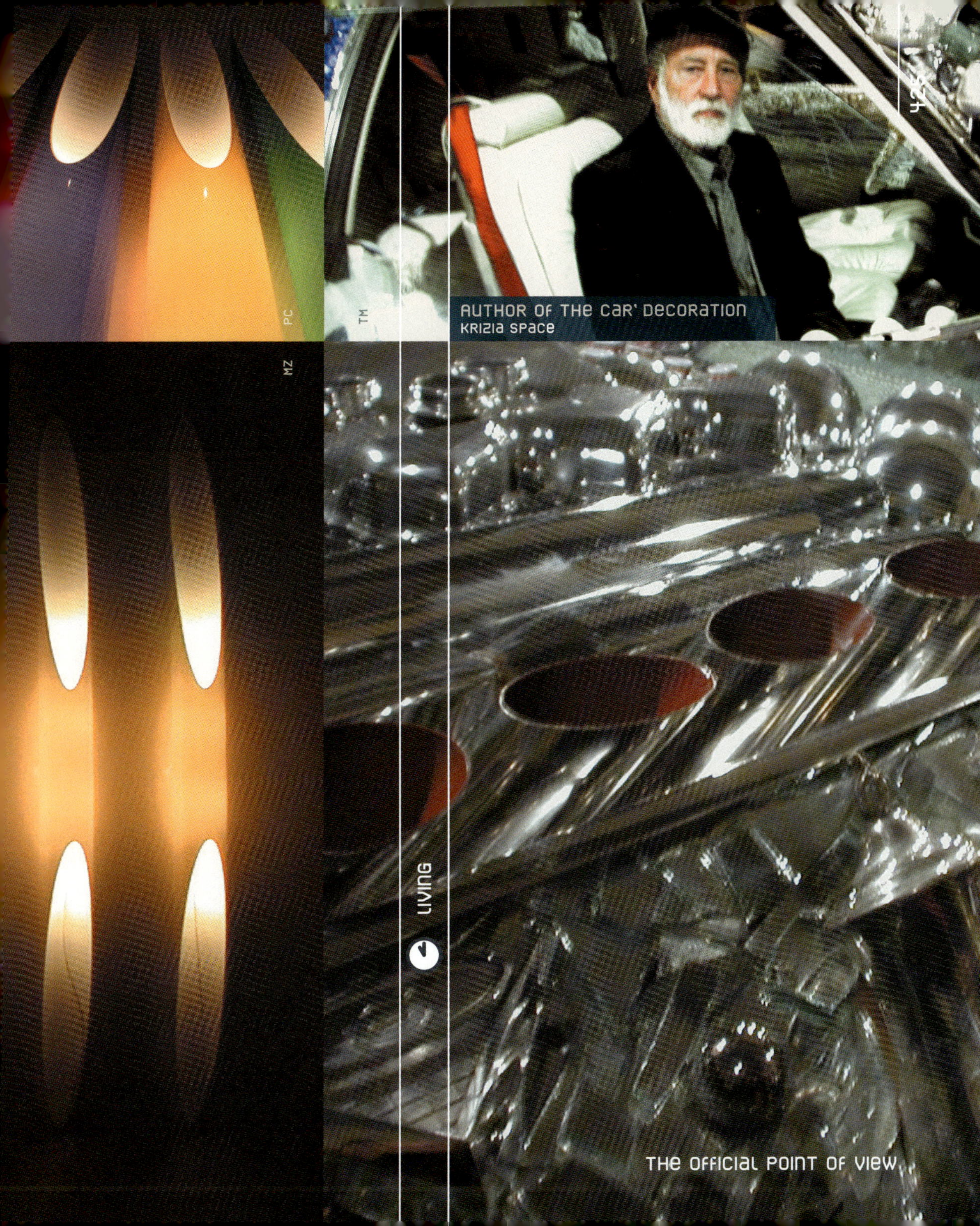
PC
TM
MZ
AUTHOR OF THE CAR' DECORATION
KRIZIA SPACE
LIVING
THE OFFICIAL POINT OF VIEW

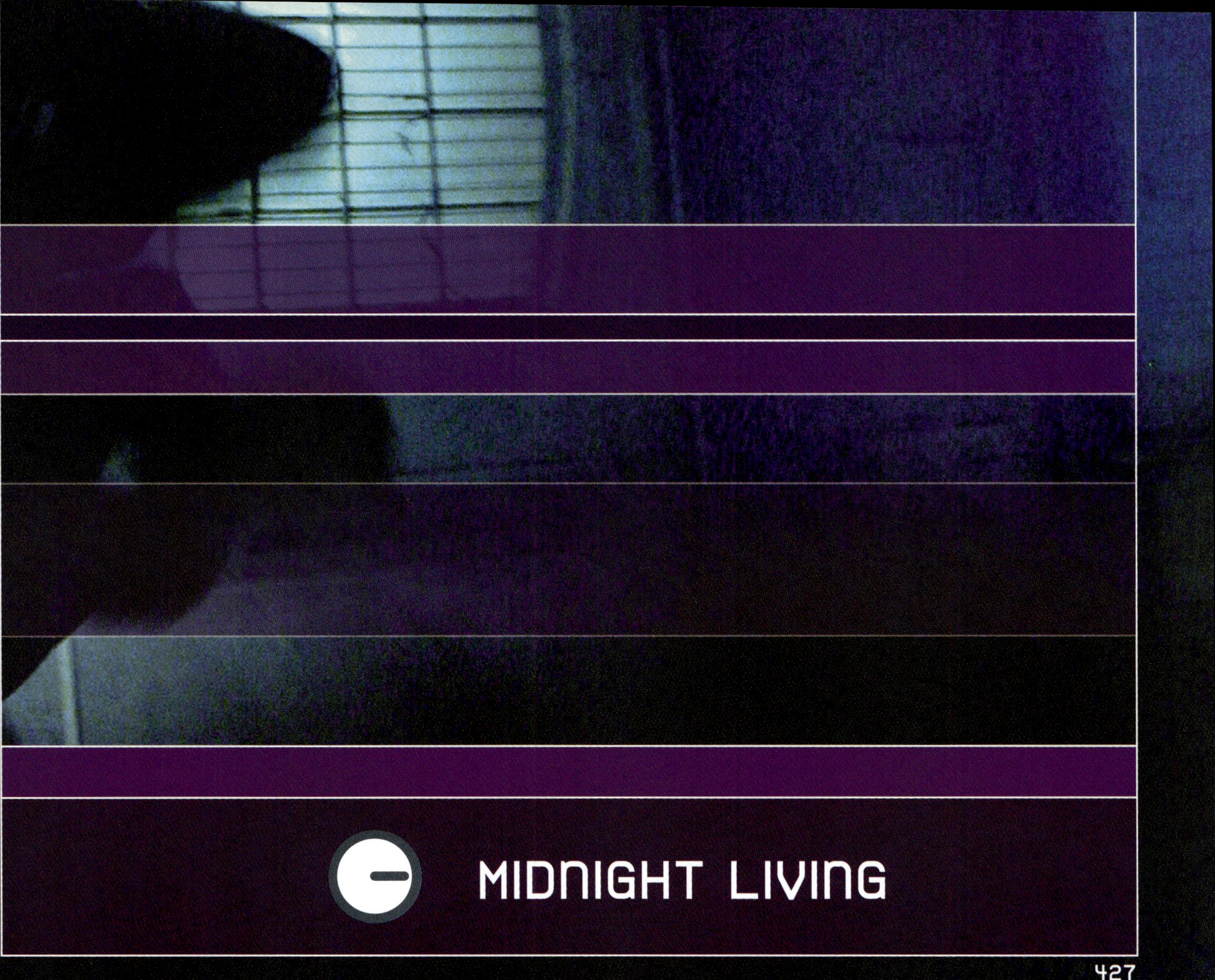

MIDNIGHT LIVING

LOOKING FOR
THE maximum
CONFORT

429
PROTO TYPOI
PC
SB
LIVING
POLTROMEC ITALIA
THE OFFICIAL POINT OF VIEW

430
THE SENTENCE INSPIRING THIS
COLLECTION IS EVITA PERON'S:
"... YOU MAY LIVE... AND DREAM."
CAPPELLINI AND EVITA PERON
CAPPELLINI

PC
Pa
SB
ESTERNI
PUCCI FOR CAPPELLINI
LIVING
THE OFFICIAL POINT OF VIEW

432
WAGNER & ASSOCIATI
SATELLITE

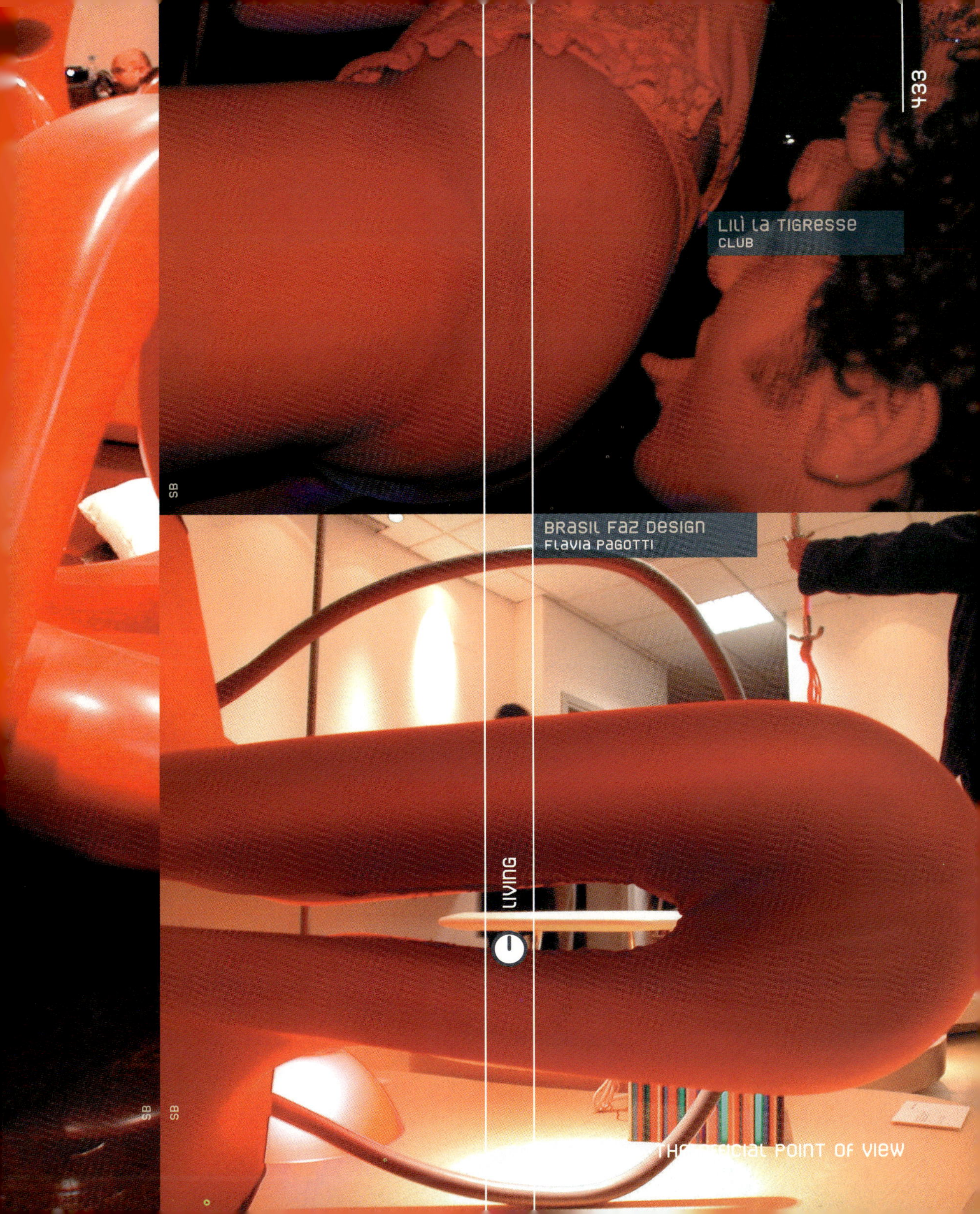

433
LILÌ LA TIGRESSE
CLUB
BRASIL FAZ DESIGN
FLAVIA PAGOTTI
LIVING
THE OFFICIAL POINT OF VIEW

solide
PLEASE TOUCH

"FORM NO LONGER FOLLOWS FUNCTION, IT FOLLOWS THE DESIGNER HIMSELF"

ANNE-LAURE GIMENEZ - ARCHITECT

LIVING

VITTORIO VALENTE FOR PIT.21

THE OFFICIAL POINT OF VIEW

Design Gallery Milano

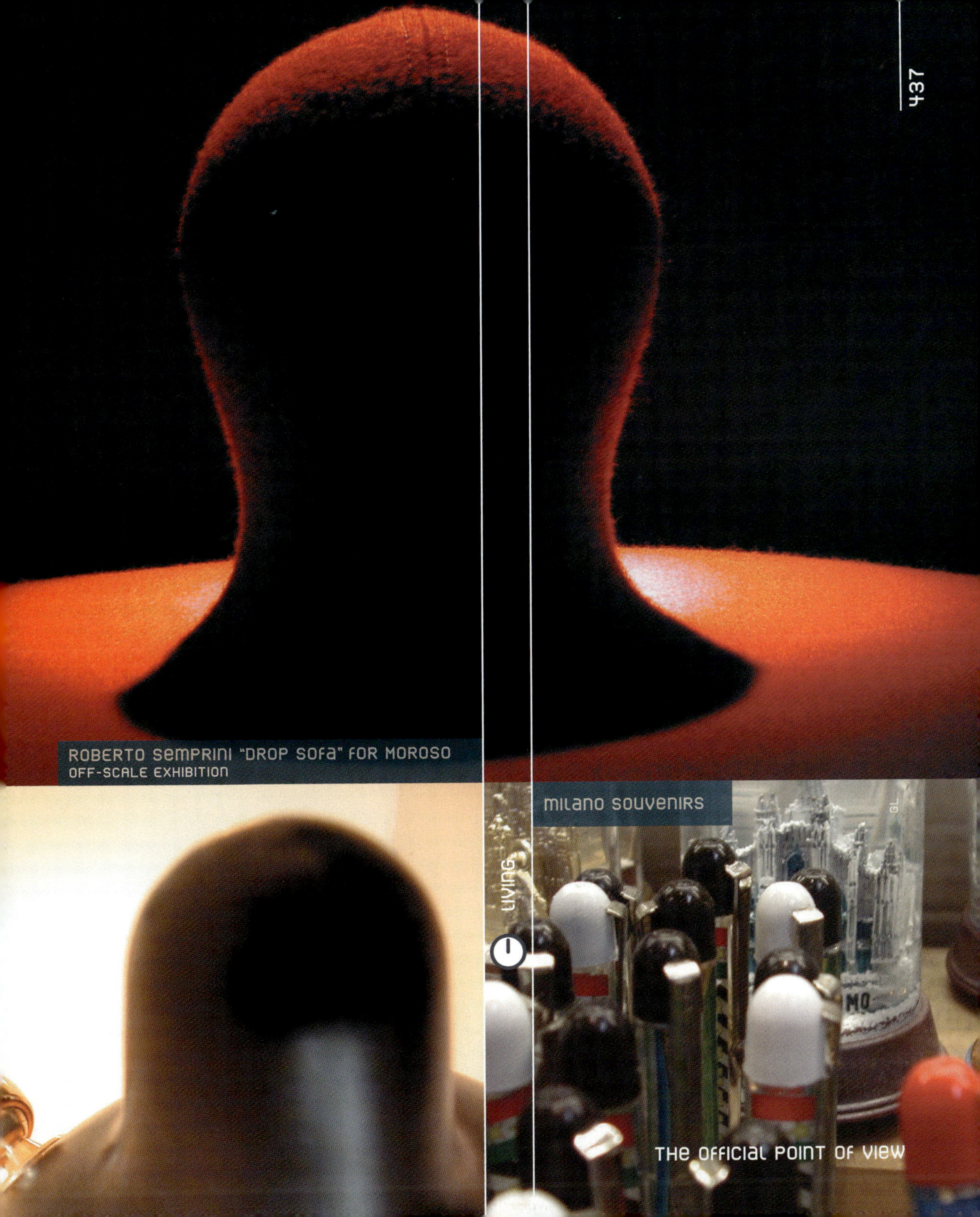

ROBERTO SEMPRINI "DROP SOFA" FOR MOROSO
OFF-SCALE EXHIBITION
milano souvenirs
LIVING
THE OFFICIAL POINT OF VIEW

DAVID + PULVIRENTI
MULTIPURPOSE TABLE

VANITY CHAIR
FRAU

KAZUYO KOMODA
PANDORA
LIVING

01 am club

CLUBBING
THE OFFICIAL POINT OF VIEW

ナナナ

445
CLUBBING
THE OFFICIAL POINT OF VIEW

"RON ARAD IS NOT AN INDUSTRIAL DESIGNER BECAUSE THE PRODUCTION PROCESS IS MISSING.
ZANUSO WAS A TRUE DESIGNER, HE WOULD DESIGN A WHATCH THAT WAS BEAUTIFUL, FUNCTIONAL AND AFFORDABLE TO EVERY POCKET. TODAY, THAT DOESN'T HAPPEN ANYMORE"

DIEGO PROFILI - ARCHITECT

TM
RR
Stazioni Cadorna
Salone Internazionale del Mobile
10 - 15 Aprile 2002
THESI
IPERBUS
CONCESSIONARIA AUTOBUS IVECO
IVECO
GL
CLUBBING
THE OFFICIAL POINT OF VIEW

MILA SCHON

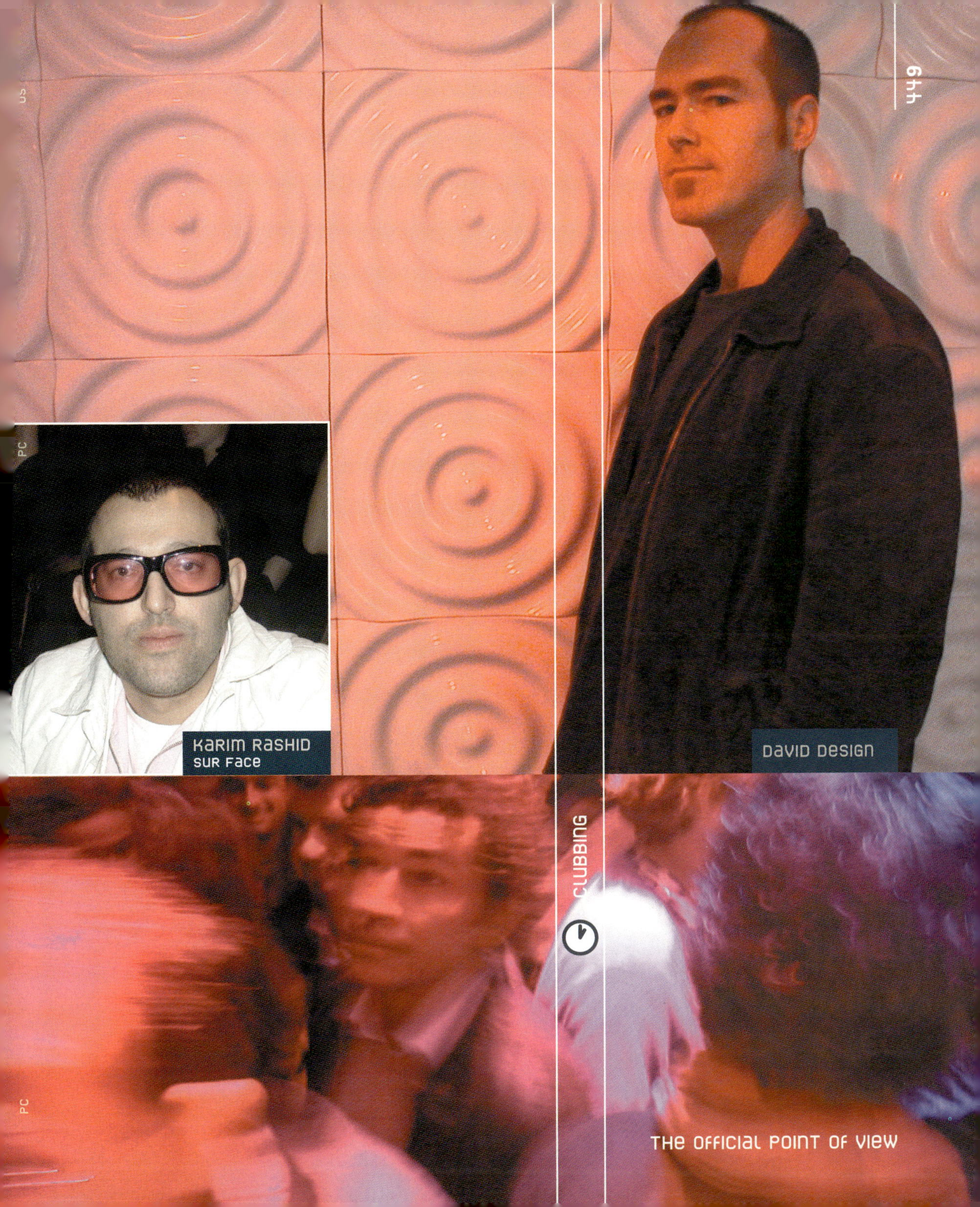
449
KARIM RASHID
SUR FACE
DAVID DESIGN
CLUBBING
THE OFFICIAL POINT OF VIEW

Denis Santachiara
Neon Lamp

451
PC
SB
Pa
CLUBBING
THE OFFICIAL POINT OF VIEW

452
DOMUS ACADEMY

453
CLUBBING
STANTON
THE OFFICIAL Paris Review

CLUBBING
DJ CaRLITO FOR DJ PeR SIGNORa
esterni
THe OFFICIaL POINT OF VIeW

esterni

457
INGO MAURER
MARCEL WANDERS
sense of wonder
CLUBBING
THE OFFICIAL POINT OF VIEW

NEW SONOR
MILANO
CLUBBING
ERRERAN1
CM/RG/IR
THE OFFICIAL POINT OF VIEW

THE OFFICIAL POINT OF VIEW

02 am BEDROOM

GREEN ROLLING FOR AUPING-MORNATA

CHRISTOPH SEYFERTH FOR AUPING-MORNATA

THE OFFICIAL POINT OF VIEW

463
BEDROOM

464
Design
THE OFFICIAL POINT OF VIEW

RON ARAD FOR CAPPELLINI
BEDROOM

496
FLOU
THE OFFICIAL POINT OF VIEW
TM

FLOU
BEDROOM
MORENO FERRARI FOR MARANGONI SCHOOL
"Navigation Garments"

single
single
single
single
single
ngo design
LOReDana LONGO "SINGLe" PILLOW
SaTeLLiTe

ISTITUTO EUROPEO DEL DESIGN
BEDROOM

"Design is global because one of the aims of design is cultural changes, and we must constantly reconsider what we want"
MARNIX OOSTERWELD - DESIGNER
zanotta
THE OFFICIAL POINT OF VIEW

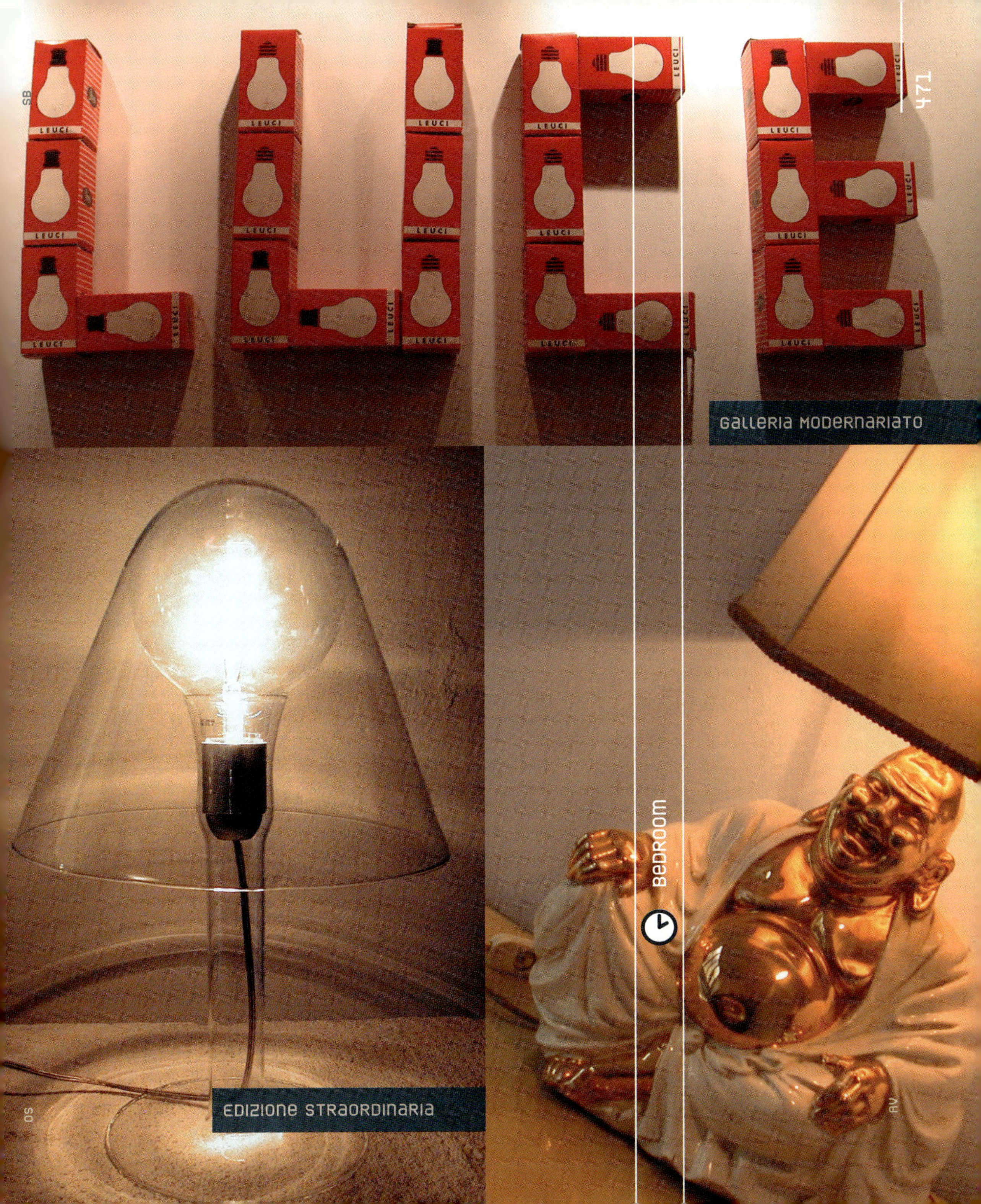

Galleria Modernariato

BEDROOM

Edizione straordinaria

THE OFFICIAL POINT OF VIEW

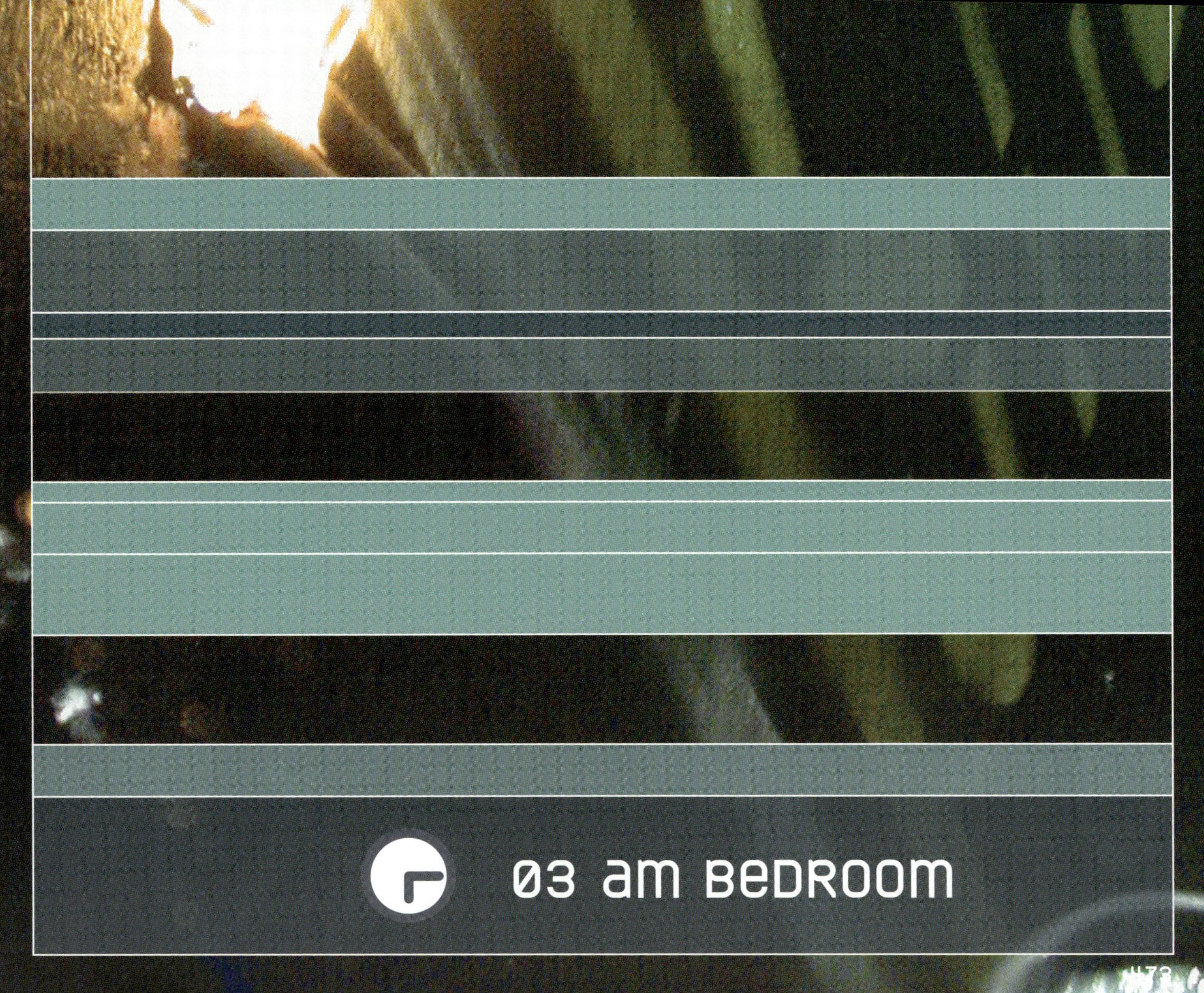

03 am BEDROOM

ナナ
THE OFFICIAL POINT OF VIEW

475
IDeas wake up in the
middle of the night
BEDROOM

"The sensorial relationship with design is getting worse with digital progress, we see a lot of presentations in dark rooms with projections, visually it is nice but it destroys the relationship with the object that should be touched, smelled, tried"
ANNE-LAURE GIMENEZ, ARCHITECT, (FRANCE)
THE OFFICIAL POINT OF VIEW

BEDROOM

cassina
L 18 LEVELS
THE OFFICIAL POINT OF VIEW

JOACHIM ENGLER
satellite
imel
479
BEDROOM
GL
GL

sturmundplastic
satellite
the official point of view

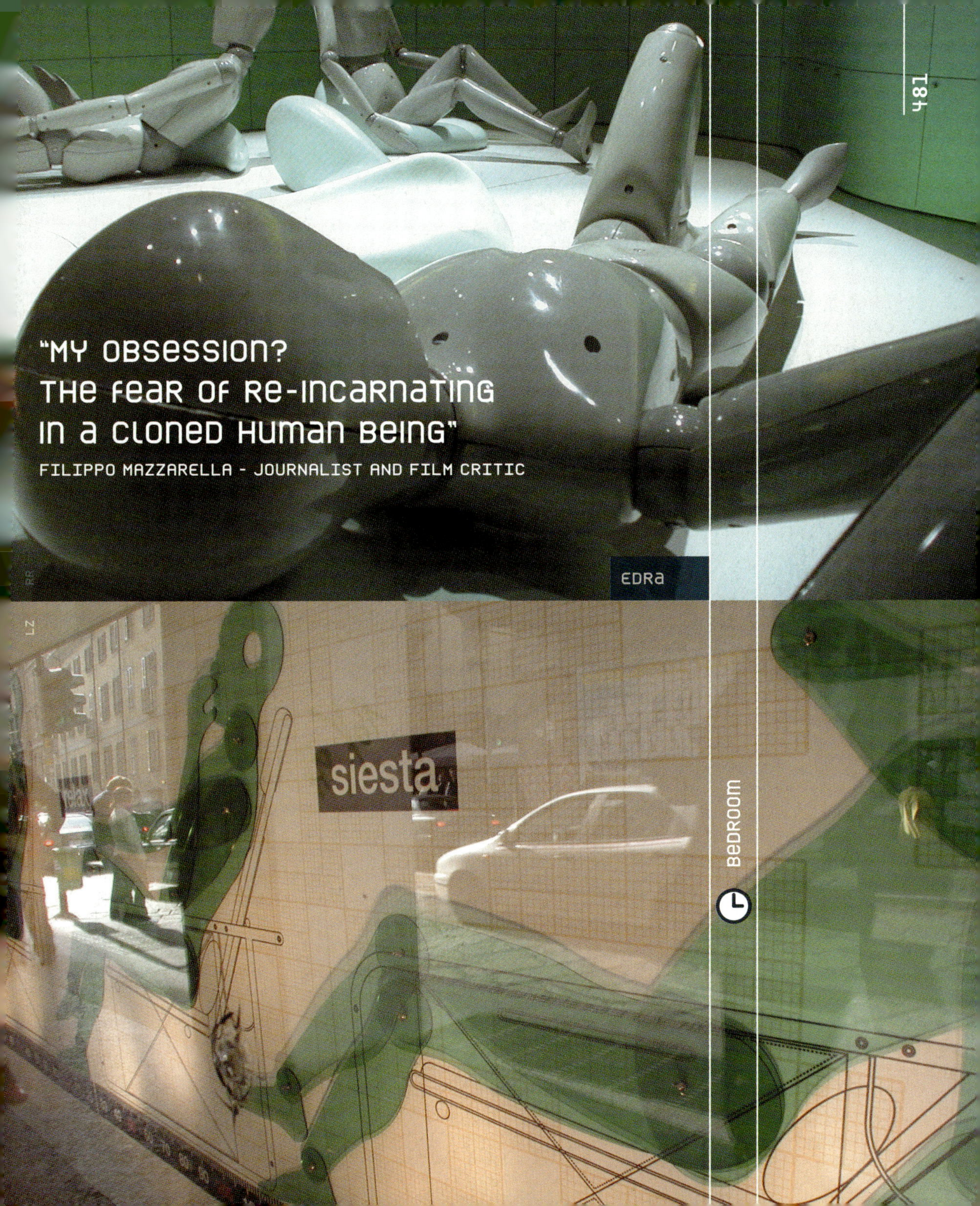
184
"MY OBSESSION?
THE FEAR OF RE-INCARNATING
IN A CLONED HUMAN BEING"
FILIPPO MAZZARELLA - JOURNALIST AND FILM CRITIC
RR
EDRA
LZ
siesta
BEDROOM

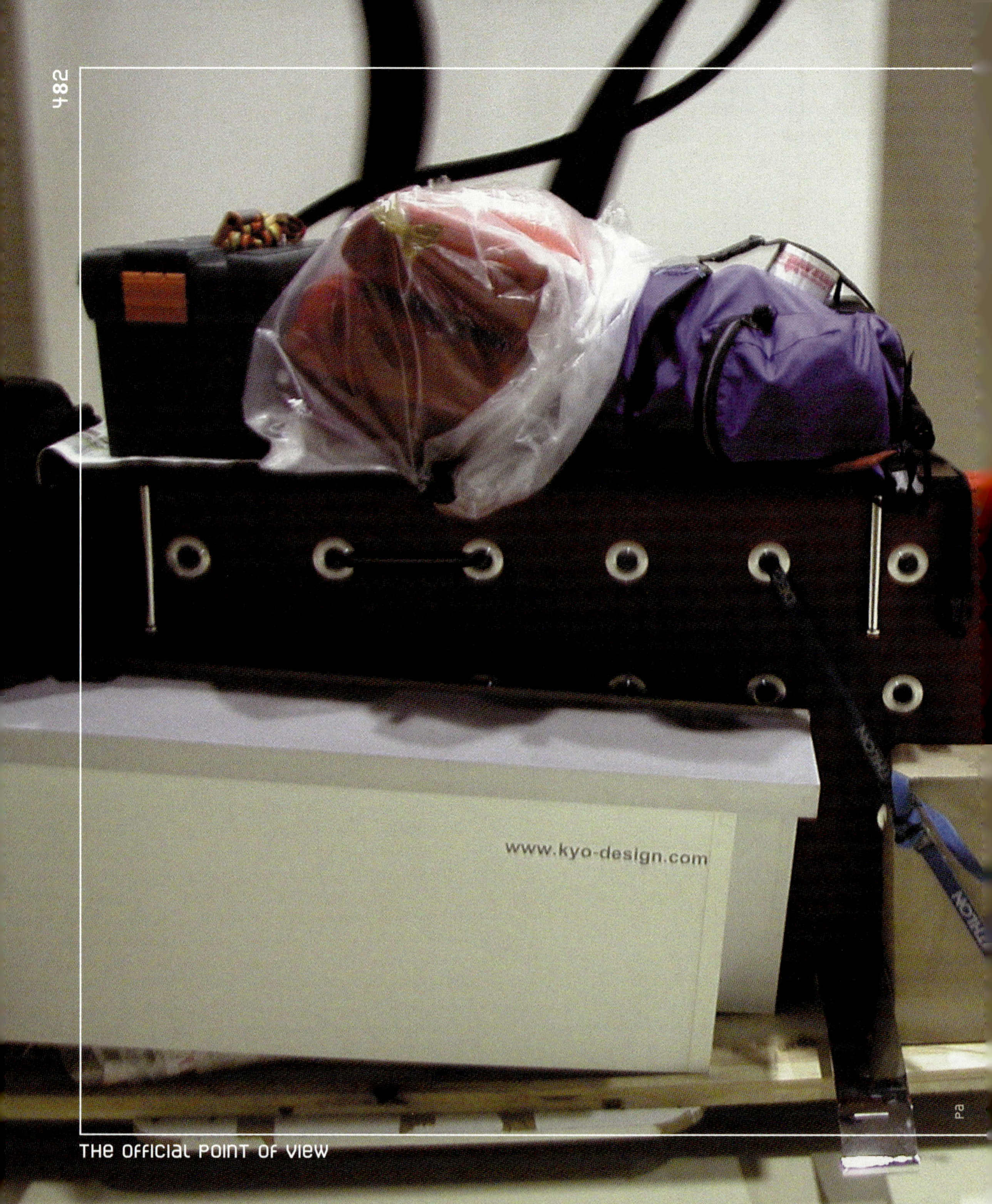
www.kyo-design.com

04 AM BEDROOM

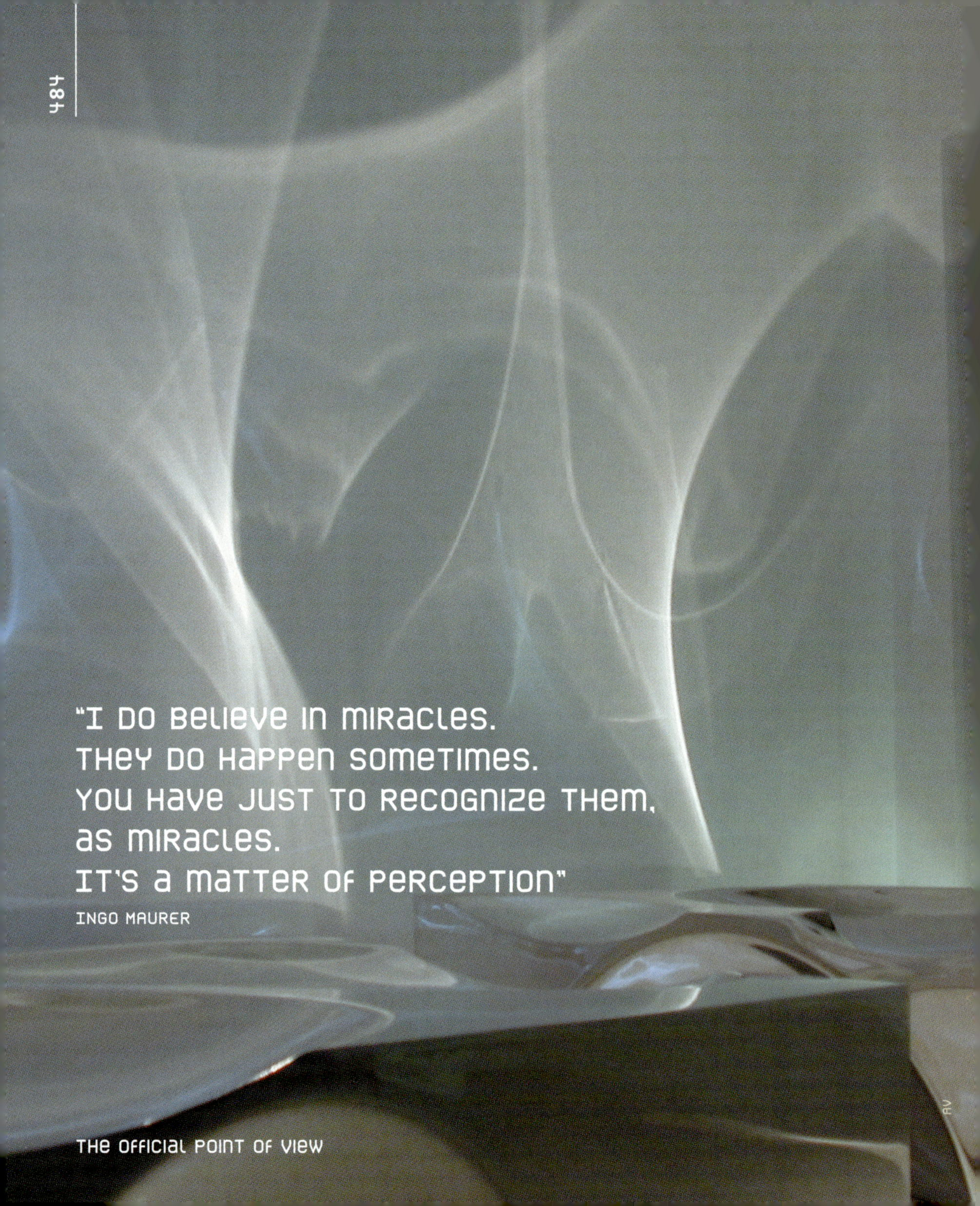

"I DO BELIEVE IN MIRACLES.
THEY DO HAPPEN SOMETIMES.
YOU HAVE JUST TO RECOGNIZE THEM,
AS MIRACLES.
IT'S A MATTER OF PERCEPTION"
INGO MAURER

DReaminG

STELLA MCCARTNEY FOR MOROSO
"OFF - SCALE" EXHIBITION

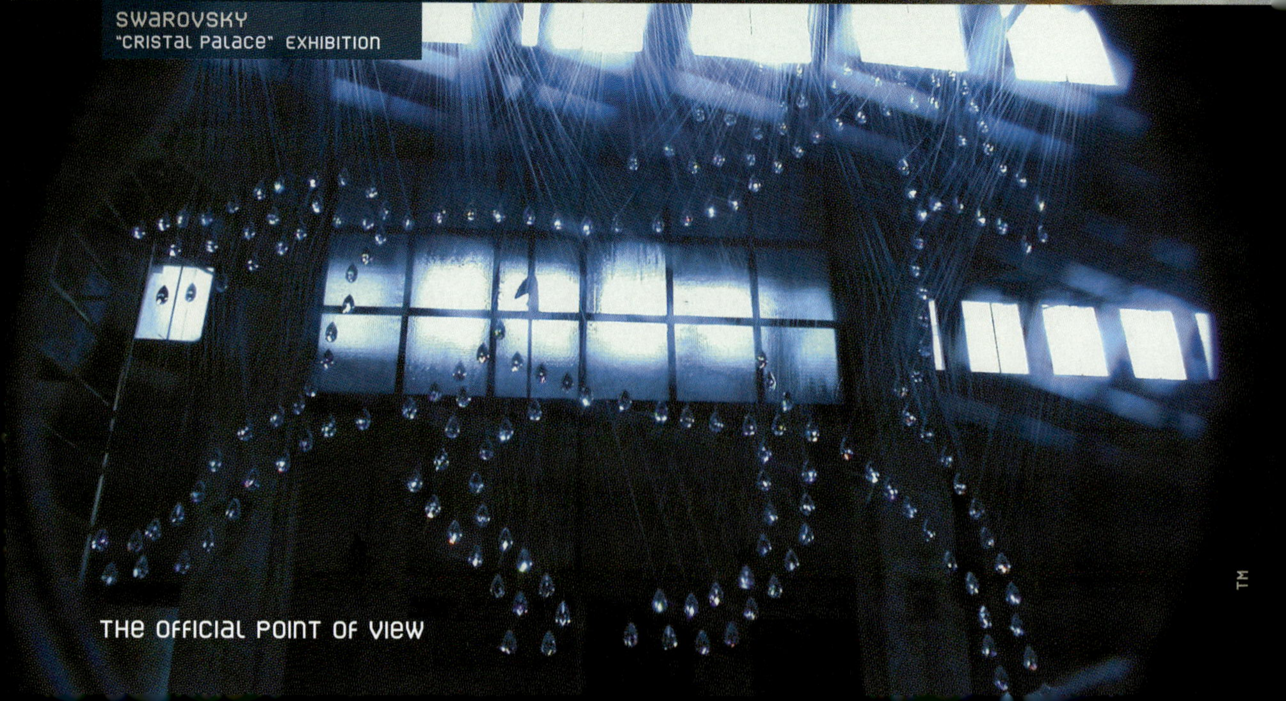

SWAROVSKY
"CRISTAL PALACE" EXHIBITION

THE OFFICIAL POINT OF VIEW

HELA JONGERIUS SWAROVSKY
"CRISTAL PALACE" EXHIBITION

DREAMING

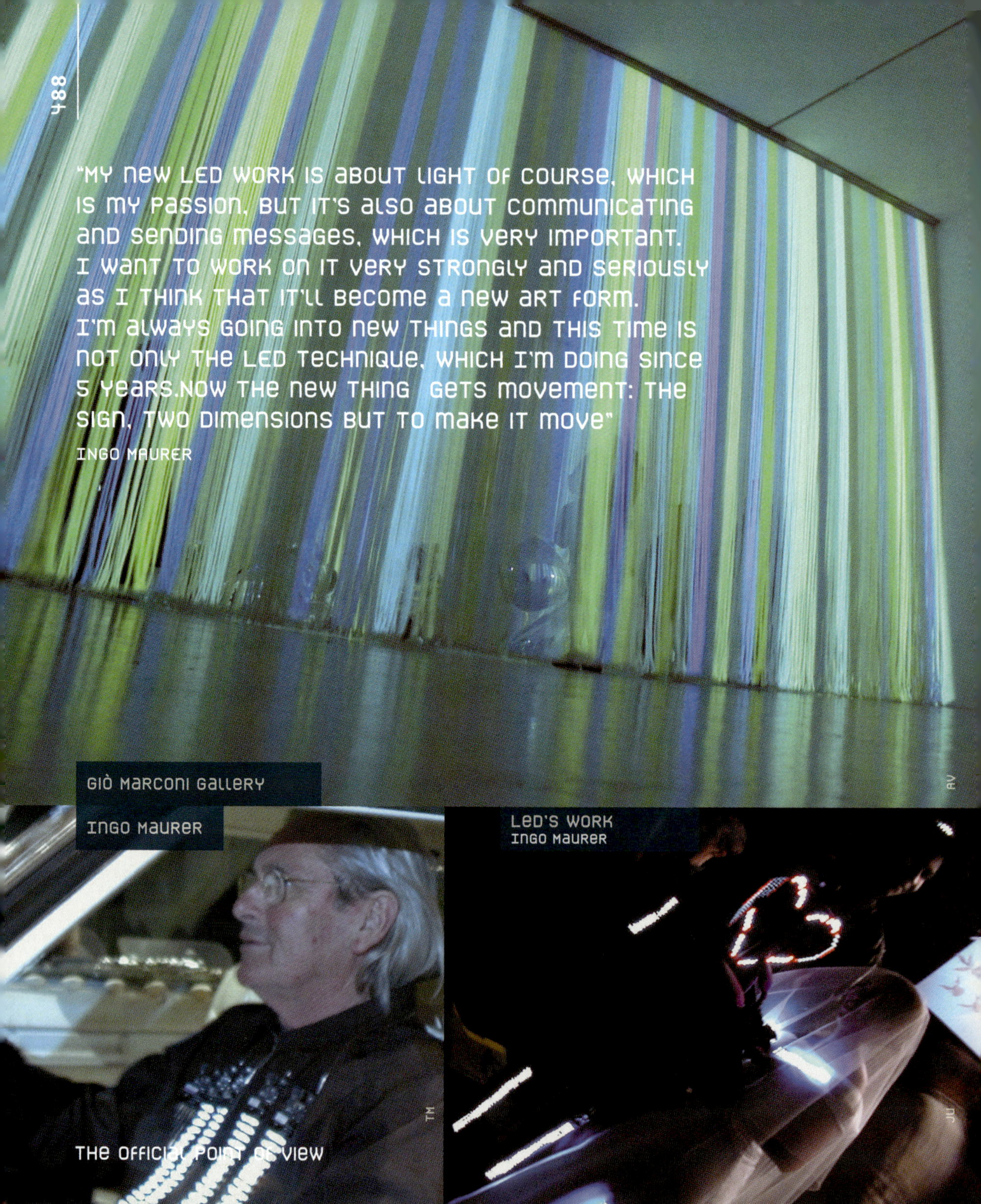
488
"MY NEW LED WORK IS ABOUT LIGHT OF COURSE, WHICH
IS MY PASSION. BUT IT'S ALSO ABOUT COMMUNICATING
AND SENDING MESSAGES, WHICH IS VERY IMPORTANT.
I WANT TO WORK ON IT VERY STRONGLY AND SERIOUSLY
AS I THINK THAT IT'LL BECOME A NEW ART FORM.
I'M ALWAYS GOING INTO NEW THINGS AND THIS TIME IS
NOT ONLY THE LED TECHNIQUE, WHICH I'M DOING SINCE
5 YEARS.NOW THE NEW THING GETS MOVEMENT: THE
SIGN. TWO DIMENSIONS BUT TO MAKE IT MOVE"
INGO MAURER
GIÒ MARCONI GALLERY
INGO MAURER
LED'S WORK
INGO MAURER
THE OFFICIAL POINT OF VIEW

DReamING

RICHARD MeIeR FOR GRanD HOTeL SaLOne
PaRIGI - ROOM

Lucellino
Ingo Maurer
THE OFFICIAL POINT OF VIEW

"DESIGN CONTAINING TRUTHFULNESS
SHOULD BE A DESIGN WHICH IS CREATED
BY A VERY HONEST, GOING STRAIGHT
FORWARD ONE AND USING THE VANITY,
WHICH IS A STRONG MOTOR OF OUR BEING,
INTO SOMETHING REALLY TRUE AND NOT
ANY GIMMICK"
INGO MAURER
DREAMING

492
MZ
THE OFFICIAL POINT OF VIEW

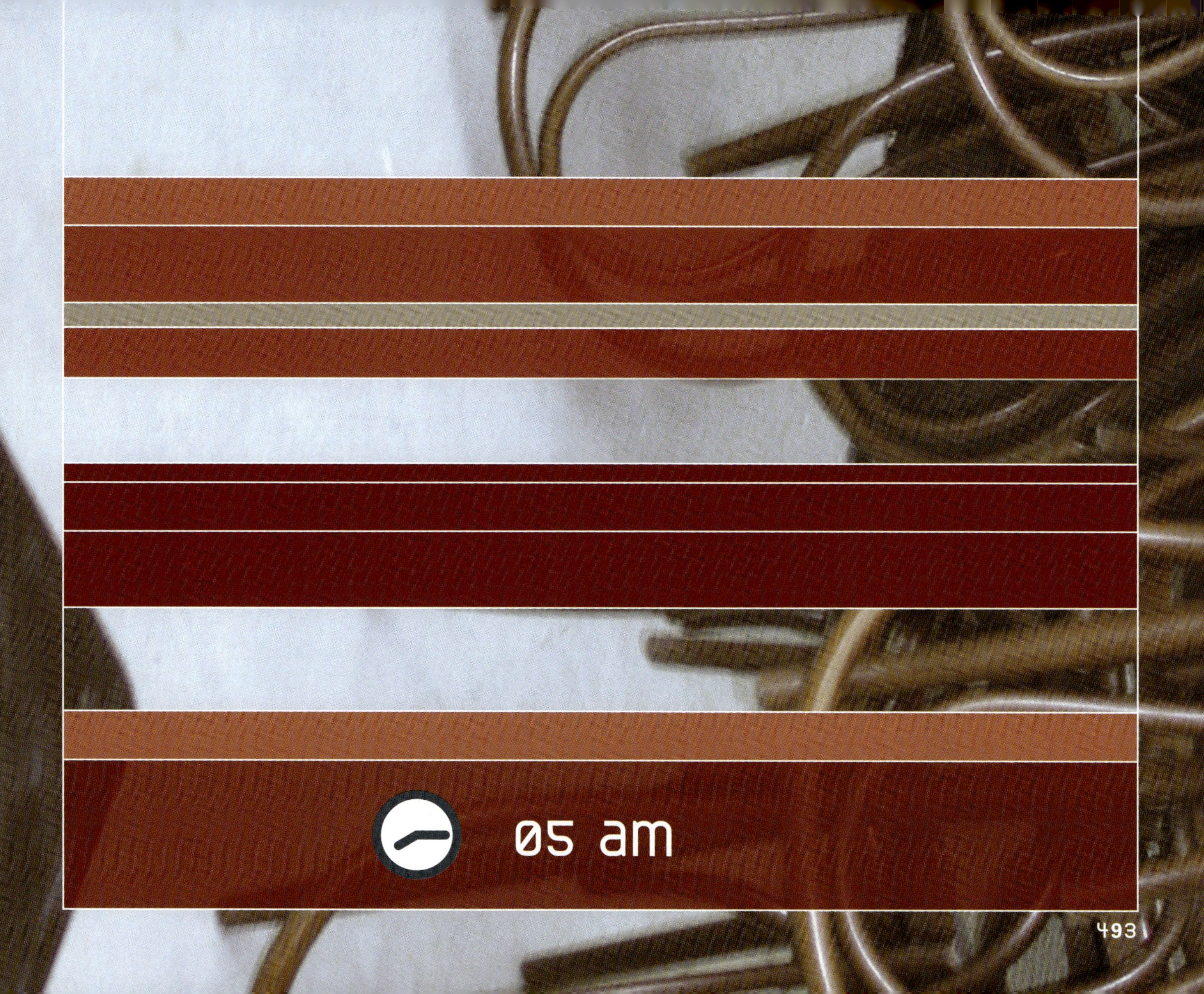
05 am

THE OFFICIAL POINT OF VIEW

495
05 am

496
THE OFFICIAL POINT OF VIEW

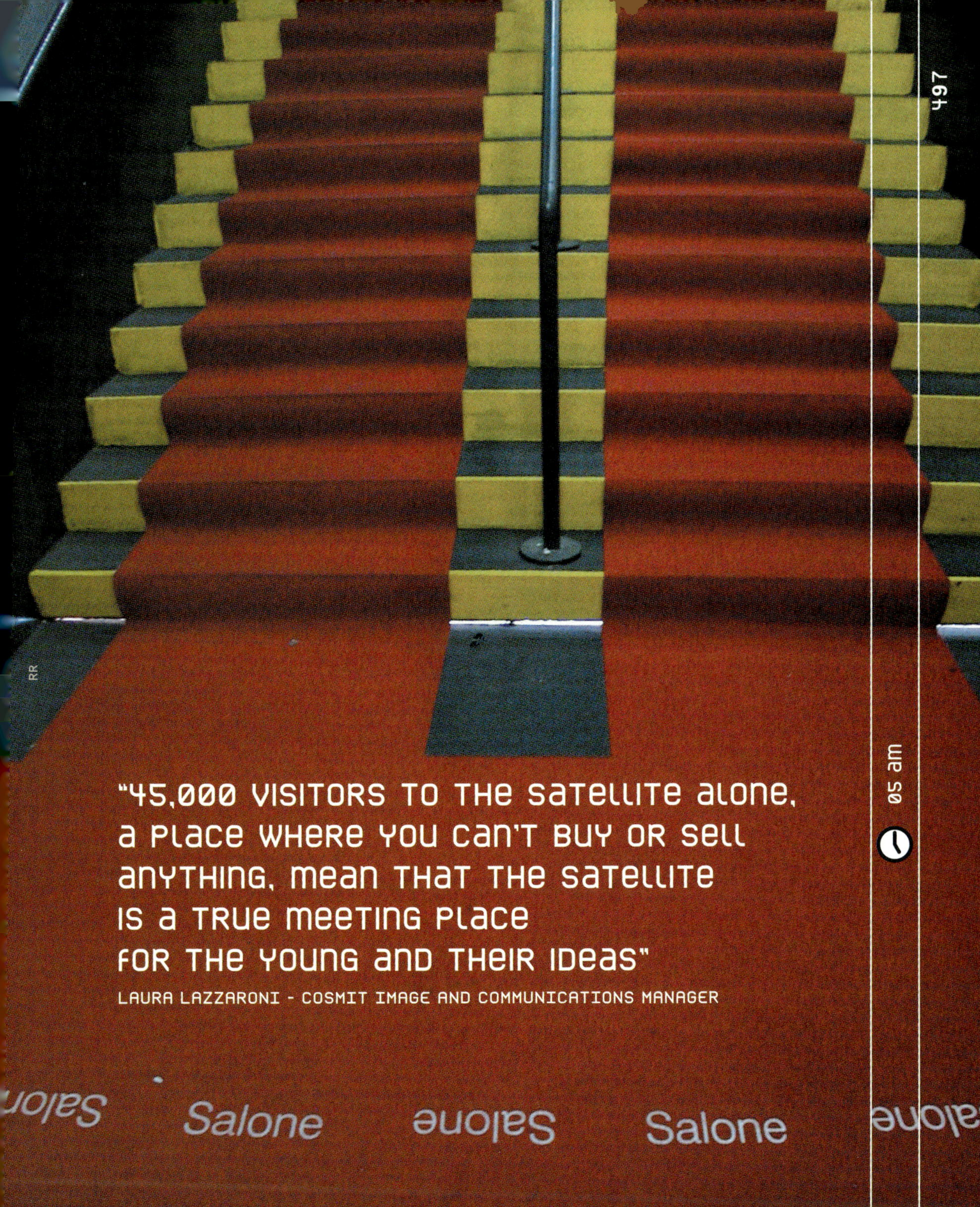
497
"45,000 VISITORS TO THE SATELLITE ALONE,
A PLACE WHERE YOU CAN'T BUY OR SELL
ANYTHING, MEAN THAT THE SATELLITE
IS A TRUE MEETING PLACE
FOR THE YOUNG AND THEIR IDEAS"
LAURA LAZZARONI - COSMIT IMAGE AND COMMUNICATIONS MANAGER
05 am
Salone

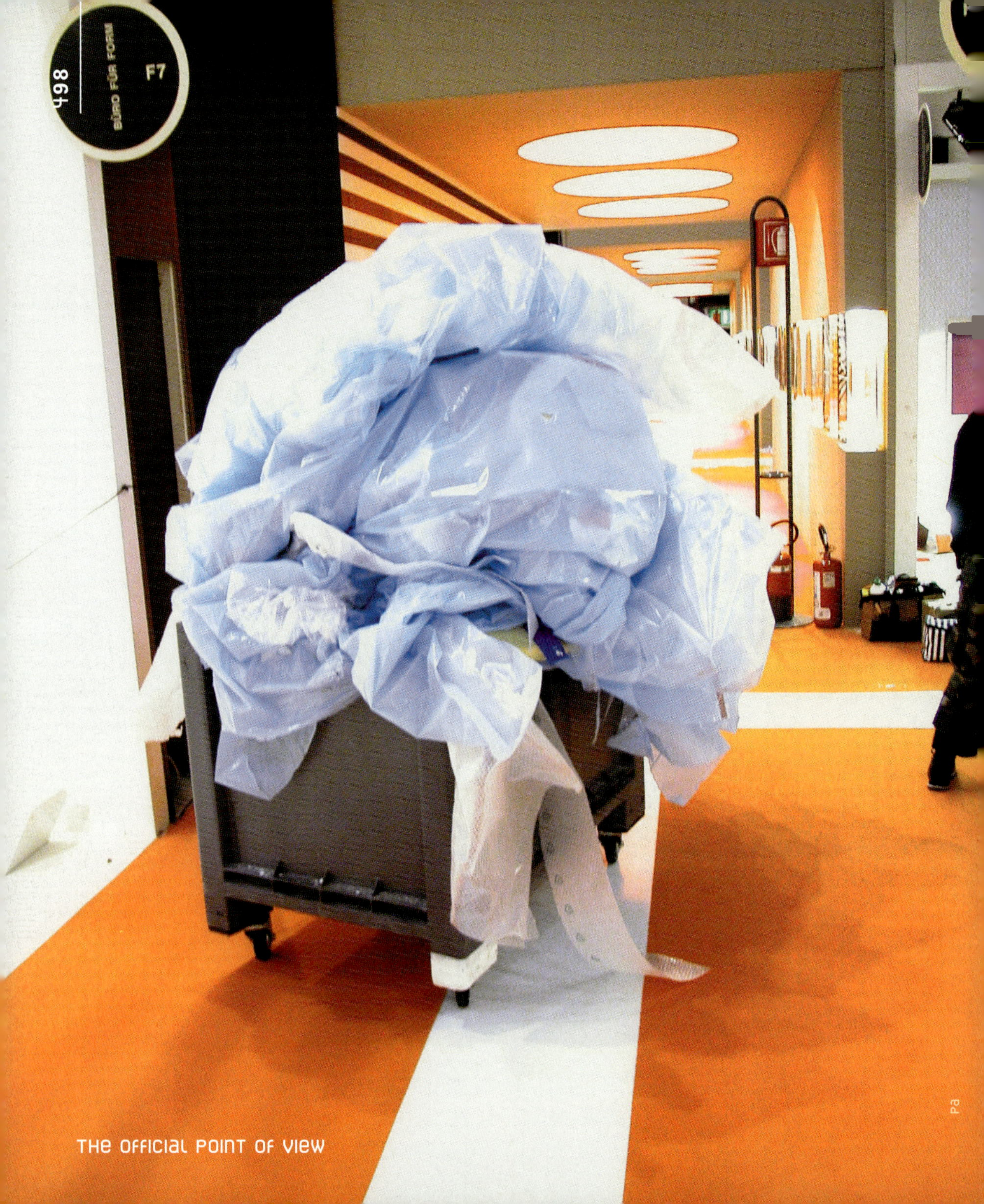

THE OFFICIAL POINT OF VIEW

499
invecta
NOLOSTAND
05 am

THE OFFICIAL POINT OF VIEW

PC
PC
MAN
IVECO
ATIKA
ø5 am

Before the Chair Became a Chair What Was It?

A Stream of Consciousness from the mind of Daniele Pignatelli

This is the story of a man, a dog and a chair, a lifetime in 4 days, a date -the 17th- for each month of every season and a season for every 17 years.

SPRING 17:

The first rays of dawn slowly rise up from out of the dark.

There is a tree, a secular olive tree right in the middle of the stage: a tree that has lived a full and intense life - you can tell from the venation of the leaves, from the cuts, grazes and the scars, from its' height and its' width - but it is still in good health: its' silver-highlighted leaves hide big juicy olives.

A ripe olive falls from a branch but before it touches the ground it gets caught in midflight by a child's hand.

The child, thrilled by his heroic gesture, runs around the huge trunk in delight, waving his hand in the air to prevent his puppy, a greyhound, from stealing the olive.

SUMMER+17:

(PITCH BLACK) NIGHT.

Flashes of lightning from a tropical storm intermittently light up the stage: the olive tree, under which the boy and his greyhound are sheltering (it is understood that they are older now, the child and the puppy from the previous scene), casts ghostly shadows.

The greyhound wearily raises his hind leg in order to relieve himself against the tree trunk just as a powerful bolt of lightning almost strikes the startled boy who barely manages to avoid being hit by the bolt which violently cleaves the olive tree in two.

The boy goes to the panting-burnt-shocked greyhound and tries to help him to lower his leg but as soon as his paw touches the ground and the boy lets go, the leg slowly but surely returns to its upraised position.

A ray of sunlight filters through the clouds and lights up the olive tree: it is in pieces and its leafy branches are lying on the ground; the boy moves in and out of the fallen branches gathering the olives.

He finds himself sitting on the maimed-trunk and even though he's experiencing this for the first time, it's nice and comfortable: he likes it and tries out various sitting positions until, overdoing it slightly, he falls.

The greyhound can't help smiling in spite of the awkward angle of his leg that simply will not go back into position.

AUTUMN+17:

(PITCH BLACK) NIGHT.

The ever-increasing sound of powerful blows.

The stage gradually lights up but a thick fog makes it difficult to see clearly.

Every now and then the fog dissolves enough for just a few instants so that what is happening can be glimpsed, creating a series of cross-fading effects or better yet the impression of a curtain opening and closing: a man can be seen, beating a huge branch with a stone into the base of the cloven trunk while the greyhound - whose

LEG HAS BEEN AMPUTATED IN THE MEANTIME - MOVES BACK AND FORWARD TO THE RHYTHM OF THE BLOWS.

THE CURTAIN OF FOG OPENS AND CLOSES ON THE MAN WHO IS PUTTING ANOTHER BRANCH BESIDE THE FIRST ONE AND FINALLY OPENS TO SHOW THE MAN SITTING ON THE MAIMED TRUNK PROUDLY LEANING BACKWARDS TOWARDS THE STRUCTURE THAT HE HAS CREATED FROM THE BRANCHES.

THE DOG SITS BACK ON THE GROUND IMITATING HIM.

WINTER+17:

ONE OF THOSE EXTRAORDINARY MORNINGS WHEN THE AIR IS SO CLEAR THAT THE TOPS OF THE FARAWAY MOUNTAINS CAN BE SEEN.

AN OLD MAN, SEEN FROM BEHIND, IS GIVING THE FINAL TOUCHES TO WHAT ONCE UPON A TIME WAS THE MAIMED TRUNK: 4 LEGS HAVE BEEN CARVED OUT FROM THE BASE AND THE BRANCHES/BACK HAVE BEEN POLISHED, TRANSFORMING IT INTO A COMFORTABLE PLACE TO REST ALBEIT IMMOBILE.

THE GREYHOUND, VISIBLY AGED, OBSERVES HIM MOTIONLESSLY ON HIS THREE LEGS.

THE OLD MAN WALKS ONCE AROUND HIS CREATION AND THEN SITS ON IT.

IT STARTS TO SNOW LIGHTLY AND ONE SNOWFLAKE, A BIT BIGGER THAN THE OTHERS, LANDS ON THE DOG'S BACK: THE DOG REMAINS MOTIONLESS AND THEN HELPLESSLY BUT SLOWLY LEANS SIDEWAYS UNTIL FINALLY HE COLLAPSES COMPLETELY.

THE WORRIED OLD MAN MOVES TOWARDS THE DOG AS THE EVER-THICKER FALLING SNOW MAKES IT INCREASINGLY DIFFICULT TO SEE.

(PITCH BLACK) NIGHT...

A SPARK BECOMES A FLAME AND THEN A FIRE, A BONFIRE, WHICH LIGHTS UP THE STAGE: BESIDE THE BLAZING MAIMED-TRUNK-CHAIR, THE OLD MAN HOLDS THE DOG IN HIS ARMS CLOSE TO HIS HEART AND THE DOG, COMFORTED BY THE WARMTH, RECOVERS ENOUGH TO GET BACK ONTO HIS THREE LEGS.

AFTER WARMING THEMSELVES WELL, THE OLD MAN AND THE DOG GAZE INTO THE FIRE THAT AT FIRST DANCED HIGH BUT THEN SLOWLY GOT SMALLER AND SMALLER UNTIL IT FINALLY WENT OUT, LEAVING THE OUTLINE OF THE UNFINISHED MAIMED-TRUNK ON

STAGE, THE SKELETON OF THE FIRST CHAIR: THE FIRE HAS FORGED SINUOUS SHAPES THAT GIVE IT PERFECT STABILITY, AN AMAZING LIGHTNESS PARTICULARLY CONSIDERING ITS' NATURAL ROBUSTNESS.

IT HAS A COLOUR THAT HAS NEVER BEFORE BEEN SEEN: OPAQUE YET SPARKLING, BLACK, THAT SHADE OF PITCH BLACK THAT CONTAINS ALL THE COLOURS IN THE WORLD.

BEAUTIFUL IN CONTRAST TO THE WHITE SNOW.

THE OLD MAN PULLS THE CHAIR FREE FROM THE GROUND IN ONE MOVE, PLACES IT BESIDE THE DOG AND SITS DOWN.

AND IN THAT PRECISE MOMENT A PROCESSION OF 17 DOZEN, 17 HUNDRED, 17 THOUSAND PEOPLE PASS BY, ATTRACTED BY THE ENORMOUS BONFIRE, AND FIND THEMSELVES NOT ONLY BEWITCHED BY THE NEVER-BEFORE SEEN OBJECT BUT ALSO WILLING TO BARTER THEIR BELONGINGS IN ORDER TO TRY IT OUT.

AND EACH PERSON, AS THEY SIT DOWN ONE BY ONE, REALISES FOR THE FIRST TIME THAT THE DOG, UNLIKE THE CHAIR, HAS ONLY 3 LEGS.

A NEW IDEA IS BORN.

DRAWING BY ERCOLE PIGNATELLI

PAVIA
The OFFICIAL POINT OF
The OFFICIAL POINT OF
GIULIA BER
FOTOREPORTER
Salone Internazionale del Mobile
Salone del Complemento d'Arredo
Eurocucina
Elmu.2002 Comfort & Technology
SaloneSatellite
Milano 10/15 aprile 2002
8.30-18.30
ALBERTO GIULIANI
0000400007
3172032001533 4525610
COSMIT spa
P.IVA 12470090154
Tessera valida per 4 ingressi
FOTOREPORTER
EMANUELE COLOMBO
0000400006
3172032001533 4525610

AUTHORS.

GIULIA BER TACCHINI -JU-

IS A DESIGNER AND CREATIVE DIRECTOR WORKING
IN FASHION DESIGN - MAINLY ACCESSORIES -
(DIOR, FERRÉ, SAZABY-TOKYO, PRADA, CUSTUME
NATIONAL, ETC) AND INDUSTRIAL DESIGN (FONTANA
ARTE, ARFLEX, HABITAT, BAROVIER&TOSO, STURM
UND PLASTIC, ETC.), RESEARCHING IN PARTICULAR
INNOVATIVE MATERIALS AND THEIR APPLICATIONS.
SHE HAS DESIGNED SILVER JEWELRY AND
TABLETOP FOR WILLIAM SPRATLING AND SHE
IS DOING RESEARCH WORK IN THE FIELDS OF
PHOTOGRAPHY, FILMSCRIPTING AND VIDEOFILM.
JULIA@THEOFFICIALPOINTOFVIEW.IT

LUCIO LUZO LAZZARA -LZ-

IS A GRAPHIC DESIGNER AND ART DIRECTOR.
HE WORKS WITH MANY INSITUTIONS AND FIRMS
FROM ALESSI TO BANG&OLUFSEN, FROM LEVI'S TO
MCCANN ERICKSSON, FROM MONDADORI TO WARNER
BROS, DESIGNING DIFFERENT KIND OF PRODUCTS,
IN A SPAN GOING FROM BOOK-JACKETS TO VIDEO-
INSTALLATIONS VIA MAGAZINE DESIGN AND TV
TRAILERS.
HE IS A TEACHER IN THE POLITECNICO DI MILANO
AND CO-FOUNDER OF THE GRAPHIC DESIGN STUDIO
ZETA_LAB, IN MILANO.
LUZO@THEOFFICIALPOINTOFVIEW.IT

PAOLO CALCAGNI -PA-

IS CO-FOUNDER OF CENTRAL PRODUCTION
AND SINCE 1990 DIRECTOR OF MUSIC AND
ADVERTISING FILMS FOR OVER 100 NATIONAL AND
INTERNATIONAL CLIENTS.
IN 1992 HE ASSOCIATED WITH THE ENGLISH
PRODUCTION FIRM VOYAGER TO PRODUCE SPOTS
FOR VODAFONE, APLETISE, PHILIPS, VOLKSWAGEN,
BRITVIC.
LATER HE WORKED FOR A NUMBER OF
INTERNATIONAL PRODUCTION FIRMS: NY-
INDIPENDENT ARTIST (USA), MIA FILM (SOUTH
AMERICA), CABELSTONE/MARCHEN FILM (D),
JOHN SPARY.ASS (GB), EDIE SAETA (SP), DANIEL
ISRAEL (AU), NEXUS FILM (JP), MONTAINI FILM (P)
DIRECTING ACTRESSES OF INTERNATIONAL FAME:
LETIZIA CASTA, MARIAGRAZIA CUCINOTTA, ISABEL
PASCO', CATHERINE ZETA JONES, PENELOPE
CRUZ.
IN THE SAME YEAR HE DIRECTED A SHORT FILM
TITLED "RADIO ANGELS" DEDICATED TO DUANE
MICHALS.
HE HAS EARNED RECOGNITIONS IN ADVERTISING
FILM FESTIVALS IN MILAN AND CANNES.
IN 1995 HE CREATED THE COMPANY ENORME
FILM ART.
PAOLO@THEOFFICIALPOINTOFVIEW.IT

RICCARDO RINETTI -RR-

IS A JOURNALIST AND A MUSIC CRITIC.
FROM 1977 TO 1982 HE WAS IN THE EDITORIAL
STAFF OF THE MAGAZINE "CIAO 2001" WHILE
WORKING FOR OTHER PUBLICATIONS LIKE
"ROCKSTAR" AND "MUSIC". HE ALSO PRODUCED
A NUMBER OF RECORDS WORKING WITH SERGIO
CAPUTO AND MIMMO LOCASCIULLI. IN 1982 HE
PUBLISHED THE BIOGRAPHY OF LUCIO DALLA FOR
THE TYPES OF GREMESE EDITORE.
FROM THE END OF 1981 TO 1994 HE WORKED
IN THE INTERNATIONAL ADVERTISING AGENCY MC
CANN ERIKSON, FIRST AS A COPYWRITER AND
THEN AS CREATIVE CO-DIRECTOR, DOING WORKS
FOR A NUMBER OF INTERNATIONAL BRANDS
(L'OREAL, GM, NABISCO ETC.). SINCE 1994 HE HAS
BEEN WORKING AS ADVERTISING FILM DIRECTOR.
HE WORKED, AMONGST OTHERS, FOR BULGARI,
POMELLATO, TIM, SONY.
AT THE SAME TIME HE CONTINUED HIS
PHOTOGRAPHIC ACTIVITY BOTH IN ADVERTISING
(POMELLATO, GIORGIO VISCONTI, OMNITEL, BIRAGHI,
BUITONI) AND IN HIS PERSONAL RESEARCH ON
BLACK AND WHITE IMAGES.
HE HAS RECENTLY BEEN FILMING FOR BANCA
SAN PAOLO IMI WITH ARTIST UGO NESPOLO AND
MARTINA COLOMBARI AND HE IS ABOUT TO FINISH
WORKING ON THE PHOTOGRAPHIC BOOK "MEGAN
SEGRETA" DEDICATED TO MEGAN GALE WITH THE
PARTICIPATION OF OMNITEL/VODAPHONE.
RICCARDO@THEOFFICIALPOINTOFVIEW.IT

PHOTOGRAPHERS.

ALBERTO GIULIANI -GL-

Born in 1975, in 1993 he started working as a fulltime photo-reporter with Grazia Neri agency. since then he has covered assignments around the world for different magazines on subjects from the forced sterilization in Peru to the recent war in Afghanistan, from the diaspora of Tibetans to daily life on Italian beaches. In 2000 he won the Canon Prize, with the project "next to nothing" about social problems from around the world.
albertogiuliani@hotmail.com

TOMMASO MANGIOLA -TM-

Born in Calabria, he now lives in Milan. He has worked with clients such Condénast, GFT, Amica, Cappellini, Armani, Prada, and with various other entrepreneurs, not as wellknown but equally interesting, such as tattooers, bakers, gardeners, tailors, entertainers, jewellers and editors.
tommasomangiola@libero.it

EMMANUEL MATHEZ -MZ-

Born in 1969, he works as a freelance photographer.
His photos appeared on the covers of many Italian records.
He has been published in magazines such as Gulliver, D Donna, Maxim, Bside, Happy Web, Pulp, DNR (American Fashion), Il Diario, Big Magazine, Urban, Carnet and so on.
Shortlisted for Kodak European Young Photographers Award 1993
Biennale Giovani Artisti del Mediterraneo '94
Shortlisted for San Carlo Borromeo Award '95
Kodak Immaginando Award 1996
mathez@tiscalinet.it

AGOSTINO OSIO -OS-

Born in 1978, he lives and he works in Milan, where he studied photography at the European Institute of Design. He mainly works in artistic photography films.
osiago@hotmail.com

SEBASTIANO PAVIA -SB-

Born in Catania in 1972, photographer, he has worked with Fabrica di Oliviero Toscani, Grazia Neri agency, Upside Down, for different companies and important international and Italian newspapers.

His photoshave been published in magazines such as Photografia, Zoom, Photo Italia, Photographies, Private, P. Polaroid, Photo Espana, and Nu Attitudini Morbose.
He has directed videos such as 'Razzismo' for MTV and "Giornalismo" for Arte' France.
sebbapavia@katamail.com

MARCO PIETRACUPA -PC-

He works in the fields of fashion photography and portraits. He graduated from the Italian Institute of Photography and he has used the themes of his artistic-photographic research to hold two private exhibitions.
He has worked for numerous CD sleeves.
His works has been published in fashion and design magazines such as Glamour, D-Repubblica, Kult, Label, Nu, Themepark and Big.
Personal art exhibition: "MONDI2" Galleria Modigliani DUE/ART.
marco.pietracupa@tiscalinet.it

ALESSANDRO VIGANÒ -AV-

Born in 1972, he lives in Milan. He studied at the NCAD in Dublin and then graduated in architecture from the Politecnico of Milano..
He is interested in different fields of creative disciplines including digital photography.
ale@zetalab.com

MARCO ARNÒ

First assistant photographer and coordination

DANIELE PIGNATELLI

Born in Milano, he graduated in film direction from CPF.
Since 1991 he has been working with several production companies directing videoclips for Italian songwriters and singers. He has also written and directed, short films, worked on TV series and theater productions. He is currently writing the script for his first feature film 'Scara Mante'.
In 2002 his short film 'Terzo' & Mondo' won several awards.
dapign@tin.it

508

ZETA_LAB

DOING THE BOOK: 23 DAYS OF WORK, 544 PAGES TO MAKE, 5 GRAPHIC
DESIGNERS, 20.000 DIGITAL PHOTOGRAPHS TO SELECT.
5 APPLE® POWER MACINTOSH G4, 44 PIZZAS, 378 COFFEES.
DESIGNED WITH ADOBE® INDESIGN 2.0, ADOBE® PHOTOSHOP.
info@zetalab.com

509
VITTORIO LINFANTE
MARCO BOLDRINI
ROBERTA ROBBIE RICCIUTII
Adobe
InDesign 2.0
THE OFFICIAL POINT OF VIEW

THanKs TO.

OUR THANKS TO ALL
THE PEOPLE WHO
HAVE SUPPORTED
THIS PROJECT:

ALESSANDRO ANDREI
MANLIO ARMELLINI
MASSIMO BASSO
MATILDE BATTISTINI
JEAN BLANCHAERT
FRANCO BOLELLI
ACHILLE BONITO
OLIVA
ELIZABETH BOURKE
DANIELE BRANDOLINO
MAURIZIO CATTELAN
MAURIZIO CAVALLI
LUCA CHECOLA
ALESSANDRA CENTINI
COSMIT
LUCIANO DALLAPE'
DANIELA DANZI

DARIO D'APRILE
DAVIDE
MAX DE LUCA
LUIGI DI CORATO
ANDREA DOJMI
ERICA ELLENA
DAVIDE FACCIOLI
LEANDRO FINC
ODOARDO
FIORAVANTI
CHIARA FUMAI
FRANCESCA FRIGINO
CLAUDIA FRIGNANI
MATTIA FRIGNANI
GIGI GIANNUZZI
ANN-LAURE GIMENEZ
MIRELLA GUIDO
PERTTI KEKARAINEN
MAITTI KOHILAKOSKI
INTER NOS
ISTITUTO ITALIANO
FOTOGRAFIA

LORENZA WEYLAND
MARVA GRIFFIN
WILSHIRE
FLAVIA FOSSA
MARGUTTI
TACO LANGIUS
LAURA LAZZARONI
TOMMASO LEVARDINI
MARIA LICCI
LUCIANA MAESTRA DI
COLORE
PAOLA MANFRIN
ELEONORA MARASCIO
ACHILLE MAURI
FILIPPO MAZZARELLA
ANTONELLA MIANTE
SIVIA MORANDI
ALBERTO MORELLI
FABIO NOVEMBRE
MARNIX OOSTERWELD
ALESSIA PALLADINI
CLAUDIO PANCHERI

LUCA PANCRAZZI
MINNA PASANEN
CAMILLA PERRUCCI
ERCOLE PIGNATELLI
MILKA POGLIANI
DIEGO PROFLI
TONI QUARANTA
ROBERTA ROCCA
FEDERICO ROSSI
VALENTINA SACHERO
DENIS SANTACHIARA
STEFANO SENARDI
KIVI SOTAMAA
GIANFRANCO TAINO
ADAM TIHANY
VALENTINA TESCARI
LEON VAN GERWEN
CORETTA VAN WIJK
ENRICA ZAGHINI

TECHNICAL SPONSORS.

9NETWEB   WWW.9NETWEB.IT   MANDARINA DUCK
ADIDAS   WWW.ADIDAS.IT   NIKON/ NITAL ITALIA
ADOBE ITALIA   WWW.ADOBE.IT   PC GRATIS
AGNOS TECH ENGINEERING   POLIPLASTICA

THE OFFICIAL POINT OF VIEW

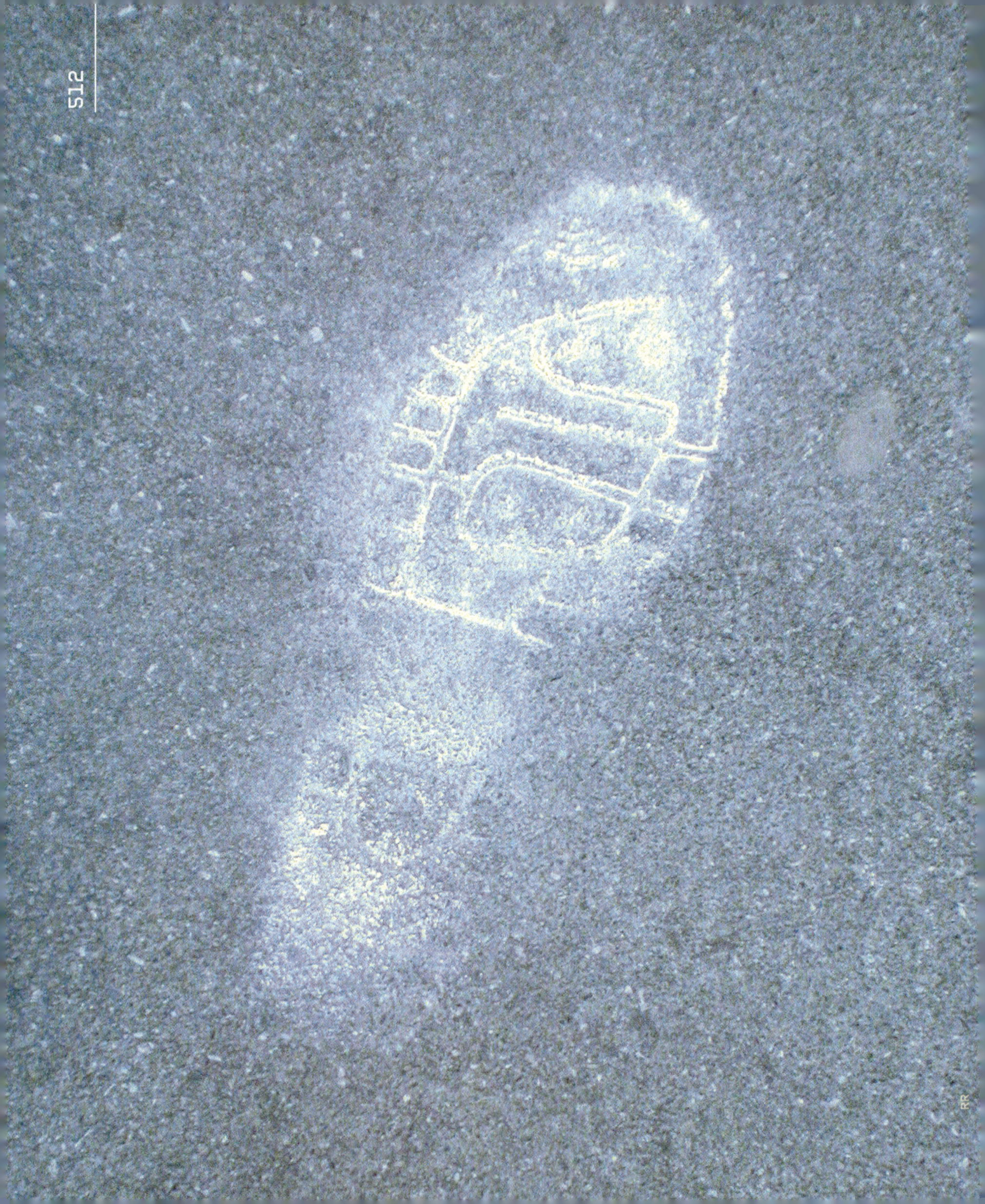

aDResses

...4!
August-Bebel-Strasse 29
06108 Halle, Germany
Tel +49 179 5268528
Fax +49 345 3881416
hack@dreipunkt4.de
www.dreipunkt4.de

A.K.I.S.
Pauksciu Tako Street 22
4043 Vilnius, Lithuania
Tel +370 2 729235
aistule@takas.lt
www.akis.w3.lt

Annemarie Adriaanse
Quai du Cheval-Blanc 16
1227 Geneva, Switzerland
Tel +41 22 3424970
Cell. +41 76 5764911
Fax +41 22 8704582
aej_adriaanse@hotmail.com
www.annemarieadriaanse.com

Adriano Design
Via Cesana 85
10139 Torino, Italia
Tel +39 0114330117
Fax +39 0114339679
studio_adriano@iol.it
www.adrianodesign.it

Agentura Carolina Ltd.
Albertov 7/3a
12800 Prague 2, Czech Republic
Tel +420 2 24301090
Fax +420 2 24301539
doubrava@carolina.cz
www.carolina.cz

Alt Design
Buweilerstrasse 16
66687 Wadern-Rathen, Germany
Tel/Fax +49 6871 5885
s.alt@alt-design.de
www.alt-design.de

Amano, Asano & Partners
Via Biancospini 19
20146 Milano, Italia
Tel +39 0242290431
Fax +39 0247717217
tadao@attglobal.net

Amok?
Via G. Regaldi 22
20161 Milano, Italia
Cell. +39 338 2684664
Fax +39 0266200150
aloschiavo@libero.it

Antenna.02
c/o Silvia Knüppel
Schützenstrasse 6
76137 Karlsruhe, Germany
Tel +49 721 3848338
furniture_fields@web.de

Apt. 5 Design, Terence Sean Yoo & Angela Tarasco
Via Colangiuli 5
75100 Matera, Italia
+39 339 4573999
+39 333 8261999
Fax +1 320 2092697 (USA)
mail@apt5design.com
www.apt5design.com

Francesco Arnone & Antonio Scordato
Via Città di Palermo 112
90011 Bagheria (PA), Italia
Tel/Fax +39 091961349
Cell. +39 335 8078617

Atlason & Lewin
226 West 25th Street # 3FE
10001 New York, USA
Tel +1 212 9474557
Fax +1 212 9474552
atlason@atlason.com
gabriellelewin@aol.com

Aura Objects
144 Daws Road
Adelaide, South Australia 5039
Tel +61 8 82750100
Fax +61 8 82764594
szappia@chariot.com.au

Enrico Azzimonti & Jordi Pigem
Via Mameli 10
21052 Busto Arsizio (VA), Italia
Tel/Fax +39 331323128
e.azz.@working .it

Alessandra Baldereschi & Lothar Windels
Viale Rimembranze 54/40
20099 Sesto San Giovanni (MI), Italia
Tel +39 022489976
Fax +39 0226225515
alessandra.baldereschi@tin.it
lotharwindel@hotmail.com

Niklas Bandobranski/ Branski HB
Nysatrav. 17
18161 Lidingõ, Sweden
Tel +46 8 7663944
Tel +46 8 6677938
branski2001@yahoo.com

Giada Barbieri
Via B. Cellini 19
20129 Milano, Italia
Tel +39 02784844
Fax +39 0276023971, Cell. +39 335 6068154
giada1@hotmail.com

Ross Beccari
Località Centovello 86
34017 Trieste, Italia
Tel/Fax +39 040225095
rossb@libero.it

Juan Benavente Valero
C/ Manuel Marti 5-3
46021 Valencia, Spain
Tel +34 963 251199
Tel +34 617 313264
juanico@juanico.net
www.juanico.net

Bianchini Rozenberg
Via Romanello da Forlì 25
00176 Roma, Italia
Tel +39 06272057
02.studio@tin.it

Big William
The Robins, Honey Lane
SL6 6RJ Hurley Berkshire, UK
Tel/Fax +44 1628 826687
andy.hale@mo.billy.com
www.mo-billy.com

ULRIK BLOMQUIST
BURMEISTERGADE 7, 5TH
1429 COPENHAGEN, DK
TEL +45 28150275
ULRIK.BLOMQUIST@TELIAMAIL.DK

BOMB-DESIGN
LESSINGSTRASSE 12
06114 HALLE/ SAALE, GERMANY
TEL +49 178 8371806
TEL +49 177 2784337
FAX +39 345 5250386
INFO@BOMB-DESIGN.DE
WWW.BOMB-DESIGN.DE

BONATO/ LUNARDON/ SANO
VIA FRANCESCO INGEGNOLI 13
20131 MILANO, ITALIA
TEL +39 0226145827
FAX +39 0226115434
SANO@STUDIOSANO.COM
WWW.STUDIOSANO.COM

BOON
ROTENWALDSTRASSE 116
70197 STUTTGART, GERMANY
TEL +49 711 6599708
FAX +49 711 6599750
INFO@BOON-DESIGN.DE
WWW.BOON-DESIGN.DE

BRAM BO
BASILIEKSTRAAT 14
3800 ST-TRUIDEN, BELGIUM
TEL +32 496 407773
FAX +32 11 592484
BRAM.BO@ATTGLOBAL.NET

BREEZE-AIR
STATIONSTRASSE 45
8003 ZÜRICH, SWITZERLAND
TEL +41 76 3461172
MMUTINGA@YAHOO.COM
WWW.MYBREEZE.ORG

RAOUL BRETZEL
VIA ROCCARASO 31
00135 ROMA, ITALIA
TEL +39 0635510312
CELL. +39 338 5058303
FAX +39 068541127
RBRETZEL@LIBERO.IT

PETER A. BÜCHELE
OBERER ACHDAMM 50
6971 HARD, AUSTRIA
TEL +43 5574 725130
FAX +43 5574 7251373
BUECHELE.P@VOL.AT
WWW.BUECHELE.COM

BÜRO FÜR FORM + µ
HANS-SACHS-STRASSE 12
80469 MÜNCHEN, GERMANY
TEL +49 89 26949000
FAX +49 89 26949002
INFO@BUEROFUERFORM.DE
WWW.BUEROFUERFORM.DE

CASIMIR MEUBELEN NV
GUIDO GEZELLELAAN 169
3550 HEUSDEN ZOLDER, BELGIUM
TEL +32 11 452535
FAX +32 11 432214
INFO@CASIMIR.BE
WWW.CASIMIR.BE

SERGIO CATALANO
VIA P. MELCHIADE 27
84018 SCAFATI (SA), ITALIA
TEL/FAX +39 0818508666, CELL. +39 338
9943470
S.CATALANO@AWN.IT
WWW.SERGIOCATALANO.IT

KAREN CHEKERDJIAN & TINNA
GUNNARSDOTTIR
P.O.BOX 11-7217
BEIRUT, LEBANON
TEL +961 3 382263
FAX +961 1 855308
KAREN@CYBERIA.NET.LB

CARMEN CHIOMENTO
VIA III NOVEMBRE 27
38057 PERGINE VALSUGANA (TN),
ITALIA
TEL +39 0461512351
FAX +39 0461982798
CELL. +39 349 7116353

DANIELA CHIONNA
VIA SALVO D'ACQUISTO 17
72021 FRANCAVILLA FONTANA (BR),
ITALIA
TEL/FAX +39 0831853102
CHIONNADESIGN@LIBERO.IT

PETER CHRISTIAN
51 ARTHUR COURT, CHARLOTTE
DESPARD AVENUE
LONDON SW11 5JA, UK
TEL +44 20 76228096
FAX +44 20 76270744
RUTHSTUART@PETERCHRISTIAN.COM
WWW.PETERCHRISTIAN.COM

CODICE 21
VIA CADORE 40
20135 MILANO, ITALIA
TEL/FAX +39 025456727

CODICE21@HOTMAIL.COM

ADRIAN COHAN
AVELLANEDA 1021, FLORIDA
1602 BUENOS AIRES, ARGENTINA
TEL +54 11 47917081
FAX +54 11 47969506
ACOHAN@CTADESIGN.COM
WWW.CTADESIGN.COM

LONN COMBS, EC ASSOCIATES
315 BERRY STREET, UNIT 208
BROOKLYN NY 11211, USA
TEL +1 347 8372820
FAX +1 718 3875611
LONNCOMBS@EARTHLINK.NET

CARLO CONTIN
VIA TAZZOLI 3
20051 LIMBIATE (MI), ITALIA
TEL +39 0299055889
FAX +39 02990573
INFO@CARLOCONTIN.IT
WWW.CARLOCONTIN.IT

ANTONIO COS
VIALE CORSICA 57/A
20133 MILANO
TEL/FAX +39 02733078
SOPHIETONIO@HOTMAIL.COM

LORENZO DAMIANI
VIA SEGANTINI 55
20035 LISSONE (MI), ITALIA
TEL/FAX +39 0392455342
LORENZO.DAMIANI@TIN.IT

FRANCESCA DAVOLI
VIA CISALPINA 22
42100 REGGIO EMILIA, ITALIA
TEL/FAX +39 0522 513187
INFO@FRANCESCADAVOLI.IT
WWW.FRANCESCADAVOLI.IT

DEEPDESIGN
CORSO MAGENTA 44
20123 MILANO, ITALIA
TEL +39 0248028725
FAX +39 0248531121
INFO@DEEPDESIGN.IT

DELINEODESIGN
VIA RISORGIMENTO 107
31044 MONTEBELLUNA (TV), ITALIA
TEL/FAX +39 0423604555
INFO@DELINEODESIGN.IT
WWW.DELINEODESIGN.IT

CHRISTIAN DELIUS & RAPHAL NUSSBAUMER
ANKERSTRASSE 3
8004 ZÜRICH, SWITZERLAND
TEL +41 1 2403333
FAX +41 1 2403334
INFO@E-FOUR.CH
WWW.E-FOUR.CH

DESIGN BY F. MAURER VIENNA
STREICHERGASSE 7, ATELIER
1030 VIENNA, AUSTRIA
TEL +43 1 512 1030
FAX +43 1 5121040
DESIGN@FMAURER.COM
WWW.FMAURER.COM

DIEZ & DE LA FONTAINE
GEYERSTRASSE 20
80469 MÜNCHEN, GERMANY
TEL +49 89 20245392
FAX +49 89 244333858
DELAFONTAINE@GMX.DE
DIEZ@MAC.COM

DISASTERDESIGN
VIA ANTONIO OROBONI 5/A
20161 MILANO, ITALIA
TEL/FAX +39 026464880
DISASTERDESIGN@TISCALINET.IT

D-NISH DESIGNWORKSHOP
MYNSTERSVEJ 7A, 3TV
1827 FREDERIKSBERG, DK
TEL +45 3379 3220
FAX +45 3379 3221
DESIGN@D-NISH.COM
WWW.D-NISH.COM

DROVE
55 LEATHER LANE
EC1N 7TJ LONDON, UK
TEL +44 207 4046511
FAX +44 207 4046512
SWRONG@DROVE-DESIGN.CO.UK
WWW.DROVE.DESIGN.CO.UK

EDI
VIA ARONCO 213
28053 CASTELLETTO TICINO (NO), ITALIA
TEL +39 0331973492
CELL. +39 347 5848681
SILVACEI@TIN.IT

RAFI ELBAZ, LIFEFORM
414 BROADWAY, 4TH FLOOR
10013 NEW YORK, USA
TEL +1 212 3431095
FAX +1 212 3432065

RAFFAEL@LFMSHOP.COM
WWW.LFMSHOP.COM

JOACHIM ENGLER
MUEHLEWEG 11
72800 ENINGEN, GERMANY
TEL +49 7121 820811
FAX +49 7121 820812
INFO@JOACHIM-ENGLER.DE
WWW.JOACHIM-ENGLER.DE

BOJE ESTERMANN
93 RUE DU FAUBOURG ST. HONORÈ
75008 PARIS, FRANCE
TEL +33 1 40069580
FAX +33 1 53307501
BOJE@REQUAEST.COM

GIUSEPPE FINOCCHIO
VIA LA MASA 25
90139 PALERMO, ITALIA
TEL +39 0916113310.
FAX +39 0916113294
CASACOMEME@CASACOMEME.IT
WWW.CASACOMEME.IT

FORM
2-5-10 JINGU-MAE, SHIBUYA-KU
TOKYO, JAPAN
TEL +81 3 57756412
FAX +81 3 57756413
ASH-BARN@FORM-TOKYO.COM
WWW.FORM-TOKYO.COM

FORSLUND/ ASBJORN/ SÖRENSEN
KEPPLERSGADE 13 4TH
2300 COPENHAGEN S, DENMARK
TEL +45 23220151

LAURENT FORT
VIA MANZONI 46
26024 PADERNO PONCHIELLI (CR), ITALIA
TEL/FAX +39 037467793

FOUNDATION 33
33 TEMPLE STREET
E2 6QQ LONDON, UK
TEL +44 20 77399903
FAX +44 20 77398989
INFO@FOUNDATION33.COM
WWW.FOUNDATION33.COM

FRANK
UNIT 7, I GLEBE ROAD
E8 4BD LONDON, UK
TEL/FAX +44 207 9234755
THOMAS.ROD@BTOPENWORLD.COM

CHRISTOPHE FRANÇOIS
31 RUE DU SABOT
59800 LILLE, FRANCE
TEL +33 3 20301538
CHRISTOPHEFRANÇOIS@KYO-DESIGN.COM
WWW.KYO-DESIGN.COM

FREMDKÖRPER
VOGELSANGER STRASSE 193
50825 KÖLN, GERMANY
TEL +49 221 9545941
FAX +49 221 543538
FREMDKOERPER@NGI.DE

FUCHS + FUNKE
SCHWEDTER STRASSE 34A
10435 BERLIN, GERMANY
TEL 49 30 44047952
FAX +49 30 44047954
FUCHS.FUNKE@WEB.DE

GARISELLI ASSOCIATI
VIA MULINO 3
42014 CASTELLERANO (RE), ITALIA
TEL/FAX +39 0536859158

GRUPPO AUREA
VIA ALA 3
95123 CATANIA, ITALIA
TEL +39 348 4532550
FAX +39 095436703

GRUPPO MIX
VIA CARLO BAZZI 51
20141 MILANO, ITALIA
TEL +39 0289503021
FAX +39 0289501462
IXISRL@TIN.IT
WWW.IXISRL.COM

GUGGENBICHLERDESIGN...
REDTENBACHERGASSE 35/11
1160 VIENNA, AUSTRIA
TEL +43 699 19241530
FAX +43 1 9241530
DESIGN@GUGGENBICHLER.AT
WWW.GUGGENBICHLER.AT

ANGELICA GUSTAFSSON STUDIO
JOHN ERICSSONSGATAN 13, NB
11222 STOCKHOLM, SWEDEN
TEL/FAX +46 8 6540300
ANG.GUS@SPRAY.SE

JIHOON HA
CHUNGGU-VILLA 607-401, MAEHWA-MAUI
YATAP-DONG 217, BUNDANG GU, SEONGNAM-SI
KYUNGGI-DO, SOUTH KOREA

TEL +82 11 2060530
JAKEHA@HOTMAIL.COM

HAPPY FINISH DESIGN
21 HILLCREST AVENUE
3101 KEW, VICTORIA, AUSTRALIA
TEL +61 3 98179780
FAX +61 3 92707300
NICKRENNIE@NETSPACE.NET.AU

HAJIME HATTA
145-4 OIKE HANE-CHO
444 OKAZAKI-SHI AICHI-KEN, JAPAN
TEL/FAX +81 564 530524
HATTAHAJIME@HOTMAIL.COM

SACHIO HIHARA
1-5-6 SHINTORI
SHIZUOKA, 420-0065, JAPAN
TEL +81 54 6520057
FAX +81 54 6520058
HIHARA@MX1.S-CNET.NE.JP

HONKAHE INTERIOR+FURNITURE
VORDERE CRAMERGASSE 11
90478 NÜRNBERG, GERMANY
TEL +49 911 2104908
FAX +49 911 2104910
INFO@HONKAHE.DE
WWW.HONKHAHE.DE

IL-STUDIO, ISABELLE LEIJN
VROLIKSTRAAT 355-C
1092 TB AMSTERDAM, THE
NETHERLANDS
TEL/FAX +31 20 6751654
ISABELLE-LEIJN@PLANET.NL
WWW.LEIJN.COM

CHARLES O. JOB
OTTIKERSTRASSE 53
8006 ZÜRICH, SWITZERLAND
TEL/FAX +41 1 3611420
JOBCHARLES@GMX.CH
WWW.CHARLESJOB.COM

CORDULA KAFKA
SCHLOSSALLEE 45
13156 BERLIN, GERMANY
TEL/FAX +49 30 4766997
CORDULA@KAFKADESIGN.DE
WWW.KAFKADESIGN.DE

BEAT KARRER
ZIMMERLISTRASSE 6
8004 ZÜRICH, SWITZERLAND
TEL +41 1 4005500
FAX +41 1 4005504
KARRER@BEATKARRER.NET
WWW.BEATKARERR.NET

KÄSS UND HECK
JÜLICHERSTRASSE 14
50674 KÖLN, GERMANY
TEL +49 221 4204821
FAX +49 221 4204823
MAIL@KAESSUNDHECK.DE
WWW.KAESSUNDHECK.DE

KEISUKE FUJIWARA/ KEISUKE FUJIWARA DESIGN OFFICE
5-10-15 HIROO, SHIBUYA-KU
TOKYO 150-0012, JAPAN
TEL +81 3 57915791
FAX +81 3 57915792
FUJIWARA@YA3.SO-NET.NE.JP

SHIRO KIYOTA, GAIA COMMUNICATION
702 KYOMACHIDAI BUILDING, 2-23 DEMACHI
860-0074 KUMAMOTO-CITY, JAPAN
TEL +81 96 3121350
FAX +81 96 3121351
GAIA-MANA@MVI.BIGLOBE.NE.JP

KNOCH
33 COURS XAVIER ARNOZAN
33000 BORDEAUX, FRANCE
TEL/FAX 33 5 56525483
KNOCH.PATRICK@VOILA.FR

MARC KRUSIN
VIALE CONI ZUGNA 23
20144 MILANO, ITALIA
CELL. +39 348 7040559
MKRUSIN@HOTMAIL.COM

LANZILLO & MARTINENGO
VIA DEI GRACCHI 9
20146 MILANO, ITALIA
CELL. +39 335 6632651
CELL. +39 349 8301770
FAX +39 02700546905
TL_CM@VIRGILIO.IT
WWW.TL_CM.3000.IT

CLARISSA DORETTE LESSMANN, CDLDESIGN
KRAUTMUEHLENWEG 8
52066 AACHEN, GERMANY
TEL +49 241 92045890
FAX +49 241 92045891
CLARISSA@CDLDESIGN.DE
WWW.CDLDESIGN.DE

LIMINAL
LARVIKSGATA 3
0468 OSLO, NORWAY
TEL 47 93094515
FAX +47 22441139

SARI@LIMINAL-DESIGN.COM
WWW.LIMINAL-DESIGN.COM

LLA.BOR
BUCHHOLZER STRASSE 9
10437 BERLIN, GERMANY
TEL +49 30 22326616
FAX +49 30 22326619
MAIL@LLA-BOR.DE
WWW.LLA-BOR.DE

LOREDANA LONGO
VIA CARLO MARX 3
95045 MISTERBIANCO (CT), ITALIA
CELL. +39 333 8960132
FAX +39 095482939
LORELOY@LIBERO.IT

LORBUS
VIA VESPRI SICILIANI 16/6
20146 MILANO, ITALIA
CELL. +39 339 5457926
MAIL@LORBUS.COM
WWW.LORBUS. COM

M.N.O.
VOLMARIJNSTRAAT 118
3021 XW ROTTERDAM, THE NETHERLANDS
TEL +31 104259696
JAN@JANMELIS.NL
WWW.MNODESIGN.NL
WWW.JANMELIS.NL

MASTRO DESIGN
VIA EMILIA S. PIETRO 22
42100 REGGIO EMILIA, ITALIA
TEL/FAX +39 0522431591
CELL. +39 335 463955
INFO@MASTRODESIGN.IT
WWW.MASTRODESIGN.IT

MARIANGELA MERONI
VIALE REPUBBLICA 76
20035 LISSONE (MI), ITALIA
TEL +39 0392457703
FAX +39 0392143838
MARIMERONI@TISCALINET.IT

ANDREA MODICA
VIA ROMA 151
20010 MARCALLO C/ CASONE (MI), ITALIA
TEL/FAX +39 029761851
ANDREA.MODICA@TISCALI.IT

MOORHEAD & MOORHEAD
83 CANAL STREET NO. 309
10002 NEW YORK, NEW YORK, USA
TEL +1 212 2198489

fax +1 212 2749471
info@mooreheadandmoorehead.com
www.mooreheadandmoorehead.com

More or Less Design
Corso dei Tintori 23
50122 Firenze
Tel/fax +39 0552477316
nicolavolpini@moreorlessdesign.dom

Benedetta Mori Ubaldini
Flat C - Crayford Road
N7 0ND London, UK
Tel +44 20 76079314
Tel +44 7941 884024
benedettamori@supanet.com

Lisa-Dionne Morris, Gasp Design
Betony Road, Enigma Business Park
WR14 1GB, Malvern, UK
Tel +44 1684 572880
fax +44 1684 577643
lisadionnemorris@yahoo.co.uk

Motels Design Group
Planie 22C
72764 Reutlingen, Germany
Tel +49 7121 479227
fax +49 7121 491943
contact@motels.de
www.motels.de

Inci Mutlu & Luca Milano
La Maison, Strada Statale 181
12030 Manta (CN), Italia
Tel +39 017586027
fax +39 017588437
mutlutasarim@superonline.com
www.incimutlu.com

Norway Says
Waldemar Thranesgt. 75 D
0175 Oslo, Norway
Tel +47 22 208362
fax +47 22 114057
moebel@c2i.net
www.norwaysays.com

Officinesantandrea snc
Contrada Rossi 6
37028 Roverè V.se (VR), Italia
Tel/fax +39 045500918

Open Spaces
Via Palermo 12
20124 Milano, Italia
Tel +39 0262690548
fax +39 0262910238

---

decarlo.gualla@tiscalinet.it

Or-bit Design
Piazza S. Alessandro 3
20123 Milano, Italia
cell. +39 347 2533399
fax +39 02875236
design@real-or-bit.com
www.real-or-bit.com

Oui, mais non
64 Rue des Tournelles
75003 Paris, France
Tel/fax +39 1 42740543
merlin@oui-mais-non.com
www.oui-mais-non.com

Pacific Edge
44 Margaret Avenue
4201 Havelock North, New Zealand
Tel/fax +646 8774684
trubridge@clear.net.nz

Plant
801 Nexus Tower 206-3 Ojang-Dong, Jung-gu
100-310 Seoul, South Korea
Tel +82 2 22741098
fax +82 2 22723426
plant@plantmade.com
www.plantmade.com

Polyline
Belgielei 4/48
2018 Antwerpen, Belgium
Tel +32 321 85397
fax +32 321 85547
info@polyline.be

Positive Industrial Design
6101 Pinecrest Drive
Los Angeles CA 90042, USA
Tel +1 323 2559130
corygrosser@hotmail.com

Putty Factory
Toftesgate 69D
0552 Oslo, Norway
Tel/fax +47 22381590
Tel +47 97016080
are.hundstuen@chello.no
www.puttifactory.com

Q01, Nicola Vittori
Via G. Bianchetti 46
31044 Montebelluna (TV), Italia
Tel +39 0423600195
cell. +39 329 4331434
jazzvit@hotmail.com

---

www.q01.it

Quinze & Milan Designers
I.Z. Klein Frankryk, 60
9600 Ronse, Belgium
Tel +32 475 892755
fax +32 55 305100
quinzemilan@hotmail.com
www.quinzeandmilan.com

Massimo Rasero
Via Saluzzo 42
10125 Torino, Italia
Tel/fax +39 011658333
massimorasero@libero.it

Recline & A to Y
Poste Restante K5, Oslo Plads 10
2100 Copenhagen, DK
Tel +45 26214145
yuriko@hotmail.com

Kai Richter
Klauprechtstrasse 20
76137 Karlsruhe, Germany
Tel +49 721 386695
richter@kairichter.com
www.kairichter.com

Satoko-Takashi
Via Buonarroti 6
20145 Milano, Italia
Tel +39 0248013901
satokoko@td5.so-net.ne.jp
mot@mac.com

Schäfer/ Hofmann
Sophienstrasse 179
76185 Karlsruhe, Germany
Tel +49 721 8301956
fax +49 721 8301958
dschaef@hfg-karlsruhe.de

Frédéric Schaumburg
13 Rue Duperrè
75009 Paris, France
Tel +33 608854189
fax +33 1 48787596
lnetfred@club-internet.fr

Eva Schildt Design
Strindbergsg. 47
11553 Stockholm, Sweden
Tel 46 73 9443187
schildteva@hotmail.com

Balz Steiger
Erlengutstrasse 2
8703 Erlenbach/ Zürich, Switzerland

TEL +41 78 8802185
FAX +41 19152185
DESIGN@STEIGER.COM
WWW.DESIGN.STEIGER.COM

SUNG DESIGN LIMITED
SUNDIAL COTTAGE, HAMPTON COURT
ROAD
KT89DA, EAST MOLESEY, SURREY, UK
TEL/FAX +44 20 89779505
INFO@SUNGDESIGN.COM
WWW.SUNGDESIGN.COM

SUPRAFIVE
C/O ARCH. CARLO-GABRIEL BLOTTO
PIAZZA E. DE AMICIS 127
10126 TORINO
TEL +39 0115096394
CELL. +39 339 6523655
FAX +39 0115083508
SUPRAFIVE@SUPRADESIGN.IT

SWISSPLUS DESIGNTEAM
AUSTRASSE 45
8045 ZÜRICH, SWITZERLAND
TEL/FAX +41 1 4614078
FABIO@GALLANA.CH
WWW.GALLANA.CH

HIROKI TAKADA/ TAKADA DESIGN
2-23 KITAEJIMACHO
510-023 SUZUKA MIE, JAPAN
TEL +81 593 862250
FAX +81 593 871203
HIROKI@TAKADADESIGN.COM
WWW.TAKADADESIGN.COM

PASCAL TARABAY & CATALINA TOBON
VIA TOLSTOI 16
20146 MILANO, ITALIA
TEL +39 3487012377
TARABAY@HOTMAIL.COM
WWW.PASCALTARABAY.COM

JÉROME TARBY & JÉROME GAUTHIER
136 RUE D'AVRON
75020 PARIS, FRANCE
TEL +33 1 40091842
FAX +33 1 42454538
JÉROME.TARBY@WANADOO.FR

THORSTEN_FRANCK
LAUTENSACKSTRASSE 21
80687 MÜNCHEN, GERMANY
TEL +49 89 57869194
FAX +49 89 57869195

THORSTEN_FRANCK@T-ONLINE.DE

KAY THOSS
HIMMELREICHALLEE 35
48149 MUENSTER, GERMANY
TEL/FAX +49 251 9829926
CELL. +49 179 2161794
MAIL@KAYTHOSS.COM

TOM BARBER DESIGN
2665 OUTLOOK DRIVE
89509 RENO, NEVADA, USA
TEL/FAX +1 775 8265991
TTBARBER@NUBELL.NET

TORH MOBLER
WILHELMSGATE 3
0168 OSLO, NORWAY
TEL +47 23367696
FAX +47 23367675
CATHRINE@TORH.NO
WWW.TORH.NO

DIEGO JAVIER TOSELLO
2 DE ABRIL 624
1748 GRAL RODRIGUEZ, BUENOS
AIRES, ARGENTINA
TEL/FAX +54 237 4840053
DIEGOTOSELLO@HOTMAIL.COM

TRONDESIGN
EDERWEG 4-6
34277 FULDABRÜCK (KASSEL),
GERMANY
TEL +49 561 928808-0
FAX +49 561 92880844
INFO@TRONDESIGN.DE
WWW.TRONDESIGN.COM

HIROSHI TSUNODA
COMERCIO 29 BAJO
08003 BARCELONA, SPAIN
TEL +34 93 3190499
HIROSHIDESIGN@HOTMAIL.COM

UMAMY
7 BAR-ILAN STEET
63826 TEL AVIV, ISRAEL
CELL. +972 58 395986
CELL +972 53 613699
FAX +972 3 5100107
INFO@UMAMY.COM
WWW.UMAMY.COM

UP NORTH
WESTYE EGEBERGSGT. 3A
0177 OSLO, NOEWAY
TEL +47 922 39767
MAIL@UPNORTH.NO
WWW.UPNORTH.NO

URBAN CAMPING
TIDEMANOSGT. 20
0260 OSLO, NORWAY
TEL/FAX +47 22 551350
CELL. +47 92 821614
URBAN.CAMPING@HOTMAIL.COM

U.S.O. DI GINO FACCHINI
STRADA TORRE TRESCA 16
70124 BARI, ITALIA
TEL +39 0805042757
FAX +39 0805042882
WWW.USODESIGN.IT

SERGE VIZCAINO
18, RUE DE LA GLACIÈRE
1060 BRUXELLES, BELGIUM
TEL +32 2 5343873
S-VIZCA@EASYNET.BE
WWW.CUBUSMOBILE.COM

VOBRO VOX
IN DER EY 29
8047 ZÜRICH, SVIZZERA
TEL +41 79 2367178
FAX +41 1 4012500
VOBROVOX@FREESURF.CH

WAGNER & ASSOCIATI SAS
VICOLO PERAZZOLO 1
35012 CAMPOSAMPIERO (PD) , ITALIA
TEL +39 0499303820
INFO@WEA.IT

KAZUHIRO YAMANAKA
UNIT 15, 109 BARTHOLOMEW ROAD
LONDON NW5 2BJ, UK
TEL/FAX +44 208 4523018
KAZ@MA.KEW.NET

Z'ATELIER DI LUISA CAPUA-MCCORMICK
VIA BORGO SANTA CROCE 4
50123 FIRENZE, ITALIA
TEL/FAX +39 0552638681
ZAZIBAR@KATAMAIL.COM

PATRICK ZULAUF DESIGN
AARBURGERSTRASSE 76
4600 OLTEN, SWITZERLAND
TEL +41 79 3434324
FAX +41 61 3211810
PATRICKZULAUF@HOTMAIL.COM

ALTERSTUDIO
Via Pinamonte Da Vimercate 4
20121 Milano
Tel +39 02 29011250
alterstudio@libero.it

ARCHILAB
Via J. Dal Verme 15
20159 Milano
Tel +39 02 69005672
www.archilab.it
archilab@archilab.it

Gae Aulenti
P.zza San Marco 4
20121 Milano
Tel +39 02 8692762

Antonia Astori Driade
Via G. Rossini 3
20122 Milano
Tel +39 02 795005

Miki Astori
Via C. Correnti 7
20123 Milano
Tel +39 02 89404251
miki.astori@tiscalinet.it

Aattak
www.aattak.com

ATTIVO CREATIVE RESOURCE
Via Privata Rutilia 10/8
20141 Milano
Tel +39 02 54116645
milano@attivocreative.com

**Karim Azzabi Design
Network**
Via Ausonio 6
20123 Milano
Tel +39 02 89421599

Emmanuel Babled
Via G. Segantini 71
20143 Milano
T+ 39 02 58111119

**Enrico Baleri
Baleri Italia S.P.A.**
Via F. Cavallotti 8
20122 Milano
Tel +39 02 76014672

BASE
Via A. Fumagalli 2
20143 Milano
Tel +39 02 8394799
info@8a5e.com
www.8a5e.com

Mario Bellini
P.zza Arcole 4
20143 Milano
Tel +39 02 89410387
atelier@bellini.it

Benza Inc.
www.benzadesign.com

Guglielmo Berchicci
Via Valparaiso 9
20144 Milano
Tel +39 02 48019284

**BRANCO STUDIO
D'ARCHITETTURA D'INTERNI
E DI DESIGN**
Via Cardinale A. Sforza 81/A
20141 Milano
Tel +39 02 89516831

**BRASS CLARE DESIGN STUDIO
D'ARCHITETTURA D'INTERNI
E DI DESIGN**
Via G.B. Bertini 19
20154 Milano
Tel +39 02 34934013

**Antonio Brizzi e Babette
Riefenstahl**
Via C. D'Adda 9
20143 Milano
Tel +39 02 89429253

Andrea Branzi
Via Solferino 25
20121 Milano
Tel +39 02 6592227
anbranzi@tin.it

Sergio Brioschi
Via G.B. Bertini 19
20154 Milano
Tel +39 02 33101454

Cambiofaccia
www.cambiofaccia.it

Mario Cananzi
Alzaia Naviglio Grande 156
20144 Milano
Tel +39 02 4239671

Chiara Cantono
Via M. Malpighi 3
20129 Milano
Tel +39 02 29518792

**CARUZZO RANCATI
ARCHITETTI ASSOCIATI**
Via G.B. Pergolesi 2
20124 Milano
Tel +39 02 66713092

Anna Castelli Ferrieri
C.so di Porta Romana 87/B
20122 Milano
Tel +39 02 5510451

Achille Castiglioni
P.zza Castello 27
20121 Milano
Tel +39 02 8053606
achillecastiglioni@libero.it

Pierluigi Cerri
Via A. Saffi 25
20123 Milano
Tel +39 02 48519800
cerri.associati@flashnet.it

Aldo Cibic Cibic & Partners
Via Varese 18
20121 Milano
Tel +39 02 6571122
aldocibic@cibicdesign.com

Antonio Citterio & Partners
Via Cerva 4
20122 Milano
Tel +39 02 7638801
citterio@mdsnet.it

CODICE 31
Via Cadore 40
20135 Milano
Tel +39 02 5456727
codice31@freemail.it

Marco Colombo Studio ABC
Via A. Stradella 13
20129 Milano
Tel +39 02 29523200

mcolombo@planet.it

DAVID DESIGN
www.daviddesign.net

MICHELE DE LUCCHI
STUDIO DE LUCCHI
Via G. Pallavicino 31
20145 Milano
Tel +39 02 43008230
sdl@studiodelucchi.it

GABRIELE DE VECCHI
Via E. Lombardini 20
20143 Milano
Tel +39 02 8323365
gabrieledevecchi@libero.it

PAOLO DEGANELLO
Via G.B. Tiepolo 30/B
20129 Milano
Tel +39 02 70009324

DERIM
www.derindesign.com

FRANCESCA DONATI STUDIO
C.so G. Garibaldi 44 20121 Milano
Tel +39 02 6590978

DDL - STUDIO D'URBINO LOMAZZI
C.so XXII Marzo 39
20129 Milano
Tel +39 02 76110543
durbilon@tin.it   x

GILLO DORFLES
P.le Lavater 3 20129 Milano
Tel +39 02 29400351

DROOG DESIGN
www.droogdesign.nl

TERRY DWAN
C.so G. Garibaldi 60
20121 Milano
Tel +39 02 6597452

CECILIA FABIANI
Via Gaudenzio Ferrari 7
20123 Milano
Tel +39 02 8393696

MARIO FALCI
Via Generale G. Govone 100
20155 Milano
Tel +39 02 33603600

GUIDO FERRANTE
Via G.B. Vico 2
20123 Milano
Tel +39 02 4815329

PAOLO FERRANTE
Via San Marco 50
20121 Milano
Tel +39 02 6575925

MADDALENA FERRARESI
V.le Pasubio 16
20154 Milano
Tel +39 02 6597999

LUIGI FERRARIO
Via Castelfidardo 10
20121 Milano
Tel +39 02 6572806
luigiferrario@luigiferrario.it
www.luigiferrario.it

MASSIMILIANO FISICHELLA
Via G. Pacini 36
20131 Milano
Tel +39 02 70638409

GIANNI FORCOLINI
C.so G. Garibaldi 89
20121 Milano
Tel +39 02 6571980

DUILIO TOMMASO FORTE
Via A. Corelli 34
20134 Milano
Tel +39 02 70208099
www.duilioforte.com

FRANCESCADONATISTUDIO
www.francescadonatistudio.com

AGFRONZONI STUDIO
Via Solferino 44
20121 Milano
Tel +39 02 6597962

GILAB
www.glab.it

JACOPO GARDELLA
Via G. Verdi 6
20121 Milano
Tel +39 02 86995581

GIUGIARO DESIGN
Via A.Grandi 21
10024 Moncalieri (TO)
Tel +39 011 6893311
www.giugiarodesign.it

GRASSI ALFONSO & ASSOCIATI
Via Lodovico il Moro 13
20143 Milano
Tel +39 02 89127624

EZIO GRASSI
V.le L. Scarampo 19
20148 Milano
Tel +39 02 4697976

GREGORIETTI ASSOCIATI
Via Montebello 27
20121 Milano
Tel +39 02 29004813

GREGOTTI ASSOCIATI INTERNATIONAL
Via M. Bandello 20
20123 Milano
Tel +39 02 4814141

HARRY & CAMILA CREATORS OF SIGNS
Via G. Meda 43
20141 Milano
Tel +39 02 8464141

HIDDEN
www.hiddenart.com

HIVE
www.hive@hivespace.com

MASSIMO IOSA GHINI
Via Gentilino 6
20136 Milano
Tel +39 02 58106183
info@iosaghini.it
www.iosaghini.it

JAMES IRVINE STUDIO JAMES IRVINE
Via G. Sirtori 4
20129 Milano
Tel +39 02 29534532
james@james-irvine.com

MAKOTO KAWAMOTO
Via dell'Aprica 8
20158 Milano
Tel +39 02 6080246
026080246@iol.it

MONKEY BOYS
www.monkeyboys.nl

KIM HIROMI
VIA G. ROMANO 17
20135 MILANO
TEL +39 02 58302113
INFO@HIROMIKIM.COM
WWW.HIROMIKIM.COM

PERRY ALAN KING
E SANTIAGO MIRANDA
VIA PRIVATA V. FORCELLA 3
20144 MILANO
TEL +39 02 8394963
KINGMIRANDA@IOL.IT
WWW.KINGMIRANDA.COM

KITA TOSHIYUKI
C.SO G. GARIBALDI 12
20121 MILANO
TEL +39 02 72023466

KOMODA KAZUYO
VIA F. FILZI 7
20124 MILANO
T 39 02 66713655
KKOMODA@MICRONET.IT

LAR CENTER
WWW.LARCENTER.COM.BR

MAARTEN KUSTERS
MK DESIGN STUDIO
VIA F. DE SANCTIS 24
20141 MILANO
TEL +39 02 89500917   MK_
DESIGNSTUDIO@YAHOO.COM

CLAUDIO LA VIOLA
P.ZZA 5 GIORNATE 10
20129 MILANO
TEL +39 02 59902621

FERRUCCIO LAVIANI
VIA E. DE AMICIS 53
20123 MILANO
TEL +39 02 89421426
LAVIANI@INTERNETFORCE.COM

UGO LA PIETRA
VIA GUERCINO 7
20154 MILANO
TEL +39 02 33608400

PIERO LISSONI
LISSONI ASSOCIATI
VIA GOITO 9
20121 MILANO
TEL +39 02 6571942

VICO MAGISTRETTI
VIA CONSERVATORIO 20   20122

MILANO
TEL +39 02 76002964

ANGELO MANGIAROTTI
VIA CESARE DA SESTO 15
20123 MILANO
TEL +39 02 89400449

ENZO MARI
P.LE F. BARACCA 10
20123 MILANO
TEL +39 02 4817315

SAMUELE MAZZA
WWW.VISIONNAIREHOMEPHILOSOPHY.COM

ALESSANDRO
E FRANCESCO MENDINI
VIA SANNIO 24
20137 MILANO
TEL +39 02 55185185
WWW.ATELIERMENDINI.IT

DAVIDE MERCATALI
RIPA DI PORTA TICINESE 13
20143 MILANO
TEL +39 02 8360220
WWW.DAVIDE.MERCATALI.COM

MASSIMO MOROZZI
MOROZZI & PARTNERS
VIA MORIMONDO 21
20143 MILANO
TEL +39 02 89128572
MOROZZI@PLANET.IT

NAVONE ASSOCIATI
VIA VARESE 18
20121 MILANO
TEL +39 02 29060748
NAVONE@TIN.IT

PAOLA NAVONE
C.SO SAN GOTTARDO 22
20136 MILANO
TEL +39 02 58104926
PAOLANAVONE@TIN.IT

JOHANNES NORLANDER
ARKITEKTUR &FORM
WWW.NORDLANDER.SE

FABIO NOVEMBRE
VIA MECENATE 76/3
20138 MILANO
TEL +39 02 504104
WWW.NOVEMBRE.IT

OFFECCT
WWW.OFFECCT.SE

GIAMPIERO PEJA
VIA GOITO 9 20121 MILANO
PEJA@PEJA.IT

PERMAFROST
WWW.PERMAFROST.NO

MICHELE PIVA
VIA PRIVATA CORNO DI CAVENTO 6
20148 MILANO
TEL +39 02 4981971

PAOLO PIVA E FRANCESCO
OBERON
VIA G. COMPAGNONI 30
20129 MILANO
TEL +39 02 70125117

PIERO PINTO
VIA G. DONIZETTI 33
20122 MILANO
TEL +39 02 782703

GIACOMO POLIN
VIA D. MANIN 3
20121 MILANO
TEL +39 02 29000162
ARCPOLIN@TIN.IT

DANIELA PUPPA
VIA SAVONA 97 20144 MILANO
TEL +39 02 4234244

ARNE QUINZE
WWW.QUINZEANDMILAN.TV

FRANCO RAGGI
VIA SAVONA 97 20144 MILANO
TEL +39 02 4234244

STEFANO REBOLI
WWW.STEFANOREBOLI.COM

UMBERTO RIVA
VIA VIGEVANO 10
20144 MILANO
TEL +39 02 89406844

PAOLO RIZZATTO
VIA BRAMANTE DA URBINO 7
20154 MILANO
TEL +39 02 3452580

ITALO ROTA
VIA M. MELLONI 35
20129 MILANO
TEL +39 02 76115332

RUDE BRAVO DESIGN
WWW.RUDEBRAVO.COM

MARC SADLER
Via Savona 97
20144 Milano
Tel +39 02 4224199
m.sadler@tin.it

SANO TAKAHIDE STUDIO SANO
Via F. Ingegnoli 13
20131 Milano
Tel +39 02 26145827
sano@sano.com
www.studiosano.com

DENIS SANTACHIARA
Alzaia Naviglio Grande 156
20144 Milano
Tel +39 02 4221727

RICHARD SAPPER
Via A. Beretta 3
20121 Milano
Tel +39 02 72023101

WILLIAM SAWAYA PAOLO MORONI
Via Andegari 18
20121 Milano
Tel +39 02 86395231
sawamoro@libero.it
www.sawayamoroni.com

LUCA SCACCHETTI
Via Marcona 12
20129 Milano
Tel +39 02 54108585 scacchetti@sca
cchetti.com
www.scacchetti.com

PATRIZIA SCARZELLA SIGLA
C.so Sempione 70
20154 Milano
Tel +39 02 31810030

LUIGI SERAFINI
Via A. Ponchielli 3
20129 Milano
Tel +39 02 29406204

JERSZY SEYMOUR
Via Vigevano 39

20144 Milano
Tel +39 02 89422105
jerszyseymour@tin.it

BENJAMIN SHAFFER
www.pantoneb.com

SNOWCRASH
www.snowcrash.se

SARAH SONG
www.sarahsongdesign.com

ETTORE SOTTSASS
SOTTSASS ASSOCIATI
Via Melone 2
20121 Milano
Tel +39 02 72599201

FLAVIA ALVES DE SOUZA
falvesdesouza@yahoo.com

GEORGE SOWDEN
C.so di Porta Nuova 46/B
20121 Milano
Tel +39 02 653089

STEW
www.stewdesignworkshop.com

SUMAMPA
www.sumampa.com

SWEDESE
www.swedese.se

MATTEO THUN
Via A. Appiani 9
20121 Milano
Tel +39 02 29000270
info@matteothun.com
www.matteothun.com

TOUCK DESIGN STUDIO.INC.
www.touckdesignstudio.com

UNIFORM
www.uniform.nl

PATRICIA URQUIOLA
Via G. Uberti 33
20129 Milano
Tel +39 02 29511012

PETER VALOIS
www.touchdesignstudio.com

NIELS VAN EIJK
www.ons-adres.nl

VIRTUALLY DESIGN
www.virtuallydesign.com

STUDIO VUDAFIERI
Via N.A. Porpora 64
20131 Milano
Tel +39 02 70635767

WUNDERKAMMER STUDIO
Via E. Lombardini 24
20143 Milano
Tel +39 02 8372781

PAOLO ZANI
Via Montevideo 4
20144 Milano
Tel +39 02 58112775
paolo.zani@tiscalinet.it
www.paolo.zani.it

MARCO ZANIN
SOTTSASS ASSOCIATI
Via Melone 2
20121 Milano
Tel +39 02 72599201

ANTONIO e PAOLA ZANUSO
Via dell'Orso 16
20121 Milano
Tel +39 02 29002115

MARCO JR. ZANUSO
Via Soncino 1
20123 Milano
Tel +39 02 8900847

ZIG ZAG
www.zigzagdesign.org

companies

ACCORNERO
Via Umberto I 1/2, 15035
Frassinello Monferrato (AL),
Italy
Tel +39 014 2933581
Fax +39 014 2928369

info@accornero.it
www.accornero.it

ADOBE SYSTEMS ITALIA SRL
Via Paracelso, 26
20041 Agrate Brianza

Tel 039 65501
www.adobe.it

DRIADE SPA
Via Padana Inferiore 12/A, 29012
Fossadello di Caorso (PC), Italy

TEL +39 0523 818618
FAX +39 0523 822628
COM.IT@DRIADE.COM
WWW.DRIADE.COM

ALESSI SPA
VIA PRIVATA ALESSI 6,
28882 CRUSINALLO DI OMEGNA (VB)
ITALY
TEL +39 0323 868611
FAX +39 0323 641605
INFO@ALESSI.COM
WWW.ALESSI.COM

ALIAS SPA
VIA L. DA VINCI 29/33, 24064
GRUMELLO DEL MONTE (BG), ITALY
TEL +39 035 4422511
FAX +39 035 4422590
INFO@ALIASDESIGN.IT
WWW.ALIASDESIGN.IT

ARC LINEA SPA
VIA PASUBIO 50,
36030 CALDOGNO (VI), ITALY
TEL +39 0444 394111
FAX +39 0444 394263
ARCLINEA@ARCLINEA.IT
WWW.ARCLINEA.IT

ARMANI / VIAMANZONI31
VIA A. MANZONI 31,
20121 MILANO
TEL +39 02 72318600
WWW.ARMANI-VIAMANZONI31.COM

AVANT DE DORMIR
VIA F. TURATI 3,
20121 MILANO
TEL +39 02 6599990
FAX +39 02 6571058
INFO@AVANTDEDORMIR.COM
WWW.AVANTDEDORMIR.COM

B&B ITALIA
CONTRACT SPA
VIA DON MINZONI 4,
20020 MISINTO (MI), ITALY
TEL +39 02 967691
FAX +39 02 96328071
CONTRACT@BEBITALIA.IT
WWW.BEBITALIA.IT

B&B ITALIA SPA
STRADA PROVINCIALE 32, 22060
NOVEDRATE (CO), ITALY
TEL +39 031 765111
FAX +39 031 795224
BEB@BEBITALIA.IT
WWW.BEBITALIA.IT

BANG & OLUFSEN ITALIA SPA
VIA MERAVIGLI 2,
20123 MILANO
TEL +39 02 7259141
FAX +39 02 72591444
ITALY_MARKET@BANG-OLUFSEN.DK
WWW.BANG-OLUFSEN.COM

BISAZZA SPA
VIA MILANO 56,
36041 ALTE (VI), ITALY
TEL +39 0444 707511
FAX +39 0444 492088
INFO@BISAZZA.IT
WWW.BISAZZA.IT

BOFFI SPA
VIA OBERDAN 70,
20030 LENTATE SUL SEVESO (MI),
ITALY
TEL +39 036 25341
FAX +39 036 2565077
WWW.BOFFI.IT

BONACINA
PIERANTONIO & C.
VIA SANT'ANDREA 20/A,
22040 LURAGO D'ERBA (CO), ITALY
TEL +39 031 699225
FAX +39 031 696151
WWW.BONACINAPIERANTONIO.IT

BONTEMPI CASA SPA
VIA DIRETTISSIMA DEL CONERO 71,
60021 CAMERANO (AN), ITALY
TEL +39 071 7300032
FAX +39 071 7300036
INFO@BONTEMPI.IT
WWW.BONTEMPIFURNITUUR.COM

ROCCO BORMIOLI SPA
VIA GENOVA 4/A,
43100 PARMA (PR), ITALY
TEL +39 0521 7901
FAX +39 0521 527821
WWW.BORMIOLIROCCO.COM

CAPPELLINI SPA
VIA MARCONI 35,
22060 AROSIO (CO), ITALY
TEL +39 031 759111
F+39 031 763333
CAPPELLINI@CAPPELLINI.IT
WWW.CAPPELLINI.IT

CASSINA SPA
VIA BUSNELLI 1,
20036 MEDA (MI), ITALY
TEL +39 036 23721
FAX +39 036 2342246

INFO@CASSINA.IT
WWW.CASSINA.IT

CINOVA SRL
VIA MISSORI 2,
20035 LISSONE (MI), ITALY
TEL +39 039 461031
FAX +39 039 480889
INFO@CINOVA.IT
WWW.CINOVA.IT

CULTI AGRATI SRL
VIA G. LEOPARDI 8,
20030 SEVESO (MI), ITALY
TEL +39 036 2551985
FAX +39 036 2551420

CYRUS COMPANY
VIA MOTTARONE 60,
21010 VOGHERA DI SAMARATE (VA)
ITALY
TEL +39 0331 224911
FAX +39 0331 721136
INFO@CYRUSCOMPANY.IT
WWW.CYRUSCOMPANY.IT

DANESE
VIA A. CANOVA 34,
20145 MILANO
TEL +39 02 34939534
FAX +39 02 34538211
INFO@DANESEMILANO.COM

DASSI MOBILI MODERNI
VIA G. MATTEOTTI 134,
20035 LISSONE (MI), ITALY
TEL +39 039 481173
FAX +39 039 464611
DMMDASSI@TIN.IT

DILMOS
P.ZZA SAN MARCO 1,
20121 MILANO
TEL +39 02 29002437
FAX +39 02 29002350
INFO@DILMOS.IT
WWW.DILMOS.COM

DOVETUSAI
VIA SIGIERI 24,
20135 MILANO
TEL +39 02 59902432
FAX +39 02 59902442
INFO@DOVETUSAI.IT
WWW.DOVETUSAI.IT

ECLECTICA CONTAINER (TERESA GINORI)
C.SO GARIBALDI 3,
20121 MILANO

TEL +39 02 876194
FAX +39 02 877810

FEG
STRADA VALASSINA, ANG. VIA PASCOLI
20034 GIUSSANO (MI), ITALY
TEL +39 036 28691
FAX +39 036 2869280
INFO@GRUPPOFEG.COM
WWW.GRUPPOFEG.COM

FLEXFORM SPA
VIA L. EINAUDI 23/25,
20036 MEDA (MI), ITALY
TEL +39 036 23991
FAX +39 036 2730555
FLEXFORM@FLEXFORM.IT
WWW.FLEXFORM.IT

FLOU SPA
VIA CADORNA 12,
20036 MEDA (MI), ITALY
TEL +39 036 23731
FAX +39 036 272952
INFO@FLOU.IT
WWW.FLOU.IT

FONTANAARTE SPA
ALZAIA TRIESTE 49,
 20094 CORSICO (MI), ITALY
TEL +39 02 45121
FAX +39 02 4512660
INFO@FONTANAARTE.IT
WWW.FONTANAARTE.IT

FOPPA PEDRETTI SPA
VIA A. VOLTA 9, 24064
GRUMELLO DEL MONTE (BG), ITALY
TEL +39 035 830497
FAX +39 035 831283
WWW.FOPPAPEDRETTI.IT

FRATELLI GUZZINI SPA
CONTRADA MATTONATA 60,
62019 RECANATI (MC), ITALY
TEL +39 071 9891
FAX +39 071 989260
FRATELLIGUZZINI@FRATELLIGUZZINI.COM
WWW.FRATELLIGUZZINI.IT

IKEA ITALIA (RETAIL)
STRADA PROVINCIALE 208 3,
20061 CARUGATE (MI), ITALY
TEL +39 02 929271
WWW.IKEA.COM

INSA
LOCALITÀ CANOVA 1,
27017 PIEVE PORTO MORONE (PV)
ITALY

TEL +39 0382 727411
FAX +39 0382 788111
INFO@INSA.IT
WWW.INSA.IT

ITALHOME LE SEDIE
L.GO C. TREVES 2,
20121 MILANO
TEL +39 02 6551787
ITALHOME@PIANETASEDIA.IT
WWW.PIANETASEDIA.IT

KARTELL SPA
VIA DELLE INDUSTRIE 1,
20082 NOVIGLIO (MI), ITALY
TEL +39 02 900121
FAX +39 02 9053316
KARTELL@KARTELL.IT
WWW.KARTELL.IT

KNOLL INTERNATIONAL
P.ZZA G. MISSORI 3,
20123 MILANO
TEL +39 02 7222291
FAX +39 02 72222930
ITALIA@KNOLL.COM
WWW.KNOLL.IT

LA MURRINA
V.LE ISONZO 11,
22078 TURATE (CO), ITALY
TEL +39 02 969751
FAX +39 02 96975211
LAMURRINA@LAMURRINA.COM
WWW.LAMURRINA.COM

LAGOSTINA SPA
VIA 4 NOVEMBRE 45,
28887 OMEGNA (VB), ITALY
TEL +39 0323 6521
FAX +39 0323 61046
INFO@LAGOSTINA.IT
WWW.LAGOSTINA.IT

LEMA SPA.
S.S. BRIANTEA 342,
22040 ALZATE BRIANZA (CO), ITALY
TEL +39 031 630990
FAX +39 031 632492
LEMA@LEMAMOBILI.COM
WWW.LEMAMOBILI.COM

MANDARINA DUCK
VIA DON MINZONI 36,
40057 CADRIANO
DI GRANAROLO (BO) ITALY
TEL +39 051 764411
FAX +39 051 766056

MATTEOGRASSI SPA
VIA PADRE ROVAGNATI 2, 22066
MARIANO COMENSE (CO), ITALY
TEL +39 031 757711
FAX +39 031 748388
INFO@MATTEOGRASSI.IT
WWW.MATTEOGRASSI.IT

MC SELVINI
VIA C. POERIO 3, 20129 MILANO
TEL +39 02 76006118
FAX +39 02 781325
WWW.MCSELVINI.IT

MH WAY
VIA PUECHER 1
VIA ROSSELLI 37,
20090 FIZZONASCO / PIEVE
EMANUELE (MI), ITALY
TEL +39 02 90781960
FAX +39 02 90724782
MHWAY@MHWAY.IT
WWW.MHWAY.IT

MOLTENI & C. SPA
VIA ROSSINI 50,
20034 GIUSSANO (MI), ITALY
TEL +39 036 23591
FAX +39 036 2355170
WWW.MOLTENI.IT

MOROSO SPA
VIA NAZIONALE 60,
33010 CAVALICCO DI TAVAGNACCO
(UD), ITALY
TEL +39 0432 577111
FAX +39 0432 570761
INFO@MOROSO.IT
WWW.MOROSO.IT

NARDI INTERNI SPA
VIA REFRONTOLO 5,
31053 PIEVE DI SOLIGO (TV), ITALY
TEL +39 0438 83546
FAX +39 0438 83021
INFO@NARDINTERNI.IT

NITAL SPA
VIA TABACCHI 33,
10132 TORINO, ITALY
TEL +39 011 8996804
011 8996225
WWW.NITAL.IT

OLTREFRONTIERA
VIA C. CATTANEO 30, 22066
VIGHIZZOLO DI CANTÙ (CO), ITALY
TEL +39 031 737311
FAX +39 031 737329
INFO@OLTREFRONTIERA.IT

www.oltrefrontiera.it

PANDORA DESIGN
Via Canonica 40,
20154 Milano
Tel +39 02 316157
Fax +39 02 34939492
www.pandoradesign.it

PC GRATIS
Via Taormina 17,
20129 Milano
Tel +39 02 6883182
Fax +39 02 66805848
pcgratis@pcgratis.it
www.pcgratis.it

**PIONEER ELECTRONICS
ITALIA SPA**
Via R. Lepetit 8,
20020 Lainate (MI), Italy
Tel +39 02 93911
Fax +39 02 9391300

PLANK
Via Nazionale 35,
39040 Ora (BZ), Italy
Tel +39 0471 803500
Fax +39 0471 803599
info@plank.it
www.plank.it

POLIFORM SPA
Via Montesanto 28,
22044 Inverigo (CO), Italy
Tel +39 031 6951
Fax +39 031 699444
info.poliform@poliform.it
www.poliform.it

POLTRONA FRAU SPA
S.S. 77, Km 74,500,
62029 Tolentino (MC), Italy

Tel +39 0733 9091
Fax +39 0733 909246
info@poltronafrau.it
www.poltronafrau.it

RIMADESIO SPA
Via Furlanelli 96,
20034 Giussano (MI), Italy
Tel +39 036 23171
Fax +39 036 2317317
rimadesio@rimadesio.it
www.rimadesio.it

SHARP ELECTRONICS SPA
Via Lampedusa 13, 20141 Milano
Tel +39 02 895951
Fax +39 02 89515900
www.sharp.it

STURM UND PLASTIC SPA
Via Coti Zelati 90,
20030 Palazzolo Milanese (MI)
Italy
Tel +39 02 99044222
Fax +39 02 99045611
www.sturmundplastic.it

SONY ITALIA SPA
Via G. Galilei 40,
20092 Cinisello Balsamo (MI)
Italy
Tel +39 02 618381
Fax +39 02 6126690
www.sony.it

TACCHINI
Via Domodossola 7,
20030 Baruccana di Seveso (MI)
Italy
Tel +39 036 2504182
Fax +39 036 2552402
tacchini@tacchini.it
www.tacchini.it

THONET VIENNA GMBH CO.
Berggasse 31, A-1090 Wien
Tel +43 1 310 200230
Fax +43 1 310 200213
www.thonet-vienna.at

TRUSSARDI HOME DESIGN
P.zza E. Duse 4, 20122 Milano
Tel +39 02 76004691
Fax +39 02 7614249

VISMARA DESIGN
Via Carducci 3, 20030
Seveso (MI), Italy
Tel +39 036 2503726
Fax +39 036 2551452
vismara@vismara.it
www.vismara.it

ZANI&ZANI SPA
Via del Porto 51/53, 25088
Toscolano Maderno (BS), Italy
Tel +39 036 5641006
Fax +39 036 5644281

ZANOTTA SPA
Via Vittorio Veneto 57,
20054 Nova Milanese (MI), Italy
Tel +39 036 24961
Fax +39 036 2451038
www.zanotta.it

**9 NET AVENUE
ITALIA SPA**
Via Torri Bianche 9,
20059 Vimercate (MI), Italy
Tel +39 039699901
Fax +39 03969990229
www.9netweb.it

SHOWROOMS

BLANCHAERT GALLERY
Via Nirone 19
20123 Milano
Italy

SPAZIO CONSOLO
Via dell'Aprica 12,
20158 Milano
Tel +39 02 66800673
Fax +39 02 68967049
spazio_consolo@libero.it

GALLERIA CARLA SOZZANI
Corso Como 10, Milano
Tel +39 02 653531
www.galleriacarlasozzani.com

LE CASE D'ARTE GALLERY
Via Gorani 8
20123 Milano
Tel/Fax +3928054071
POST DESIGN
Via Moscova 27, Milano

Tel +39 02 6554731
postdesign@tiscalinet.it

UNDERSTATE
Viale Crispi, Milano
Tel +39 0262690435
www.understate.it

CCADEMIA DI
OMUNICAZIONE
Ia Savona 112/a
0144 MILano
el +39 02 4815232
ax +39 0223006200
WW.HDemIa.IT

DI - ASSOCIAZIONE PER IL
ISEGNO INDUSTRIALE
Ia Bramante Da URBINO 29
0154 MILano, ITaLY
el +39 02 33100241
ax +39 02 33100878
WW.aDI-DeSIGN.ORG

COLE DES BEAUX-ARTS
 Rue Des Beaux-ARTS,
3000 BORDeaux, France
el +33 5 56334911
ax +33 5 56314623
COLe.BXARTS@maIRIe-BORDeaux.FR

OMUS ACADEMY -
RUPPO WEBEGG
Ia Savona 97,
0144 MILano, ITaLY
el +39 02 42414001
39 02 4222525
WW.DOMUSACADEMY.IT

GENESIO-ISTITUTO NUOVE
TECNOLOGIE
VIa PIeTRASANTA 14,
20141 MILano
TeL +39 02 55230369
Fax +39 02 55230410
WWW.GeNeSIO.ORG

ISTITUTO EUROPEO DI
DESIGN
VIa A. SCIeSA 4 ,
20135 MILano, ITaLY
WWW.IeD.IT

ISTITUTO EUROPEO DI
DESIGN
VIa G.POMBa 17,
10123 TORINO, ITaLY
TeL +39 011 8125668
Fax +39 011 835720
WWW.IeD.IT

ISTITUTO ITALIANO DI
FOTOGRAFIA
VIa BUGATTI 3,
MILano

ISIA _ ISTITUTO
SUPERIORE PER LE
INDUSTRIE ARTISTICHE

VIa DeGLI ALFANI 58,
50121 FIRenze, ITaLY
TeL +39 055 218836
Fax +39 055 218740
WWW.ISIa.IT

MARANGONI SCHOOL
VIa M.GONzaGa 6,
20123 MILano
TeL +39 02 861090
Fax +39 02 89010611
INFO@ISTITUTOMARANGONI.COM
WWW.ISTITUTOMARANGONI.COM

POLITECNICO DI MILANO
VIa G. DURANDO 38/A,
20158 MILano, ITaLY
TeL +39 02 23995961
Fax +39 02 23995977 LDI@maIL.POLIMI.IT

UNIVERSITA' DI GENOVA
STRaDONe S.AGOSTINO 37, 16123
GeNOVa, ITaLY
TeL +39 010 2095731
Fax +39 010 2095905
WWW.aRCH.UNIGe.IT

DI - ASSOCIAZIONE PER IL
ISEGNO INDUSTRIALE
Ia Bramante Da URBINO 29,
0154 MILano, ITaLY
el +39 02 33100241
ax +39 02 33100878
DI@essaI.IT
WW.aDI-DeSIGN.ORG

OSMIT SPa
ORO BUONAPARTE 65, 20121
ILano, ITaLY
el +39 02 725941
ax +39 02 89011563
WW.COSMIT.IT

EDERLEGNO - ARREDO
ORO BUONAPARTE 65,
0121 MILano
el +02 806041
el +02 80604392

FLGMILANO@FeDeRLeGNO.IT
WWW.FeDeRLeGNO.IT

FIERA MILANO
INTERNATIONAL SPa
PaLazzINa FMI LaRGO DOMODOSSOLa
1 , 20145 MILano
TeL +39 02 485501
Fax +39 02 43995259

I.C.E. - ISTITUTO COMMERCIO
ESTERO
C.SO MaGeNTa 59
20123 MILano, ITaLY
TeL +39 02 4813847
Fax +39 02 48005523
ICe.MILano@ICe.IT
WWW.ICe.IT

PRESS OFFICES

COSMIT _ UFFICIO STAMPA;
COSMIT EVENTI
FORO BUONAPARTE 65,
20121 MILANO, ITALY
TEL +39 02 8065141
FAX +39 02 86996211 PRESS@COSMIT.IT

COSMIT FONDAZIONE COSMIT
EVENTI - SALONESATELLITE
FORO BUONAPARTE 65,
20121 MILANO, ITALY
TEL +39 02 72594860
FAX +39 02 72594289

INTER NOS ERICA CALVI
PIAZZA S.AMBROGIO MILANO
TEL +39 02 8900632
WWW.INTERNOSAGENCY.COM
INTERNOS@FASTWEBNET.IT

MARIA LICCI PRESS OFFICE
VIA BRIOSCHI 26
20136 MILANO, ITALY
TEL +390289408589
FAX +390289427651

RECAPITO MILANESE
MILANO
TEL +39 02 89422269
RECAPITO@INAME.COM

SPAZIO CONSOLO
MILANO
TEL +39 349 2373598
INFO@CONSOLOPRODUZIONI.IT

PUBLISHER/AGENCIES

ANSA - AGENZIA NAZIONALE
STAMPA ASSOCIATA
P.ZZA CAVOUR 2, 20121 MILANO,
ITALY
TEL +39 02 76087222
FAX +39 02 76087220

ASSOCIATED PRESS -
REDAZIONE FOTOGRAFICA
P.ZZA CAVOUR 2, 20121 MILANO,
ITALY
TEL +39 02 76002000
FAX +39 02 76002626

ADN-KRONOS
P.ZZA CAVOUR 2, 20121 MILANO,
ITALY

TEL +39 02 76000901
FAX +39 02 784304

DESIGN DIFFUSION NEWS
VIA LUCANO 3, 20135 MILANO, ITALY
TEL +39 02 5516109
FAX +39 02 5456803

ABITARE SEGESTA SPA
CORSO MONFORTE 15   20122
MILANO, ITALY
TEL +39 02760901
FAX +39 02 76090301

DOMUS
VIA MAZZOCCHI 1, 20089 ROZZANO
(MILANO), ITALY

TEL +39 02 82472300
FAX +39 02 82472386

EDIZIONI CONDÈ NAST
P.ZZA CASTELLO 27, 20121 MILANO,
ITALY
ELEMOND SPA
VIA TRENTECOSTE 7 20134 MILANO
TEL +39 02 215631
FAX +39 02 26410847

ELLE DECOR
VIA A. RIZZOLI 2, 20132 MILANO, ITALY
TEL +39 02 25843380
FAX +39 02 25843862

©GIULIA BER TACCHINI
©PAOLO CALCAGNI
©LUCIO LUZO LAZZARA
©RICCARDO RINETTI

©2002 ENORME FILM ARTS SNC
MILANO, ITALY

THE OFFICIAL POINT OF VIEW
VIA NERINO, 8
ITA-20123 MILANO, ITALY
TEL +39 02 7200 1166
INFO@THEOFFICIALPOINTOFVIEW.IT

ISBN 88-900822-0-8

PRINTED IN ITALY BY
GRAFICHE LEARDINI
S.MARTINO B.A. (VR)

DISTRIBUTED WORLDWIDE BY
ACTAR
ROCA I BATLLE, 2-4
08023 BARCELONA, SPAIN
TEL +34 93 418 7759
FAX +34 93 418 6707
INFO@ACTAR-MAIL.COM